W9-AVL-721

Conference Center Planning and Design

RICHARD H. PENNER

Conference Center Planning and Design

A GUIDE FOR ARCHITECTS, DESIGNERS, MEETING PLANNERS, AND FACILITY MANAGERS

WHITNEY LIBRARY OF DESIGN
An imprint of Watson-Guptill
Publications/New York

For B.H.P. and in memory of A.J.P.

Frontispiece: Tarrytown House, Tarrytown, New York. (Photo: Bo Parker)

Part 1 opener: Scanticon-Minneapolis, Plymouth, Minnesota. (Photo: George Heinrich)

Part 2 opener: Scanticon-Denver, Englewood, Colorado. (Photo: Tim Hursley)

Copyright © 1991 by *Restaurant/Hotel Design International.*

First published in 1991 in New York by Whitney Library of Design
an imprint of Watson-Guptill Publications
a division of BPI Communications, Inc.,
1515 Broadway, New York, N.Y. 10036

Library of Congress Cataloging-in-Publication Data
Penner, Richard H.
  Conference center planning and design / by Richard H. Penner.
  p.   cm.
  Includes index.
  ISBN 0-8230-0911-4 (hardcover):
  1. Convention facilities—United States. 2. Architecture,
Modern—20th century—United States. I. Title.
NA6880.5.U6P46 1991
725′.91′097309048—dc20   90-22581
                                           CIP

Manufactured in Singapore

First printing, 1991

1 2 3 4 5 6 7 8 9/95 94 93 92 91

Preface

Two of the largest industries worldwide are education and tourism. Within these broad categories, the specific areas of adult education and the hotel business come together in the design and operation of conference and training centers. As this specialization grows in prominence, there will be an increasing need for facilities designed to meet the particular needs of the various continuing education fields.

One cannot be, in a single book, both comprehensive in scope *and* exhaustive in treatment. An earlier book, *Hotel Planning and Design*, coauthored with Wally Rutes, dealt with the full range of lodging properties but, as a result, devoted only a handful of pages to dedicated conference facilities. Other monographs have illustrated the more prominent hotels and resorts but, unfortunately, have emphasized illustration at the expense of text, and have dealt only superficially with conference centers as a specialized lodging type. With increasing business concerns for recruiting, training, and retaining qualified staff, professional development seminars, and continuing education, both business and academia have come to recognize the need to develop specialized conference and training centers.

The term "conference center" has different connotations around the world. In some coun-

tries, it is what we in the United States consider to be a *convention center*, a large complex for major exhibitions and trade shows; in others, it is a theater facility or *cultural center*, emphasizing auditoriums for lectures and artistic performances, perhaps with a few smaller meeting rooms and dining areas; some may confuse it with a *convention hotel*, with many hundreds of rooms and oriented to groups of a thousand people or more. As treated in this book, however, a *conference center* is a specially designed lodging property conceived to provide an effective environment for small conferences, meetings, and training programs. All aspects of the facility design—not just the meeting core, but also the residential, dining, recreational, and support areas, as well as professional conference services—are planned to enhance the goals of the meeting.

I had several objectives in undertaking this study and, during the past two years, additional goals took shape. My chief interest was in discovering how conference centers differ from more generic hotels in their program, planning, and design. As I got more involved with the topic, I began to investigate the differences between various categories of centers—say university or corporate or resort—in both their market requirements and their facilities. In addition, I hoped to trace the growth of this specialized hotel property over the past forty years and, more specifically, over the past decade.

The major goal of this book is to convey an understanding of the differences between conference centers and hotels and among the several types of conference and training centers. It is important that owners and developers, architects and designers, hotel and conference center operators, and meeting planners and trainers all recognize the opportunities and constraints inherent in this specialized building type. Each influences its design. Each approaches a project, whether new construction, adaptive reuse, renovation, or merely refurbishment, with different goals and biases. More important, though, is to understand conference centers from the perspective of the ultimate consumer, the conference attendee. I hope that the projects illustrated here assist the wide range of people involved in conference centers to better define their objectives in the planning of new projects or the modification of existing ones.

Many people greatly influenced this work. Paul Weintraub, then publisher, and Mary Jean Madigan, editor and current publisher, of *Restaurant/Hotel Design International* magazine approached me with the opportunity to write this book. I must thank them both for their encouragement and interest.

The leadership of the International Association of Conference Centers (IACC) has cooperated from the beginning. Executive Director Tom Bolman invited me to attend the 1989 annual conference in Snowbird, Utah, and association president Sam Haigh and executive committee members Andy Dolce, Marjorie Farley, Emily Bowden, George Cedeno, Ron Naples, Tom Silvestri, Ginny Stott, and Bob Twomey—among others—have offered ideas and suggestions.

The project analyses presented in the following pages—more than seventy different centers are illustrated and many more are described—are based to a large degree on the study of their architectural plans, as well as on tours and interviews with the project architects, management, and guests. Projects that illustrate or exemplify certain points particularly well are isolated in specially designed "feature" pages. Many architects and designers patiently and repeatedly responded to my requests for plans, data, and photos. While these sources are too numerous to mention in a complete listing—I hope the publication of their projects offers some satisfaction

—I must acknowledge the frequent help of Paul Broches, Robby Cox, Jerry Davis, Bob DiLeonardo, Alan Goldberg, Bob Hillier, Ken Hurd, Jay Larson, Steve Loos, Joe Rabun, Joel Spaeth, and Don Wudtke.

In addition to architects and designers, the developers and corporate management companies provided frequent assistance, especially in making available plans and programs. Immense help came from Glen Schostak, formerly of Scanticon Corporation, Dennis Johnson and Bruce Burkhalter of Benchmark, and Richard Joaquim of International Conference Resorts. I am further indebted to Coleman Finkel, Walter Green, Terry Harwood, and Frank Stone. Individual consultants offered important insights. I want to acknowledge the help of David Arnold and Geoff Kirkland, recently of Laventhol and Horwath, who provided data on financial performance, Bill Eaton and Ray Petit of Cini-Little International, and Owen Rabourn.

During the past two years, many students at Cornell's School of Hotel Administration assisted with the data collection and research. Most important are Jennifer Eyster, for the analyses of conference center plans and facilities characteristics, Leslie Mahoney, for the space program analyses, and Mary Mathew, for preparing many of the drawings in the book; others include Uta Birkmayer, Liz Ronayne, and Diana Pang. Valued secretarial help came from Marion Stallings and Marge Sharpsteen.

At Watson-Guptill, senior editor Cornelia Guest championed the proposal and saw it through the initial steps. Paul Lukas tirelessly dedicated weeks to the editing and production phases and Bob Fillie prepared the fine design and layout. They are all to be thanked beyond words.

Much of the travel, text preparation, and acquisition of artwork occurred during a sabbatical leave from my teaching duties at the School of Hotel Administration at Cornell. I thank former dean Jack Clark for his support of the project, and colleagues Michael Redlin, David Stipanuk, Jack Corgel, and Jan deRoos for assuming additional teaching responsibilities during this period. And above all else, my family deserves special thanks for bearing with the late nights and never-ending deadlines that a project of this scope entails—the way I schedule it.

RICHARD H. PENNER
Ithaca, New York
January, 1991

Contents

PART TWO. DESIGN GUIDE

Foreword

Small meetings represent the fastest growing segment of the United States hospitality market today. Moreover, this has been the case for the past twenty years, during which time this segment has more than doubled in size, representing more than 220 million room-nights in 1989.

Along with this growth has come a dramatic increase in the pressure to make these meetings more productive. One result has been the emergence of the conference center, a very specialized hospitality product aimed directly at satisfying the needs of small meetings.

Because of the specialized purposes of conference centers, they are indeed very different from hotels, resorts, and other types of lodging facilities. The differences are physical, operational, and philosophical—some subtle, some quite apparent—but all directly impact the conference center design and contribute to its unique character.

Dick Penner has done a terrific job here in providing a comprehensive review of how these differences translate to the programming and design requirements of conference centers. He supports this with detailed case studies, provides background information about the meeting industry and the evolution of meeting facilities, and addresses the many issues and concerns of both customer and operator as they relate to conference center design.

Whether you are a developer, architect, interior designer, operator, or meeting planner, you will find this planning handbook an extremely valuable source of information.

Sam D. Haigh
President, International Association of Conference Centers (IACC)

President, Doral Hotels & Resorts Management Corporation

PART ONE

CONFERENCE CENTER TYPES

CHAPTER 1

Introduction

The hospitality industry today is in the midst of a period of great innovation, as operating companies and entrepreneurial developers modify facilities and refine management techniques to meet the demands of new markets and remain competitive. This period can be seen as part of a larger progression. The mid-1950s marked the explosion of roadside motor inns, as the postwar economy expanded and Americans increasingly traveled over the newly constructed interstate highway system. A decade later, in the late 1960s, the opening of the Hyatt Regency Atlanta initiated the growth of the convention hotel business and signaled the increasing value of design and architecture as a marketing tool. Half a generation later, the industry exploded again with the introduction of all-suite properties and additional growth at both the economy and luxury ends of the market.

At the same time, in the early 1980s, the conference center industry marked its presence with the maturing of several influential properties and the establishment in 1981 of the International Association of Conference Centers, or IACC. Although important conference properties existed earlier—the Arden House,

operated by Columbia University in Harriman, New York (1950), the Harrison Conference Center in Glen Cove, New York (1968), the New England Telephone Training Center in Marlboro, Massachusetts (1974), and Scanticon in Princeton, New Jersey (1979), to name a few— it wasn't until the 1980s that conference centers became truly competitive and demonstrated a successful product that would show increasing acceptance and continued growth.

To define our discussion, a *conference center* is a specially designed hospitality property dedicated to providing an environment most conducive to effective conferences and meetings, especially for groups of between twenty and fifty people. The conference center provides a distraction-free, dedicated, comfortably furnished, and fully equipped facility with the added important feature of a professional staff trained to provide a high level of service to the meeting planner and conference attendees. At such a center, all aspects of the facility design, the conference support services, the food and beverage program, and the recreational amenities enhance and further the goals of a meeting.

The development of conference properties was matched by a corresponding period of

Doral Arrowwood, Rye Brook, New York. Located north of New York City, this resort conference center has successfully blended weekday high-level executive meetings and transient business with weekend recreational packages. This can be attributed in part to the siting and also to the building design, which segregates the guestrooms and features the sports and fitness components. (Architect and interiors: The Hillier Group; photo: Jim D'Addio.)

substantial growth in the number of (and attendance at) meetings, from the smallest workshops to the largest national conventions. Various studies by the trade press and independent research organizations show that while all segments of this market are increasing, the smaller corporate management, training, and sales meetings are growing the fastest. For example, while the number of association meetings—usually the meetings with the largest attendance—increased 26 percent from 1979 to 1989, corporate meetings increased by 31 percent, to about 850,000 annually, with an attendance of nearly 60 million people and expenditures of over $9 billion.

THE SMALL MEETINGS MARKET

The conference center industry is now at a point where its specialized lodging product has gained wide acceptance; the experience of the 1980s has educated both the meeting planners and the attendees. At the same time, the demand for quality small-conference venues is rapidly increasing. Recent studies of the number of small corporate and association meetings project that there will be 682,700 conferences with fewer than fifty people held in the United States in 1990, with an additional 42,600 held by American organizations overseas (Table 1–1). In addition to these small meetings, which ideally are held in the more intimate, better-serviced conference centers, the properties frequently accommodate groups as large as two hundred to three hundred people. By most estimates, however, conference and training centers currently host fewer than 2 percent of the meetings held.

Most experts expect that the number of small conferences and training programs will continue to grow, even during periods of economic downturn. Why? There are many reasons, including the following:

☐ Corporations are facing an increasingly competitive environment, and their employees are challenged to understand new manufacturing, marketing, and financial techniques and concepts.
☐ Adapting to foreign management principles will increase the demand for advanced business programs.
☐ Legal and regulatory issues will necessitate educational seminars.
☐ Companies' increasingly computerized systems and controls will make it necessary for them to train employees in order to be effective.

☐ Training and management meetings will continue to expand, leading planners to seek the ideal setting at a well-designed and professionally managed conference center.

The most common type of small meeting is the *training program*, often incorporating a high level of audiovisual support. Some companies may feature fairly standard video presentations, while others involve the trainees in intensive role-playing exercises and group sessions, which may be videotaped and played back for critique and discussion. While these events average only a few days, many training programs can last several weeks. And although the average class size is about twenty-five, many training meetings include as many as

TABLE 1-1. PROJECTED 1990 CORPORATE AND ASSOCIATION MEETINGS

Meeting Type	Total Meetings	Small Meetings[a]
Corporate meetings		
Training seminars	243,900	190,200
Management meetings	198,300	150,700
Professional–technical	111,500	70,700
Regional sales meetings	108,100	77,800
Incentive trips	76,000	40,300
National sales	40,600	15,400
Other	88,400	52,300
Total corporate meetings	886,880	596,900
Association meetings		
Educational seminars	72,900	23,300
Board meetings	38,800	31,000
Professional–technical	31,000	14,600
Regional–local	27,800	10,800
Other	16,100	6,900
Total association meetings	186,600	86,600
Overseas meetings		
Total corporate and association	69,700	42,600

[a]Fewer than fifty participants.
Source: M. Concorso, *The Small Meetings Market*, pp. 4–5, based upon *The Meetings Market '90*, Meetings and Conventions Magazine/Reed Travel Group.

thirty to fifty people. Depending on the degree of involvement of the human resources and training personnel from the company's headquarters, the training sites may be selected because of proximity to the corporate office. As companies recognize the increasing importance of training, many are bypassing the proximity issue by building their own dedicated training centers, frequently with lodging and extensive classroom and meeting support areas. While these tend to have between 250 and 450 rooms (and might require an investment in excess of $100 million), a few corporations operate substantially larger facilities. Educational programs also may be carried out in nonresidential corporate training centers or in executive conference centers, as well as in traditional hotels.

Management meetings include executive conferences and management development sessions. These generally range from about two days to five days (occasionally longer) and are designed for groups of ten to fifty. The meetings may be highly intensive, and recreation and social activities often are scheduled to offer an opportunity for relaxation. As a result, managers usually select resort or suburban conference centers with extensive recreational facilities.

Professional and technical meetings are similar to the training and management meetings. They usually last two to three days and vary in group size depending upon the topic and sponsor. Many are held at universities, with the faculty of business, management, or engineering schools serving as seminar instructors; however, all types of conference centers attract at least some small number of technical meetings.

Regional and national sales meetings are ideally held at conference centers because of the need for highly sophisticated audiovisual presentations and the desire to keep the attendees focused on the session theme. These meetings generally last three to four days and vary in size, with national meetings reaching as large as several hundred attendees. Sales meetings have many objectives, among them increasing employee motivation and enthusiasm, familiarizing employees with new product lines or sales strategies, and reasserting corporate goals and philosophies. Many larger sales meetings are held in hotels and resorts, but the small and midsize regional meetings are ideal for conference centers.

Other types of meetings are also good candidates for using conference centers. Incentive trips, which usually last about a week, generally are held at major resort hotels or popular destinations. Companies offering incentive trips as a reward to sales or management personnel tend to include business meetings during the event, although their intensity and rigor varies. Resort conference centers, especially those with on-site golf or skiing, and properties near preferred destinations offering other activities are best positioned to attract this business. Product introductions, smaller association meetings, and other specialized types of conferences, while not out of the question, are a less important part of the conference center market—these often involve hundreds of people, may be fairly short in duration, and do not generate the food and beverage and rooms revenue essential to supporting the more expensive conference center operations.

CONFERENCE CENTER FACILITIES AND SERVICES

Although conference centers have been in existence for a century as sites for meetings or retreats, it was not until 1950 that a facility dedicated to high-level professional meetings was created. After the Harriman family donated the Arden estate north of New York City to Columbia University, the school renovated the main house, constructed additional guestrooms and an amphitheater, and established an operational program to provide the types of services conferees now expect.

In the late 1960s, entrepreneurs renovated other estates outside New York to create the Harrison property on Long Island and the Tarrytown Executive Conference Center in Westchester County. These early properties, as well as notable examples in Scandinavia, created a physical, operational, and philosophical concept that now has become the modern conference center.

Planning Considerations. There are significant physical differences between the designs of conference centers and those of more traditional hotels and resorts. Many of these differences are related to the conference center's principal planning objective, which is to separate the conference and training areas from the other functions in order to eliminate distractions and intrusions during a meeting. Dining, lounge, banquet, and recreational areas usually are located away from the meeting wing, in connecting structures, or even in separate buildings. Other objectives include the architectural massing and careful siting of the facility to enhance the residential scale and create a feeling of closeness with the environment. Roadways, parking areas, and surrounding activity are screened. Moreover, the architects must design a particularly efficient building: given the extra floor area devoted to conference and recreational facilities in comparison with hotels, it is essential that conference centers be tightly planned. For example, the guestroom wings should be organized along double-loaded corridors, and service areas should be compactly arranged, since neither extra food pantries nor long service corridors can be economically justified.

Other planning and design distinctions are specific to the conference core. They include the following:

☐ The meeting space, whether in the form of classrooms, breakout rooms, amphitheaters, or other special-purpose rooms, is exclusively dedicated to conferences; such social functions as banquets and receptions are scheduled in other areas of the building. These rooms usually are assigned and dedicated to a single user group throughout its stay.

☐ Each of the conference rooms is specially designed and equipped to enhance the meeting purpose: spacious, daylit, high-ceilinged rooms incorporate the ideal types of lighting, audiovisual systems, furnishings, and individual climate controls to support a productive meeting.

☐ Assembly and refreshment areas are provided throughout the conference core, providing opportunities for frequent informal gathering and allowing the meeting planner and instructor great flexibility in scheduling breaks.

☐ In addition, such support functions as rest rooms, telephones, and offices for the conference services staff are conveniently located nearby.

The other functional areas support the conference focus. Guestrooms are designed for work and study; additional lounges and case discussion rooms may be provided on the guestroom floors. Most centers provide a lavish conferee dining room and, often, an alternative dining room, usually an upscale specialty restaurant; also, it is becoming common to add a more casual room with an informal snack menu. The recreational areas are considerably more extensive than in most hotels: the typical conference center will include an indoor pool, exercise and aerobics rooms, racquetball courts, and locker and spa facilities.

Operational Systems. Equally important to the success of a conference or meeting are the types of services that the conference center provides: conference coordinators assist the meeting planner with arrangements during the weeks leading up to the conference; the conference concierge provides the meeting participants with information, messages, and such business-center services as typing, faxing, copying, and express mail; audiovisual technicians not only provide and, if necessary, operate the audiovisual equipment, but they may even produce custom video- or audiotapes for a particular session, or as a record of the meeting; and many centers have their own closed-circuit television production studio, graphics print shop, and photographic darkroom.

Most conference centers price their facilities based on the *complete meeting package*, or CMP. This offers the meeting planner a single daily rate including lodging, three meals, conference rooms, refreshment breaks, and standard audiovisual support. The only extras are for special event dinners, such specific audiovisual requests as the production of a tape, and golf greens fees. A key element in this pricing is the inclusion of a conference dining room where meeting attendees have the flexibility to dine when they choose, sit in groups as they wish, and select from a lavish buffet. Among other advantages, this allows the participants to continue their intensive discussions without interruption as they move from classroom to dining room to breakout.

The CMP also allows for continuous refreshment breaks, which permit the instructors increased flexibility about when to schedule a break. The refreshment centers usually feature a wide selection of hot and cold beverages, rolls and fruit in the morning, and various snacks in the afternoon. This typical arrangement of the conference dining room and the continuous breaks necessitates fewer decisions by the meeting planner in terms of cost, schedule, and exact number of attendees. It also offers more flexibility and choice to the attendees themselves, and gives the center operator greater certainty in planning staffing and food purchasing.

TYPES OF CONFERENCE CENTERS

Conference centers fall into distinct categories. These distinctions are based for the most part

Chaminade at Santa Cruz, Santa Cruz, California. Converted from a former parochial school overlooking Monterey Bay, Chaminade was the first executive conference center to open on the west coast. Set on an 80-acre (32.4-hectare) site, the property includes eight conference rooms, breakout rooms, dining, and lounge areas in the original mission-style structure, and 152 oversized guestrooms in a series of residential buildings nearby. (Architects: Tom Heagle, Neil Lindstrom; photo courtesy of Chaminade.)

The Statler Hotel and Marriott Executive Education Center, Cornell University, Ithaca, New York. The centerpiece of the new university hotel and conference facility, the Marriott amphitheater accommodates 90 attendees at custom millwork tables shaped to fit the hexagonal space. The room offers extensive audiovisual, computer, and recording capabilities. (Architect: The Architects Collaborative; interiors: Kenneth E. Hurd and Associates; photo: Ed Jacoby.)

on the ownership, market orientation, and usual mix of facilities. Of course, many conference centers exhibit the characteristics of several different categories; many of the corporate conference centers, for example, compete with executive properties by soliciting general meetings. Also, like most businesses, conference centers can mature and grasp the opportunity to compete in new markets. Doral Arrowwood, for instance, has evolved from a corporate center—originally built by Citicorp—to an executive property and now to a strong resort orientation. Table 1–2 identifies the principal types of conference centers, the typical meetings they attract, and their general physical characteristics.

The *executive conference center* is the most typical midrange facility (although not necessarily midprice). It is oriented toward corporate meetings, including both training and management development. Such centers feature a relatively large number of conference rooms—only the largest corporate training centers have more. Most executive centers are located in the suburbs around the larger cities, such as New York, Washington, Atlanta, and

GE Management Development Institute, Croton-on-Hudson, New York. Used for training since the early 1950s, the GE conference center includes a new 140,000 square foot (13,020 square meter) residential, dining, and recreational facility, completed in 1987. The dramatic dining room leads to a series of terraces, offering opportunities for informal gathering. (Architect: Shepley Bulfinch Richardson and Abbott; photo: Wheeler Photographics.)

TABLE 1-2. CONFERENCE CENTER CHARACTERISTICS

Type of Center	Typical Meeting Uses	Facility Characteristics
Executive	Mid- and upper-level training and management development; management planning; sales meetings	Suburban locations; 225–300 midsize to large guestrooms; multiple dining and beverage outlets; moderate number of mid-size conference rooms; large number of breakout rooms; moderate recreational facilities
Resort	Mid- and upper-level management meetings; incentive trips; sales meetings	Resort destination or suburban locations; 150–400 large rooms; multiple dining and beverage outlets; small to moderate number of conference rooms; additional banquet rooms; extensive recreational amenities (especially outdoors)
Corporate	Technical and sales training for low- and mid-level employees; management development meetings; outside conferences if company policy permits	Suburban or headquarters locations; 125–400 rooms of varying sizes; limited dining alternatives; extensive training or conference rooms to meet corporate objectives; specialized rooms; auditorium; moderate to extensive recreational facilities
University	Executive education for middle managers; scientific meetings and continuing education programs	On-campus location; 50–150 small to midsize rooms; limited dining and beverage options; small to moderate number of conference rooms; amphitheater; auditorium (at continuing education centers); recreation located elsewhere on campus rather than as formal part of center
Nonresidential	Low- and mid-level employee education; middle and upper management development	Urban or corporate headquarters location; no guestrooms; one limited-service dining room–café; generic conference and breakout rooms; limited special-purpose rooms; no recreation
Not-for-profit	Religious, educational, and government staff training; association and foundation meetings	Often at remote location; 25–100 rooms; single dining room; small to moderate number of generic conference rooms; large multipurpose room; limited recreation (primarily outdoors)

Chicago. With increasing competition and land costs, the main concern of both developers and operators should be whether a proposed facility has the potential to attract weekend conferences or social business, both of which are necessary to ensure profitability.

Many of the *resort conference centers* have evolved from executive properties by marketing and promoting their recreational facilities. They are designed for the same type of management meetings, as well as for sales and incentive groups. Resort conference centers vary in size but most new properties are in the 300- to 400-room range, in order to support the recreational infrastructure. Usually they have somewhat less meeting space than do executive centers, but more food and beverage and recreational facilities. New resort centers are being built in both suburban locations and the more traditional resort destinations, such as Arizona and California. These often are joint-venture developments because of the extreme cost in acquiring the land and building the center and recreational amenities. In addition to these new properties, existing resort operators are adding conference center buildings to extend their seasons, and attract additional markets.

Corporate conference and training centers are physically the largest of the several categories and a few existing properties have as many as 1,000 rooms. Although many corporations have built facilities with 100 to 150 rooms, new entities tend to be in the 200- to 400-room range. Corporate centers contain much more conference space than do other types because of the need to meet very specific training needs. Many major corporations, especially those in telecommunications, insurance, pharmaceuticals, and financial services, are struggling with the decision of whether to build their own residential or nonresidential centers, or to rent space from executive centers or at other sites. Fortunately, they all realize the importance of training and employee development to their success.

University conference facilities meet three different needs: the most luxurious are designed for dedicated business school executive education programs; others provide for campus visitors and educational conferences, or for growing continuing education programs. The university centers generally are no larger than 150 rooms, and feature amphitheaters or an auditorium as well as the more typical conference rooms. These centers exist because the large research universities realize that their reputations are, in part, dependent on the types of executive and adult education programs they run, and on their abilities to bring business executives to campus on a regular basis.

The *nonresidential centers* most often are corporate operated, either for low- and mid-level training or for upper-level management development. They may be constructed near the corporate headquarters or at a site convenient to the training department. Most contain fairly standard conference rooms and may be available to the public for day meetings, depending on the corporate policy.

The most highly variable group are the *not-for-profit centers*, which may be owned by religious or educational organizations, associations and foundations, research centers, or private humanitarian and arts groups. Their facilities reflect the differing missions of their respective owner groups and offer the public or specific interest groups the opportunity to meet in, for example, a spectacular mountain setting or near a historic landmark.

The following chapters discuss each of the conference center types and illustrate a variety of planning and design solutions. Later chapters investigate the various complex programming and planning issues of the individual functional areas, including guestrooms, public areas, conference core, and recreational facilities.

CHAPTER 2

Executive Conference Centers

The interest in the conference center as a specialized lodging type has grown out of the recent popularity of these properties for high-level executive meetings. While not-for-profit retreats were established by such groups as the YMCA and the Scouts in the early 1900s, most business meetings continued to be held in corporate offices or hotels. In the early 1950s Columbia University established Arden House at the former Harriman estates north of New York City, but restricted its use for the most part to the university's own business school and advanced management programs. However, business leaders who were exposed to the specialized meeting facilities, high level of services, and distraction-free setting began to seek out similar centers. Harrison, a conference center development and management company, established a number of properties, first in an expanded mansion at Glen Cove on Long Island (1968), then later in Connecticut and outside Chicago. In Tarrytown, New York, a private developer renovated the former Biddle estate beginning in 1964, adding new wings for additional lodging, to create the Tarrytown House Executive Conference Center; a more recent remodeling occurred in 1988.

While this was taking place in America, the Danish engineering and medical associations recognized the need for improved meeting facilities in Scandinavia. In 1969, they opened the first Scanticon facility, dedicated to providing superior meetings in an innovative environment, reflecting Danish architecture at its best. The resulting center at Aarhus is smaller than its more recent American counterparts and has 110 guestrooms and fourteen conference rooms, the largest seating up to 250, in addition to the usual complement of dining, beverage, and recreational amenities. Its popularity inspired Scanticon founder Jorgen Roed to explore the potential for a similar property in the United States, and led to the eventual construction of Scanticon-Princeton, which opened in 1979.

The success of these several projects encouraged others: Citicorp developed Arrowwood north of New York City, and Equitable Insurance built the Peachtree Executive Conference Center south of Atlanta. These early-1980s projects set the standard for growth in the executive conference center segment over the latter half of the decade—growth that is expected to continue through the 1990s.

Harrison Conference Center of Glen Cove, Glen Cove, New York. Established in 1968 in an early-1900s Georgian mansion, the expanded Harrison property now includes 27 meeting rooms, 200 guestrooms, and an expansive recreation center overlooking the manicured 55-acre (22.3-hectare) estate. (Architect: Charles Adams Platt; photo courtesy of Harrison.)

SITE AND MARKET CONSIDERATIONS

Executive conference centers are conceived and built to provide service for a specific lodging and meeting need: the small group that seeks a dedicated facility with a high level of service. Some projects that have matured and evolved into executive centers were initially constructed principally for single clients, or were corporate training facilities; now they seek a mix of conference and transient business during the week and the more price-conscious meetings and social or personal markets during weekends and holiday periods. Therefore, executive centers include more elements of the typical hotel—including guestroom club floors and suites, speciality or gourmet restaurants, and larger multipurpose conference rooms—than do other conference center types.

There are important differences in the types, sizes, and orientations of executive conference centers. The most prominent type are independent (although often operated by a professional management company), for-profit entities with 200–300 rooms. In addition, there are a number of distinctive smaller properties, some with as few as twenty rooms, which offer the exclusivity of an *executive retreat*. And recently, in order to better serve the meetings market, commercial hotels have been designed with distinct and separate conference cores and existing hotels have built full-service conference additions. These *ancillary conference centers* generally have more rooms than do most executive properties but include dedicated conference facilities and services designed to attract the executive conference market.

Unlike hotel projects, which often begin with a specific site and then proceed with a market analysis, the typical executive conference center is initiated by a developer who perceives a need in a particular region. The developer's first step, then, is to commission a market study to identify and segment the different types of meeting business, locate several suitable sites, and establish the potential for appealing to a wide range of interests, including transient lodging guests, food and beverage and catering business, and weekend-resort–urban-getaway business. The lodging market mix at the strongest conference center locations should represent at least 60 percent meetings; the remaining 40 percent should be a combination of individual transient and resort or weekend markets. This market mix results from attracting between 90 and 100

Legend

1. Entrance
2. Concourse
3. Reception
4. Administration
5. Coatroom
6. Lounge
7. Restaurant
8. Kitchen
9. Conference room
10. Audiovisuals
11. Auditorium
12. Breakout room
13. Guestroom

Scanticon-Aarhus, Aarhus, Denmark (above). Scanticon established the European model of the dedicated conference facility in 1969, combining specialized meeting rooms incorporating high levels of service and technology in a dramatic exposed-concrete structure. (Architect: Friis and Moltke; photo courtesy of Scanticon.)

Scanticon-Princeton, Princeton, New Jersey (right and below). This project combines 37 conference rooms, 300 guestrooms, and five food and beverage outlets in a striking Scandinavian structure surrounding a cobblestone entry courtyard and extending into the enveloping woods of the busy Forrestal Center. (Architect: Friis and Moltke with Warner Burns Toan and Lunde; interiors: Friis and Moltke with Enicho Deichmann; interior photo: Ron Solomon; exterior photo courtesy of Scanticon.)

percent conference business during the week and 15 to 20 percent during the weekend.

The earliest executive centers, developed in the 1970s and early 1980s, hoped to succeed by focusing almost exclusively on small corporate meetings. However, although these facilities gained rave reviews and earned high marks for service, the meetings business cannot support a facility year-round; it is imperative to develop other markets for weekends and for the less popular conference weeks, including those around major holidays. Private executive conference centers, operating without the subsidies that corporate training departments contribute to their company-owned centers, therefore must find ways to fill the frequent valleys in the business meeting calendar. Doral Arrowwood, for one, has developed a highly successful weekend resort business, which often results in sell-outs in the summer.

Trends in the meetings industry have an immediate influence on the success of conference centers. For instance, Corporate America is changing its conferencing schedule to better reflect the personal preferences of its employees. Week-long meetings used to commence with a Sunday check-in, but many planners, instead of fighting employee disapproval, now organize meetings around a Monday-morning arrival. Conference centers have few options for gaining alternative business over the lost Sunday night. Indeed, in markets with few other sites for executive meetings (and hence few options for the client), the center's sales staff may insist on Sunday arrivals, offering concessions on food and beverage or other

amenities but maintaining the additional night's revenue.

An important part of this larger market mix is the weekend business, consisting of price-sensitive conferences (educational and religious groups and associations, for example) and recreational weekenders (often urbanites seeking a minivacation close to home with upscale dining and recreational choices). These latter guests do not utilize the conference core but nonetheless enjoy the resort amenities in the remainder of the facility. Accordingly, the center's architectural and interior design treatments must not be too institutional or commercial (as are the designs of many educational or corporate training facilities); the design scheme instead must play up the more casual aspects of lodging and dining.

PROGRAM AND PLANNING CONSIDERATIONS

Unlike the corporate and university conference facilities, at which the training or educational agenda can help to determine the exact mix and type of conference rooms and corporate officers can mandate operational policies for food and beverage outlets or fitness facilities, executive conference centers must provide a greater variety of spaces (actually a greater duplication of meeting areas) in order to accommodate the varying needs of training, management development, sales, or other types of business conferences. Too often the program for the ubiquitous "hotel and conference center" differs little from that of a suburban hotel: a multipurpose meeting and ban-

Henry Chauncey Conference Center, Princeton, New Jersey. Operated by the Educational Testing Service since 1973, the center serves meetings related to training, instruction, research, and learning in a series of pitched-roof structures with its 100 guestrooms arranged in clusters of eight, most with balconies overlooking the 400-acre (162-hectare) campus. (Architect: Warner Burns Toan and Lunde; photo: James Parker.)

TABLE 2-1. EXECUTIVE CONFERENCE CENTER CONCEPTUAL REQUIREMENTS

Project Aspect	*Aims and Requirements*
Sitting	Separate visually the center from surrounding roads and buildings; create a park-like setting; preserve the environment and create protected views of the surrounding landscape
Guestrooms	Design the rooms for single occupancy during the week but, because of the weekend recreational market, plan for some double occupancy; rooms should be similar in feel to first-class hotel rooms but with special attention to the work area and such work amenities as phone and computer capability; consider the need for commons areas
Lobby	Create character that reinforces the image of the business meeting setting; clearly organize circulation so that visitors can easily locate conference wing, dining, and banquet areas
Restaurants	Design the conference dining room to allow for expected meeting capacity plus 10%; include a specialty restaurant oriented to the local business community; also add a small gourmet restaurant only if a market niche is available locally; lobby lounge should have capability to divide for small private receptions
Conference rooms	Provide a multipurpose conference room (flat-floored auditorium or junior ballroom) for full capacity; ballroom or banquet room for special meal functions; amphitheater, if needed, to differentiate from competition. Principal focus is 1,000-ft^2 (93-meter^2) and larger conference rooms and large number of breakout rooms
Conference support	Include a large prefunction room near the principal conference room and smaller break areas near each group of meeting rooms; provide access to outdoor terraces if possible; locate conference services at the conference core; determine need for high-level audiovisual, graphics, and other systems
Recreation	Provide an indoor pool (outdoor if weather permits), racquetball courts, exercise, aerobics, lockers, and a sauna

quet room that can be subdivided into several smaller rooms; perhaps a few additional meeting rooms; one or two uninspired restaurants; limited fitness facilities; and so forth. In contrast, IACC-member executive conference centers offer soundproof meeting rooms, a minimum of fifty square feet of conference space per guestroom, conference dining rooms, audiovisual capability and support staff, and additional conference services.

The project development team, especially the developer-owner, architect, and operator, must establish operational and conceptual design criteria early in the planning process. These project requirements (Table 2–1) help define and focus the later planning and design decisions by bringing together the owner's objectives, the preliminary market information, the site criteria and constraints, the operator's experience, and the architect's conceptual abilities into a single report. It is important to organize a preliminary meeting—perhaps over several days—at which the team can establish a single, unified set of project objectives; often, the contributions of consultants from such key areas as food service, landscape, interiors, and audiovisuals may be included.

Executive Centers. The executive conference center is in a difficult position competitively: Although it has superior facilities for small meetings of all types, it is much less

TARRYTOWN HOUSE
EXECUTIVE CONFERENCE CENTER

Among the first American conference centers when it opened in 1963 in Tarrytown, a suburb north of New York City, Tarrytown House was transformed in a 1988 renovation that greatly expanded the dining capacity of the 1895 Biddle House. The addition—the brightly daylit Winter Palace, seating up to 175—was constructed on a former outside terrace. Other remodeling included moving the registration and office functions to the Carriage House to regain additional meeting rooms for the 120-room property; converting another mansion on the 26-acre (10.5-hectare) site, the 1840 King House, into a 10-room executive retreat; and extensive landscaping. (Architect: Harman Jablin; interiors: MacDonald Design Group; photos: Bo Parker.)

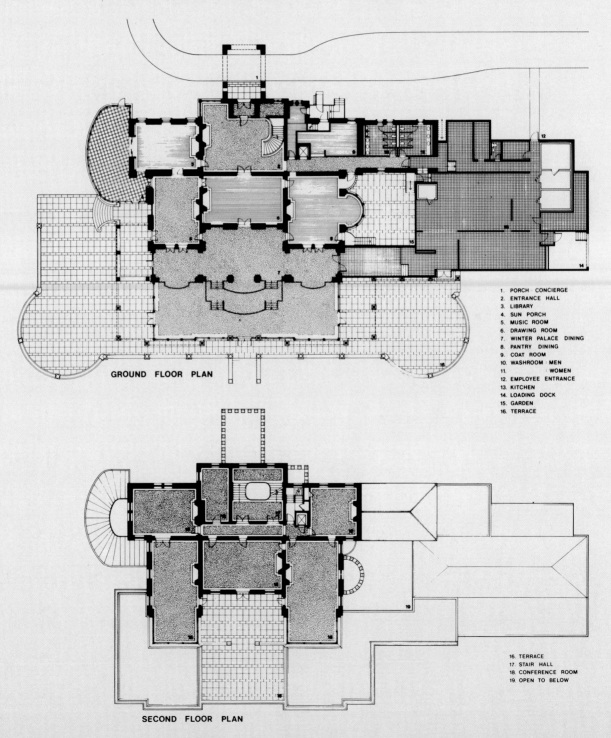

GROUND FLOOR PLAN

1. PORCH CONCIERGE
2. ENTRANCE HALL
3. LIBRARY
4. SUN PORCH
5. MUSIC ROOM
6. DRAWING ROOM
7. WINTER PALACE DINING
8. PANTRY DINING
9. COAT ROOM
10. WASHROOM MEN
11.   WOMEN
12. EMPLOYEE ENTRANCE
13. KITCHEN
14. LOADING DOCK
15. GARDEN
16. TERRACE

SECOND FLOOR PLAN

16. TERRACE
17. STAIR HALL
18. CONFERENCE ROOM
19. OPEN TO BELOW

suited than are hotels to larger groups and private functions and may be perceived as less attractive to transient business guests. Developers must be certain that feasibility and site issues are fully explored before investing large sums of money in a proposed project. Although conference centers are similar in many ways to more traditional commercial hotels, especially suburban properties, developers must analyze the site characteristics and specific market conditions with full recognition of the important differences between hotels and conference centers. They must emphasize these differences in order for conference centers to adequately differentiate themselves and fully establish their presence.

Executive centers perform strongest in actively growing commercial and upscale residential communities, convenient to interstate highways and a major airport. Scanticon, the Princeton, New Jersey, developer and management company has established a list of preferred location criteria, including:

☐ Four million square feet (372,000 square meters) of occupied office space no more than ten minutes away

☐ A large concentration of high-end residential properties no more than ten minutes away

☐ A major highway no more than five minutes away

☐ A substantial town center (to provide shopping, restaurants, and other options) no more than fifteen minutes away

☐ A major airport no more than an hour away, and closer if possible.

The site, perhaps on the edge of an office park, must reinforce the resort image. One way to accomplish this seemingly impossible task is to allocate sufficient ground area to the conference center so that it is enclosed in woods or set on the edge of a pond. Scanticon has been careful to protect its conference centers: Princeton is on a fifteen-acre site; the Minneapolis and Denver facilities feature protected view corridors, one over a wildfowl marsh, the other with views toward the snowcapped Rocky Mountains.

Conference centers require substantially more area than do traditional hotels. Table 2–2 illustrates the allocation of space at several of the more prominent executive facilities built within the last decade. For most projects the total area ranges between about 950 and 1,025 square feet (88.3 and 95.3 square meters) per room. (The smallest property, Peachtree, has

planned a conference addition of 20,000 square feet [1,860 square meters].) The additional floor area—typical hotels are in the 650 to 800 square feet (60.4 to 74.4 square meters) per room range—is allocated to conference space and related assembly and support functions, more spacious dining areas, and complete fitness facilities.

The more typical executive conference centers have 200–300 guestrooms of about 300 to 350 net square feet (28 to 32.5 net square meters) each, with a small number of larger suites. The rooms, with corridors and support areas increasing the space to 500 to 525 *gross* square feet (46.5 to 48.8 gross square meters) per room, encompass just over half of the total project area.

Lobby, dining, lounge, and other public facilities are about 10 percent of the total facility. The lobby often is about 15 square feet (1.4 square meters) per room, with the conference dining area between 15 and 25 square feet (1.4 and 2.3 square meters) per room and the total of all the restaurants and lounges about 30–50 square feet (2.7–4.6 square meters) per room. The food outlets make an important contribution to the conference objectives by providing the opportunity for participants to discuss the sessions and expand their friendships. At the market-driven executive centers, the food and beverage offerings are a key competitive tool.

Most important among the facilities is the conference core, which averages 200–250 square feet (18.6–23.2 square meters) per room and comprises about 20 percent of the project area. Although the majority of this is salable meeting space, as much as a third to a half of the space is devoted to conference assembly and such support functions as conference services, audiovisual rooms, and storage. Executive centers usually feature a ballroom or large banquet space, to accommodate special conference functions as well as local business. Because the principal market, though, is groups of fewer than one hundred people, most of the conference area is devoted to medium and large (1,000–2,000 square feet [93–186 square meters]) conference rooms and breakout rooms (200–500 square feet [18.6–46.5 square meters]).

Recreational facilities may vary from a full-fledged health and fitness center, such as at the Scanticon-Minneapolis property (72 square feet [6.7 square meters] per room), to a fairly typical indoor pool and exercise room, a range of from 6 to less than 2 percent of the project area. Most executive centers include a pool,

TABLE 2-2. EXECUTIVE CONFERENCE CENTERS, SAMPLE PROGRAMS IN SQUARE FEET (SQUARE METERS)

	Hamilton Park Florham Park, NJ (219 guestrooms)	Radisson Ypsilanti, MI (233 guestrooms)	Scanticon Minneapolis, MN (244 guestrooms)	Peachtree Peachtree City, GA (254 guestrooms)	Scanticon Princeton, NJ (292 guestrooms)	Westfields Westfields, VA (342 guestrooms)
Guestrooms	110,200 (10,249)	118,300 (11,002)	126,500 (11,765)	120,100 (11,169)	137,700 (12,806)	172,100 (16,005)
Public areas	19,700 (1,832)	24,500 (2,278)	24,400 (2,269)	25,500 (2,371)	42,300 (3,934)	31,300 (2,911)
Conference areas	43,800 (4,073)	53,900 (5,013)	61,200 (5,692)	38,600 (3,590)	60,100 (5,589)	74,700 (6,947)
Administrative areas	8,500 (790)	2,800 (260)	8,400 (781)	7,100 (660)	3,700 (344)	8,700 (809)
Back-of-house areas	21,000 (1,953)	24,600 (2,288)	53,900 (5,013)	23,900 (2,223)	47,000 (4,371)	45,900 (4,269)
Recreation	11,800 (1,097)	3,200 (298)	17,700 (1,646)	9,900 (921)	7,100 (660)	5,000 (465)
Total	215,000 (19,995)	227,300 (21,139)	292,100 (27,165)	225,100 (20,934)	297,900 (27,705)	337,700 (31,406)
Average per room	982 (91)	975 (90)	1,198 (111)	886 (82)	1,020 (95)	987 (92)

aerobics and exercise rooms, at least two racquetball courts, sauna, and lockers.

Schematic planning follows traditional organization, with the lobby acting as a central hub of the public, conference, and lodging sections. Most developers and operators want to expose the public to as much of the center as possible and therefore route all traffic through the lobby rather than providing a separate conference or function entrance, as in many hotels. (However, if local catering business is anticipated and the site permits, there may be separate ballroom access.) Because conference schedules often preclude extensive recreational activity, some centers promote the sports complex to the community, and often the recreational facilities are sited to allow public access for this purpose.

Executive Retreats. A few executive centers offer the meeting planner an unusual alternative for small conferences. The executive retreats, some with only twenty or so rooms and limited public facilities, often are located in converted estates or on remote rustic sites. In fact, many of the larger and more prominent executive conference centers (Harrison Glen Cove, Harrison Lake Bluff, Tarrytown House, and Graylyn) were established on former estates with just such limited facilities and later grew to meet the needs of the maturing conference market.

One typical executive retreat is located outside of Buffalo, where local hoteliers in 1988 established Beaver Hollow in the former Bethlehem Steel corporate retreat and refurbished it to serve business clients seeking an exclusive and private setting. The thirty-two room property is available only to a single customer at one time, assuring confidentiality and uninterrupted use of the three meeting rooms. The dining room is dominated by a massive stone fireplace and beamed ceiling and offers access to a dining and assembly terrace overlooking the wooded grounds and small lake. Situated on 140 acres, the distraction-free setting focuses the conferees' attention on the business of the day.

Many retreats offer unique features. The Garrett Creek Executive Conference Center in Paradise, Texas, provides twenty-six rooms in a facility that combines the ambience of a working ranch with the services of a first-class conference retreat. Near Tucson is the thirty-room Sunspace Ranch, located on 2,300 acres (930.7 hectares) in the foothills of the Santa Catalina mountains. The conference center includes Biosphere II, a 2.5-acre (1-hectare), glass-covered ecology research project, which is the focus of many of the conference groups. More traditional is the Henry Chauncey Conference Center in Princeton, operated by the Educational Testing Service, a 100-room facility that includes the Laurie House, a beautifully restored farmhouse that can accommodate up to fifteen people in a private setting and on a totally independent schedule.

These miniature conference centers, offering a secluded setting for a business meeting or staff retreat, create the residential environment conducive to a productive meeting. The dining room often becomes the center of activ-

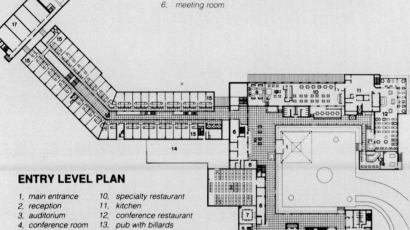

CONFERENCE WING SECTIONS

1.	banquet room	7.	conference lobby
2.	restaurant	8.	office
3.	restaurant lobby	9.	service corridor
4.	conference room	10.	reception
5.	control room	11.	conference restaurant
6.	meeting room		

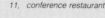

ENTRY LEVEL PLAN

1.	main entrance	10.	specialty restaurant
2.	reception	11.	kitchen
3.	auditorium	12.	conference restaurant
4.	conference room	13.	pub with billards
5.	control room	14.	earth covered terrace
6.	offices	15.	hotel guest rooms
7.	board room	16.	atrium
8.	fireside lounge	17.	racquetball courts
9.	bar	18.	swimming pool

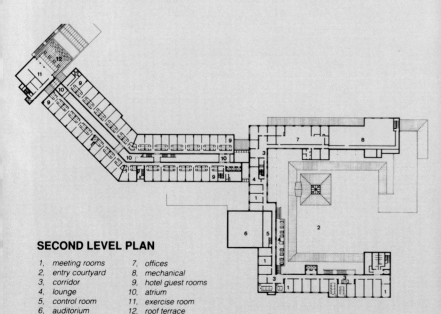

SECOND LEVEL PLAN

1.	meeting rooms	7.	offices
2.	entry courtyard	8.	mechanical
3.	corridor	9.	hotel guest rooms
4.	lounge	10.	atrium
5.	control room	11.	exercise room
6.	auditorium	12.	roof terrace

SCANTICON - MINNEAPOLIS

Like the earlier Princeton property, the second Scanticon center is organized around an arrival court marked by a sweeping porte cochere, with the several dining and beverage outlets situated to the north side of the lobby and the 300-person auditorium and 31 additional conference and breakout rooms located on the south. The most spectacular space is the six-story residential atrium, with the 240 guestrooms arranged along single-loaded corridors on either side, connected by bridges across the interior street leading to the fitness center. The room decor reinforces the character of the public spaces, with strong solid colors and custom wood casepieces. The 70,000 square foot (6,510 square meter) recreational complex includes an indoor pool, four racquetball courts, and aerobics and exercise rooms. Located within a suburban office park northwest of Minneapolis, the 21-acre (8.5-hectare) site initially was not seriously considered because of the extensive wetlands; however, the architects conceived a scheme to protect the marshes and, in fact, situated the dining rooms, lounges, and half the guestrooms to take advantage of the open vistas. (Architect: Friis Moltke Larson with BRW Architects; interiors: Klenow Deichmann and Overbye with Daroff Design; photos: Ron Solomon.)

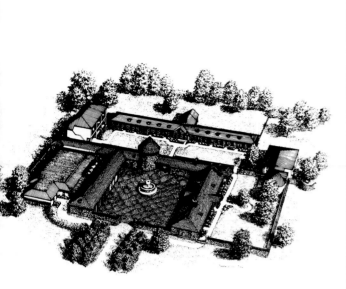

Graylyn Conference Center, Winston-Salem, North Carolina. Opened in 1984 following a four-year restoration and conversion, Graylyn features a Norman Revival building designed in 1928 by local architect Luther S. Lashmit for tobacco executive Bowman Gray, whose family donated the 55-acre (22.3-hectare) property to Wake Forest University in 1972. The main building houses 45 guestrooms, many of them wood-paneled and furnished with antiques, and a variety of luxurious public spaces. The Mews—formerly service spaces including the stable, forge, and hen houses—were renovated in 1989 to create additional lodging and conference space. The stone quadrangle offers many unique rooms, predominantly king-bedded, some with fireplaces, all opening onto balconies, private patios, gardens, or the cobbled courtyard. In total, Graylyn offers 94 rooms, four major conference rooms with extensive audio-visual features, 18 additional meeting and breakout rooms, and three elegant dining rooms. (Architect: Luther S. Lashmit; photos: Smith/Weiler/Smith.)

ity, the location for morning and afternoon breaks, cocktails, and evening gatherings. Such a dining room may offer fewer food choices than would be available at a larger center, but the cuisine usually is outstanding.

The few meeting rooms are fully equipped with the standard audio-visual systems. Recreation options vary depending on the site: fishing and jogging along the nature trail at Beaver Hollow, horseback riding at Garrett Creek, mountain climbing at Sunspace Ranch, bicycling at the Laurie House. Tennis or basketball may be available at the center, with golf privileges usually nearby.

Ancillary Conference Centers. The conference center industry, which has set high standards for accommodations, meeting rooms, dining, and recreation, as well as high expectations for conference services and technical assistance, is naturally dubious of the quality of conferences hosted by properties self-termed *hotel and conference centers*. Nevertheless, there are many properties that strike a balance between a typical full-service transient and convention hotel and an executive conference center, with the latter carefully set off in separate wing or on particular floors. Unlike many of the executive conference centers discussed earlier—which, although convenient and accessible, are intentionally distant from highways and airports to protect the setting—some developers and operators have established executive conference center facilities at airport and suburban hotel locations. Such centers must offer sufficient separation from the hotel operations in order for the conference center to have a distinct identity and a low level of distractions.

One of the first centers of this type was the Dallas–Fort Worth Airport Hilton, which opened in 1983. The 400-room hotel includes a separate two-story conference center wing housing three amphitheaters, fifteen meeting and breakout rooms, and a dedicated conference dining room and lounge. More recently, in 1986, Hilton created Conference Center 1 on the ground floor of the 420-room Woodfield Hilton near Chicago's O'Hare Airport. Located under the guestroom structure, where its layout is existing columns and limited ceiling height, the center includes fourteen conference rooms (the largest two of about 1,100 square feet each), two board rooms, and a small private dining room adjoining them. Newer still is the Atlanta Airport Hilton, at which a separate entrance give access to eight

conference rooms, a 150-seat amphitheater, and full conference support services.

A relatively new type of hotel conference center opened in mid-1990 in midtown Manhattan: a large urban hotel with a dedicated executive conference center, vertically stacked on four floors. Located within the luxury 638-room Hotel Macklowe, the conference center offers high-quality conference rooms, the typical buffet-service conference dining, and full conference services in a high-density, urban location. It is distinct from other hotels and conference facilities, which usually are one of several types: convention hotels with huge multipurpose ballrooms oriented to large groups, commercial hotels with small meeting and banquet rooms positioned to attract transient business, non-residential centers with no lodging focuses toward the shorter day meetings, and suburban executive conference centers, which do not offer the convenience of the downtown location.

DESIGN CONSIDERATIONS

Among the most important design challenges is differentiating the executive conference center from the surrounding hotel competition. While this goal can be partially accomplished by providing additional conference space and by siting the project on more generous and fully landscaped suburban tracts, often as part of a larger office park development, the design of the individual functional areas must reinforce the image of a business meeting center. Some critics find this environment too harsh, too institutional or commercial; architects or designers therefore may be called upon to soften the look to attract the other market segments.

Guestrooms. The executive conference centers that have been built recently in the United States are very similar in terms of the number of rooms and the overall quality of the lodging. The individual units are larger than those in corporate and university centers, slightly smaller than those in resort properties. Because of the growing emphasis on transient and weekend business, the 300 to 350 square foot (27.9 to 32.5 square meter) rooms feature either a king or two double beds. Because of the high levels of single occupancy, the emphasis should be on king beds. The designer must remember, though, to provide room elements that support the conference theme, including a superior work area, an oversized desk, two phone lines (to allow for computer connections), and high lighting levels.

EXECUTIVE CONFERENCE CENTERS   33

This midtown Manhattan center opened in 1990, with a self-contained conference center located on four lower floors of the 52-story Hotel Macklowe. Access is gained from separate lobby elevators or a marble-clad grand stair leading to the conference foyer. The 100,000 square foot (9,300 square meter) meeting center includes 33 dedicated conference rooms equipped with complete audiovisual capability, a videoconferencing facility, and a business center. The conference dining room subdivides into four private rooms when special groups require additional privacy. The property also includes the landmark Hudson Theater, which is available for special presentations and such events as the 1990 World Chess Championship. (Architect and interiors: Perkins & Will; exterior and meeting room photo: Elliott Kaufman; lobby photo: Jim Morse.)

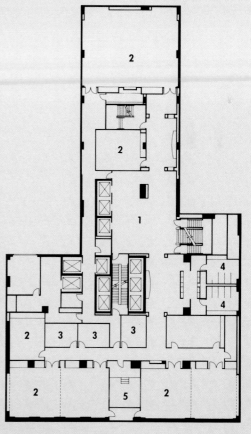

Legend
1. Conference foyer
2. Conference room
3. Breakout room
4. Toilets
5. Audiovisuals

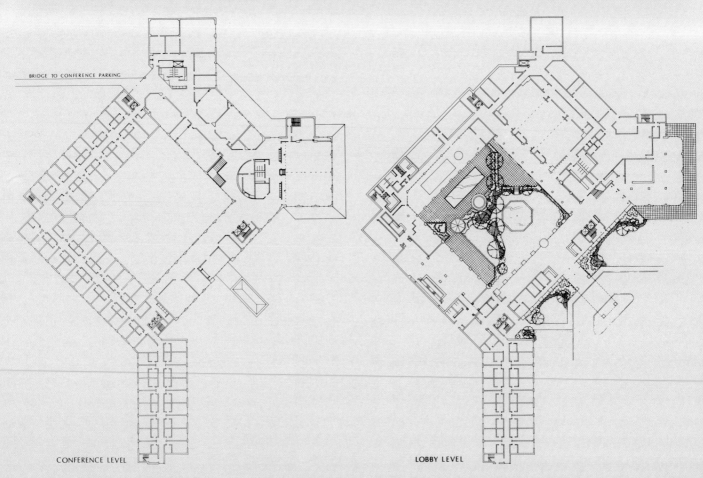

BRIDGE TO CONFERENCE PARKING

CONFERENCE LEVEL

LOBBY LEVEL

HAMILTON PARK
EXECUTIVE CONFERENCE CENTER

Located in Florham Park, New Jersey, west of New York City, Hamilton Park was conceived to meet the needs of the suburban corporate market, as determined by local focus groups who helped establish the conference room mix and specialized features. Three of the rooms incorporate rear-screen projection; another is permanently equipped as a computer lab. Opened in late 1988 on 13 acres (5.3 hectares) at the edge of Fairleigh Dickinson University, the low-rise project contains 219 guestrooms, including 23 suites, as well as a number of dialogue centers, where participants can gather informally. Many of the public spaces are oriented around a central courtyard, which, in addition to the outdoor pool, doubles as extended prefunction space and outdoor lounge seating. A second lounge and game room provide a social center adjoining the fitness complex. (Architect and interiors: Richard J. Cureton; photos: Jerry Pecknold, Jeff Cowan.)

Executive centers do not emphasize informal gathering as do corporate and university centers, where group work is expected. However, the developer and designer should be alert to opportunities to provide either commons areas (perhaps near the elevator lobby or at the joint between low-rise wings) or adequate lounge seating within the guestrooms for informal discussions. The latter is difficult to accomplish, given the budgetary pressures the larger room bays tend to create on the project. Therefore, siting the commons areas within the guestroom wing, as is the case at Hamilton Park, is more practical.

If it appears that a higher number of informal meeting places are necessary, the design team should look for other solutions. It may be possible to provide a small number of breakout rooms, furnished as a meeting space, within the guestroom block. While this arrangement is less convenient during the day for groups moving from large sessions to small breakouts, it should not be a major problem for groups to walk to a remote location. The main advantage of this scheme is that these rooms provide a real amenity in the evening, providing attendees with access to a small meeting space close to their rooms. Alternatively, full guestroom bays, each with a bathroom and furnished as a suite living room, might connect to one or two bedrooms. While there is little call for suites in executive conference centers, the middle room can be used flexibly, either as a commons area open to all guests or as a breakout room assigned to a specific meeting group, but still be available for suite accommodations, particularly as part of special weekend promotional packages.

The suite-hotel trend so prominent in first-class and midprice markets has not overtaken the conference center industry. Again, given the high cost of providing and equipping the conference core, developers usually cannot justify additional floor area in the guestrooms. The Northland Inn in Minneapolis, however, built on the model of an Embassy Suites hotel, complete with its midrise atrium, glass elevators, and 450 square foot (41.8 square meter) suites, illustrates just such a project. Early in its development, the lowrise wing was completely redesigned to accommodate the special conference and banquet needs of an executive conference center.

Public Areas. The conference center lobby provides the first opportunity for creating a special mood to reinforce the property's meet-

ing focus. Most executive centers, unlike larger hotels, make a point of routing all guests through the center lobby to create an awareness of the complete facility, rather than using a separate conference foyer for day business. The Scanticon projects establish a Danish theme that is prevalent throughout each of the centers, extending into the guestroom and recreational wings as well. Hamilton Park and Doral Arrowwood, both suburban New York properties, duplicate the feel of a suburban hotel but with a less highly decorated look. In each property, the design approach establishes an initial character that continues throughout the other public areas and conference space.

The food and beverage outlets need to be designed flexibly to accomodate meeting groups, transients, and social functions. For example, part of the lobby lounge is often set aside for small group parties. Many centers develop a lounge with two or more separate parts, an arrangement that easily permits special functions without discriminating against the individual guest. The architect and designer should consider the possibilities for creating small distinct areas, such as raised platforms, sunken seating wells, fireplace lounges, and so forth. Similarly, the dining rooms should permit sections to be separated for private parties. (See Scanticon-Minneapolis, earlier in this chapter.)

The conference dining room typically is set up with several hot and cold buffet tables, including a grill at which breakfast and lunch items are cooked to order, and is usually designed with several distinct eating areas so that

Northland Inn Executive Conference Center, Brooklyn Park, Minnesota. The first all-suite conference center, the 230-room Northland Inn is modeled after Embassy Suites, with dining areas and lounges occupying the multistory lobby atrium. The property features two ballrooms, an amphitheater, a boardroom, and 7 conference and 11 breakout rooms in a two-story conference wing. (Architect and interiors: Wudtke Watson Associates; photo by the author.)

small groups can be seated together with some sense of privacy and exclusivity. The atrium at the Northland Inn houses its conference dining room, which also extends under the guestroom structure. The result is a series of dining spaces—some, open pavilions in the lobby; others, more private areas in the lower-ceilinged section.

Executive centers need to provide for such special events as opening cocktail receptions, theme parties, and final dinners, which are common features of high-profile meetings. Rather than using private dining rooms or portions of the ballroom, many meeting planners prefer to schedule these events in the specialty or gourmet dining room. These rooms should be designed to take up to forty people and still provide a high-quality dining atmosphere for

the other patrons. The banquet functions are particularly important, as they create opportunities—not only for generating additional revenues, but for establishing a memorable experience that makes the conference center attractive for repeat business.

Conference and Training Areas. The conference space in executive centers is generally used for management development, executive training, and sales meetings, with an emphasis on interactive management education.

Most executive properties incorporate one or two larger rooms in excess of 2,000 square feet (186 square meters), several medium-size rooms, and a large number of breakout rooms. Most common are conference rooms designed for twenty-five to forty people (requiring

TABLE 2-3. EXECUTIVE CONFERENCE CENTERS, CONFERENCE CORE SPACE PROGRAMS IN NET SQUARE FEET (NET SQUARE METERS)[a]

	Hamilton Park Florham Park, NJ (219 guestrooms)	Radisson Ypsilanti, MI (233 guestrooms)	Scanticon Minneapolis, MN (244 guestrooms)	Peachtree Peachtree City, GA (254 guestrooms)	Scanticon Princeton, NJ (292 guestrooms)	Westfields Westfields, VA (342 guestrooms)
Ballroom	1 @ 4,700 (437)	1 @ 6,800 (632)	1 @ 3,800 (353)	1 @ 5,400 (502)	1 @ 3,000 (279)	1 @ 9,200 (856) 1 @ 7,800 (725) 1 @ 5,300 (493)
Large conference[b]	1 @ 4,400 (409)	1 @ 2,100 (195)	1 @ 4,200 (391)	1 @ 3,200 (298)	1 @ 5,000 (465) 1 @ 3,000 (279) 1 @ 2,400 (223) 2 @ 1,900 (177)	None
Medium conference[c]	1 @ 1,400 (130) 2 @ 1,200 (111) 2 @ 1,100 (102)	1 @ 1,225 (114) 2 @ 1,000 (93)	2 @ 1,400 (130) 1 @ 1,150 (107)	None	2 @ 1,200 (112)	None
Small conference[d]	2 @ 975 (91) 1 @ 700 (65)	3 @ 725 (67)	4 @ 975 (91) 1 @ 750 (70)	2 @ 975 (91) 2 @ 775 (72)	2 @ 900 (84)	4 @ 700 (65) 1 @ 575 (53)
Breakout	4 @ 450 (42) 3 @ 275 (26)	2 @ 375 (35) 3 @ 225 (21)	5 @ 375 (35) 14 @ 275 (26) 2 @ 175 (16)	2 @ 375 (35) 4 @ 250 (23)	10 @ 450 (42) 2 @ 300 (28) 14 @ 225 (21)	None
Boardroom	1 @ 625 (58)	1 @ 725 (67)	2 @ 750 (70)	1 @ 700 (65) 1 @ 375 (35)	2 @ 700 (65)	1 @ 800 (74)
Amphitheater	None	1 @ 3,600 (335)	None	1 @ 3,000 (279)	None	1 @ 2,550 (237)
Auditorium	None	None	None	None	None	None
Computer/special	None	1 @ 1,625[e] (151[e])	None	None	None	None
Total conference	20,025 (1,862)	21,675 (2,016)	24,175 (2,248)	17,925 (1,667)	31,050 (2,888)	29,025 (2,699)
Total assembly	9,400 (874)	11,300 (1,051)	9,600 (893)	5,400 (502)	9,500 (884)	15,100 (1,404)
Total support	4,700 (437)	5,300 (493)	10,500 (977)	6,400 (595)	9,100 (846)	12,200 (1,135)

[a]Some program areas are rounded and averaged to simplify the presentation.
[b]Larger than 1,500 square feet (139 square meters).
[c]Between 1,000 and 1,500 square feet (93 and 139 square meters).
[d]Between 500 and 1,000 square feet (46 and 93 square meters).
[e]Computer classroom

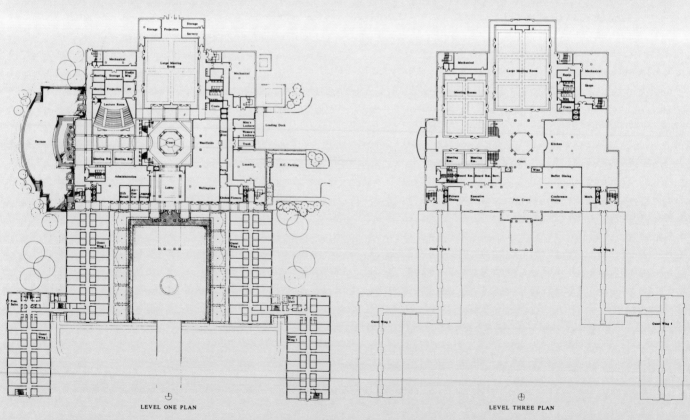

LEVEL ONE PLAN

LEVEL THREE PLAN

Located in Westfields, Virginia, only minutes from Washington's Dulles International Airport, the elegantly finished and furnished Westfields is situated in the midst of a new 1,100-acre (445-hectare) corporate park. The exterior replicates the feel of colonial Virginia and its large estates. Since opening in 1989, the 340-room conference center has catered to the numerous government and association meetings in the region. The lobby rotunda dominates the interior and establishes a "sense of place" that visually connects the lounges on the ground floor, the restaurants on the upper level, and the conference spaces, which include three large multifunction rooms, the 200-seat Lincoln Forum, a "classified briefing auditorium" with complete front and rear projection and simultaneous translation capabilities, seven smaller conference rooms, and five conference suites. The health facility on the lower level includes an indoor pool, an exercise room, and a complete health spa; eight outdoor tennis courts are nearby. (Architect: Perkins & Will; interiors: Chandler Cudlipp; photos: Peter Vitale, courtesy of International Conference Resorts.)

about 1,000 square feet, or 93 square meters), each of which might need up to four to six breakout rooms, putting great pressure on the space program and gross area requirements. Although many operators and conference planners disdain movable partitions, one solution is to accept some subdivisibility in the breakouts, perhaps dividing a 600 square foot (55.8 square meter) room, just big enough for smaller meetings, into two spaces for small group sessions.

Few executive conference centers contain amphitheaters, because they must offer a high degree of flexibility for the wide range of customer programs they attract. While helpful for differentiating the property from competitors, many developers feel that amphitheaters cost too much to build for the use they receive. Most developers of executive conference centers prefer to invest in additional multipurpose conference rooms and breakout rooms. Examples of conference core space programs are illustrated in Table 2–3.

A key question always is the relative importance of audiovisual systems and other technological backup. Some operators believe that every room should have full audiovisual capability; most owners, however, accept the compromise of providing built-in video and projection systems only in selected spaces, probably the two or three largest meeting rooms. Service to the other conference areas is provided by portable equipment, making use of hard-wired connections among the spaces. The decision is based on comparing the capital and operating costs of the two options: for one, there is a substantial cost for providing the dedicated space, purchasing the systems, and maintaining the equipment, costs that can never be realistically recovered from rental fees; the expectation is that the system will generate additional business at higher rates. For the other, the main expense is the comparatively lower cost of portable equipment, its maintenance, and the labor to move it to and from rooms as requested by the customers.

Scanticon fully equips their executive centers with a projection room between each pair of conference rooms and a major audiovisual distribution room at the "auditorium," a flat-floored multipurpose conference room used for large lecture sessions (both theater- and classroom-style), exhibits, and occasional receptions. The Scanticon projects in Princeton and Minneapolis each have about 4,000 square feet (372 square meters) dedicated to audiovisual, graphics, and projection rooms;

Doral Arrowwood has a similar amount of space. The more common allocation is 1,500 to 1,800 square feet (139.5 to 167.4 square meters).

Many of the executive conference centers include a boardroom, usually a high-profile space because of its upgraded finishes and furniture. Many owners believe such rooms to be less necessary in executive conference centers because of the facilities' overall high-quality, built-in systems and the soundproofing of the standard meeting rooms, factors that make a formal boardroom less essential. When present, the boardroom may adjoin a private anteroom or lounge and have its own private toilets, telephones, pantry, and other services.

Assembly and prefunction areas are divided among the conference areas so that the larger rooms, especially, have break spaces nearby. Including the area devoted to serving refreshments, these should be big enough to comfortably accommodate the full capacity of the largest conference room. While the break areas need to provide open space for informal gathering, they should also contain enough seating to allow for extended conversations. When possible, the foyer or break areas should open onto terraces, so that the groups can move outside in good weather.

A few executive centers feature a conference lounge, where attendees can meet without the distractions common in the prefunction areas. The lounge should be furnished with a combination of couch and chair groupings and at least one small conference table or two writing desks. Such a room might also be used by speakers as a quiet room for last-minute preparations, although it is preferable to set aside one or two small offices for this purpose. At other times, these offices might be provided to the visiting meeting planner.

The conference concierge is now a feature in practically all conference properties but was first developed in executive centers. The concierge, or conference coordinator, works at a kiosk or desk at the entrance to the conference core or at some similarly central location. This person answers questions, passes on messages, handles minor secretarial duties (including copying, sending faxes, and typing incidental work), and can summon assistance, such as audiovisual technicians or other staff. The concierge is supported by the conference planners assigned to each meeting. They require individual offices, three or four in most projects, either in the conference wing or among the sales offices.

Recreation Facilities. Recreational amenities are essential to establishing a relaxed learning atmosphere, especially for lengthier programs. The earliest executive conference centers had little more than an indoor pool and small exercise area, but current facilities include racquetball courts, major exercise and aerobics rooms, jogging tracks, and lockers with saunas or steam rooms. Often the meeting planners schedule fitness programs as part of the conference, in response to the corporate concerns for health and to provide a more active component to the day's meeting schedule. Some of the more recent projects provide a larger number of racquetball or squash courts, more substantial spa facilities, a casual restaurant or snack bar, and give greater design emphasis to the entrance to the health club, sometimes making it available to limited public use during the day. (See Doral Arrowwood, Chapter 3, and Scanticon-Minneapolis, earlier in this chapter.)

The Houstonian Hotel & Conference Center, Houston, Texas. Located near downtown on a 22-acre (8.9-hectare) campus, the Houstonian is an urban resort combining 300 guestrooms, 17 suites, 34 meeting rooms, and extensive fitness facilities, including health programs tailored to a particular meeting. (Architect: KWA; interiors: Mary Anne Bryan; photo: Steve Brady.)

Peachtree Executive Conference Center, Peachtree City, Georgia. Located south of Atlanta, Peachtree offers 254 guestrooms and a complete conference wing with two ballrooms, an amphitheater, and a variety of smaller conference and breakout rooms, many opening onto dedicated terraces or overlooking the landscaped grounds. (Architect: Rabun Hatch & Associates; interiors: Jeffrey Howard; photo courtesy of Rabun Hatch.)

CHAPTER 3

Resort Conference Centers

Meeting planners increasingly are recognizing the value of balancing an intensive meeting program with recreational activities or team-building exercises. Catering primarily to corporate and business clients, resort conference centers are ideal settings for management development meetings, marketing or sales meetings, new product launches, and incentive trips. While some attract a national audience, many new properties are marketed most heavily on a regional basis. For companies influenced by a meeting's transportation costs, the regional resort conference centers can offer an amenity package that far outstrips competing executive properties. Many analysts anticipate continued growth in the resort segment, especially on the outskirts of northern cities where much of the business originates—areas that don't yet have a full complement of resort properties.

This optimistic outlook continues despite the additional capital costs required for land and recreational facilities. The reason is simple: Competition is so keen for the high-end business meeting and the weekend and off-season vacation market that the recreational facilities and extra amenities of resort confer-

ence centers are critical to a property's ability to attract business. Indeed, not only are new resort centers being developed, but executive centers are adding resort facilities and amenities to better compete with them. In addition, many existing resorts are adding conference facilities to attract the small meetings market, further blurring the distinctions among different lodging types aiming to attract both recreational and meeting markets.

The evolution of the resort conference center can be traced back to the early 1970s. Harrison, a conference center management company, opened a conference center and inn at Heritage Village in Southbury, Connecticut, in 1971, offering a combination of extensive meeting facilities with a country-club setting, complete with golf and tennis. The next year, the Scottsdale Conference Resort opened in Arizona and established the early standard for resort conference facilities, partly because of its size (352 rooms and forty-five meeting rooms) and superior location. One of the finest resort properties, The Woodlands Inn Resort and Conference Center opened in 1974 on the edge of an artificial lake created within an oak and pine forest outside Houston. Part of a mixed-use residential, office, and recreation

Scottsdale Conference Resort, Scottsdale, Arizona. Opened in 1972, the Scottsdale resort combines spacious meeting rooms, multiple dining outlets, magnificent sports offerings (including two 18-hole golf courses), and oversized guestrooms. Slightly separated from the main complex are 12 five-bedroom *casitas*, providing a more secluded setting for small, private meetings. (Architect/designer: Chandler Cudlipp; photo: Peter Vitale, courtesy of International Conference Resorts.)

development on twenty-five thousand acres (10,116 hectares), the Woodlands Inn has gone through a series of renovations and expansion projects, the latest in 1989.

Among the most prominent and successful of all resort conference centers is Doral Arrowwood, located thirty minutes north of New York City. Built by Citicorp in 1983 for corporate training, the property evolved to compete first with nearby executive centers and, more recently, through the increased promotion of its recreational amenities (including a nine-hole golf course and large fitness center), with resort conference centers nationwide. Its success is a model to which many other projects aspire.

SITE AND MARKET CONSIDERATIONS

Resort conference centers are being developed at a wide range of locations: national and regional destinations, suburban locations, and as the centerpieces of larger land developments. In the first example, developers check existing resort destinations for characteristics making them suitable as conference properties: a nearby major airport; a substantial regional population base; varied shopping, cultural, or other nonrecreational attractions; and a suitable four-season climate. While major destinations like Palm Springs and Scottsdale offer one level of opportunity, less prominent ones such as Hilton Head, South Carolina, and Napa Valley, California, may provide a wider range of possibilities with less competition from major resorts. Some such destinations already have the resort infrastructure. For example, Benchmark opened The Resort at Squaw Creek early in 1991, in Squaw Valley, California, the site of the 1960 Winter Olympics. Combining equal numbers of guestrooms and suites, it offers a full complement of both winter and summer recreational activities in a spectacular mountain setting.

The most common setting for a resort conference facility is a suburban location, which must meet exactly the same site-selection criteria as do sites for executive centers. It may be selected because of its proximity to corporate offices, highways, or an airport, or for its natural beauty; regardless, it is essential that the site be sufficiently large and appropriate for resort development. Doral Arrowwood, for example, is within one mile of the Pepsico headquarters and two miles of General Foods, and practically adjoins the growing Westchester airport. But most importantly for its concept, the 100-acre (40.5-hectare) site establishes a sense of

Harrison Conference Center/Inn, Southbury, Connecticut (top left). After expanding in 1987, Harrison now includes 163 guestrooms, 27 conference rooms (four with rear projection), an 85-seat amphitheater, and a spectacular indoor fitness center. Outdoor enthusiasts can use the two golf courses, lighted tennis courts, pools, and jogging trails, all part of Heritage Village. (Photo courtesy of Harrison.)

The Woodlands Executive Conference Center and Resort, The Woodlands, Texas (center left). The relaxing environment of The Woodlands is enhanced by the two-story guestroom lodges, each with only 16 rooms, and the emphasis on recreation. Much of the 50,000 square feet (4,650 square meters) of dedicated meeting space adjoins the indoor tennis courts and health spa complex. (Architect: Edward Durell Stone; photo courtesy of Edward Durell Stone.)

Ojai Valley Inn and Country Club, Ojai, California (bottom left). Gracefully spread over 200 acres (80.9 hectares), this 218-room resort in 1987 added a conference center with eight meeting and boardrooms and a ballroom for over 500, surrounded by spacious terraces, and designed to complement the original 1923 Spanish-style inn. (Architect: DMJM; photo courtesy of Ojai Valley Inn.)

The Resort at Squaw Creek, Squaw Valley, California. This conference resort offers 418 rooms, almost half of them suites, in a spectacular mountain setting. The lobby features a massive stone fireplace; similar rugged design elements are incorporated into other public facilities. The conference rooms are located on the lower level, adjoining the conference dining room; two large ballrooms on the lobby floor support meetings as well as other group business. (Architect: Ward Young; interiors: Simon, Martin-Vegue, Winkelstein, Moris; rendering courtesy of Squaw Creek.)

seclusion, offers views of the wooded landscape, and has a small golf course. Convenient to Manhattan, the combination of setting and recreational amenities contributes to its success as a weekend resort. Outside Denver, Scanticon has constructed a 300-room resort conference center with marvelous meeting facilities, as well as four restaurants, three lounges, and recreational facilities highlighted by the popular Inverness golf course.

Some projects, primarily recent ones, are built as the centerpieces of larger developments. Outside Williamsburg, Virginia, adjoining its theme park and brewery operation, Anheuser-Busch has developed two thousand acres around the Kingsmill Conference Center, including a PGA championship golf course, sports club, and several hundred home sites. And near Austin, Barton Creek offers 154 oversized rooms in a spa and golf conference resort, again with additional residential development.

In addition to these resort conference center strategies, such major resorts as the Greenbrier, the Broadmoor, and LaCosta recently

have added conference centers to extend their seasons and compete with newer meeting properties, as have more intimate resorts in many parts of the country. For example, the Ojai Valley Inn in California, an elegant 60-year-old golf resort hidden in the mountains ninety minutes from Los Angeles, has added a conference building in the same stucco wall and red tile roof style as the original Spanish Mission-style complex.

As the resort conference center has grown in popularity and success, its market penetration has increased in several key segments. Originally intended to service the executive meeting at which recreational amenities were essential, today the facilities attract a wide variety of groups, including trade associations, academic institutions, professional seminars, and government organizations. The seasonal character of resorts influences their eventual economic success, however, and the additional investment in conference facilities and equipment, as well as the recreational amenities, often strains even the most conservative budget.

DORAL ARROWWOOD

Arguably one of the most successful conference centers, Doral Arrowwood is situated on 114 acres (46.1 hectares) in Rye Brook, New York, just 30 minutes north of New York City. Since opening in 1983, it has evolved from a corporate to an executive—resort center, a move made possible by its effective conference design and ability to integrate leisure activities into both the meeting day and the weekend. Its 276 guestrooms are located in two five-story wings extending beyond the recreational complex, effectively separating them from the conference and

food and beverage functions. A large audio-visual and media center is located at the entrance to the main conference core, including 15 meeting and breakout rooms and a 120-seat amphitheater; two separate conference areas each contribute an additional seven rooms, frequently used for more private meetings. Arrowwood also offers an unusually varied food and beverage program, with conference, gourmet, and private dining rooms, as well as lounges and a pub—game room. (Architect and interiors: The Hillier Group; photos: Jim D'Addio.)

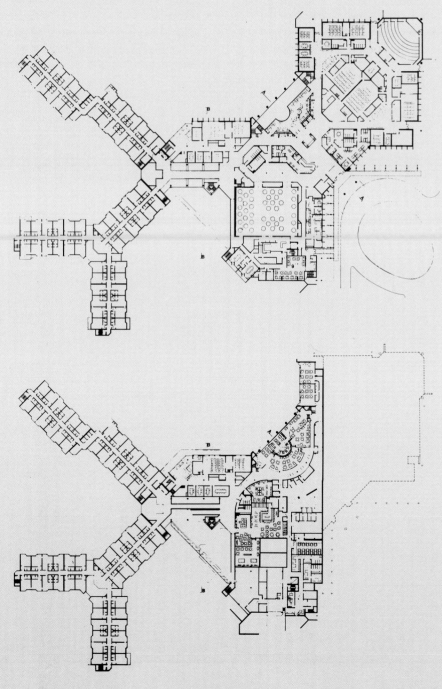

PROGRAM AND PLANNING CONSIDERATIONS

The site development issues are paramount for a resort center, and among the development team's first tasks should be a critical analysis of the opportunities and constraints of the physical site. The more seemingly problematic features often offer the most potential: Low-lying, marshy areas might be turned into a pond; ravines could be dramatically bridged with the approach road; or rock outcrops could be used to anchor such outlying recreational facilities as a golf or tennis club.

Early on, the site analysis should identify the optimum location for the main conference center building, based on views, accessibility, or reduced construction time or cost. The schematic site plan should include strategies for locating the approach and service drives, take into account the general massing of the building, determine whether the guestrooms will be part of the main structure, account for the parking and receiving areas, and identify locations of the recreational facilities. This generally requires the full cooperation of most of the development team—certainly the developer, architect, land planner, and operator—and possibly many of the other consultants.

Resort conference centers offer a number of conceptual opportunities that would be unusual at other types of properties. For example, the residential units are sometimes developed at a remote location, or the conference, dining, and recreation areas are separated into distinct buildings. This can lead to unique conceptual requirements, many of which are identified in Table 3–1. These need to be discussed thoroughly with the entire team, so that the design, engineering, operational, environmental, and investment objectives are addressed.

Generally, for resort conference centers, development of the site, recognition of opportunities inherent in the landscape, and discussion of resulting site goals (enhance views, hide parking or receiving, create dramatic approach, and so on) take precedence over the actual planning of the facility. This arrange-

LaCosta Hotel and Spa, Carlsbad, California. With 482 guestrooms and suites, LaCosta has a longstanding reputation for its resort and spa facilities. In 1987 the property added a 50,000 square foot (4,650 square meter) conference center, highlighted by an 8,000 square foot (744 square meter) ballroom, a 180-seat conference theater, and nine other meeting, breakout, and boardrooms. (Architect: WZMH; photo courtesy of LaCosta.)

TABLE 3-1. RESORT CONFERENCE CENTER CONCEPTUAL REQUIREMENTS

Project Aspect	Aims and Requirements
Siting	Develop the entry driveway to enhance guests' arrival; provide a major statement at the entry; hide parking and service functions; provide most guestrooms with a view; provide public areas with views of grounds or recreation
Guestrooms	Anticipate double occupancy for social and vacation business and mixed single and double occupancy for conferences; provide large room spaces each with oversized bathroom, clothes storage, seating and dining space; provide a terrace or patio where appropriate
Lobby	Establish "sense of place," tieing resort setting to conference theme; use local materials; organize circulation to aid visitors' movement through the project
Restaurants	Position conference dining room for views overlooking grounds; size specialty and gourmet restaurants based on market needs; provide lounges and informal dining at the recreational centers and an entertainment lounge for long-stay centers (especially ski resorts)
Conference rooms	Provide subdivisible ballroom necessary for meetings and social functions; also provide an amphitheater and a moderate number of meeting and breakout rooms
Conference support	Design foyer and break areas to open to the outside; locate conference services at conference core; provide basic audiovisual support but limited high-tech features
Recreation	Provide large complex with at least one major sport; provide additional outdoor activities (pool, tennis, etc.) if site and climate warrant; provide the usual health club, lockers, and so on indoors

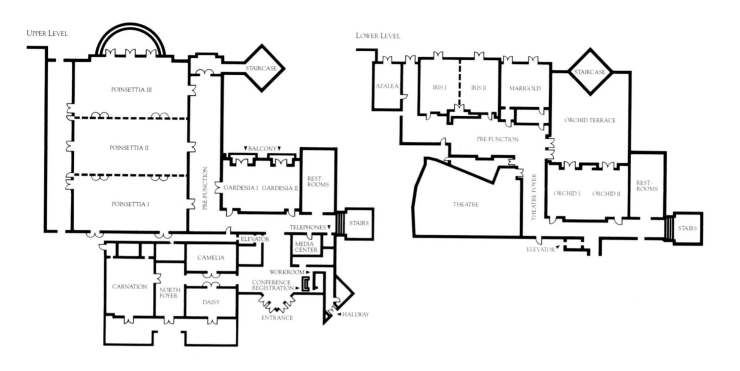

UPPER LEVEL

POINSETTIA III

POINSETTIA II

POINSETTIA I

PRE-FUNCTION

STAIRCASE

▼BALCONY▼

GARDENIA I GARDENIA II

REST-ROOMS

TELEPHONES▼

STAIRS

ELEVATOR

MEDIA CENTER

WORKROOM▶

CAMELIA

CONFERENCE REGISTRATION

CARNATION

NORTH FOYER

DAISY

ENTRANCE

▼HALLWAY

LOWER LEVEL

AZALEA

IRIS I IRIS II MARIGOLD

STAIRCASE

ORCHID TERRACE

PRE-FUNCTION

THEATRE

THEATRE FOYER

ORCHID I ORCHID II

REST-ROOMS

STAIRS

ELEVATOR▼

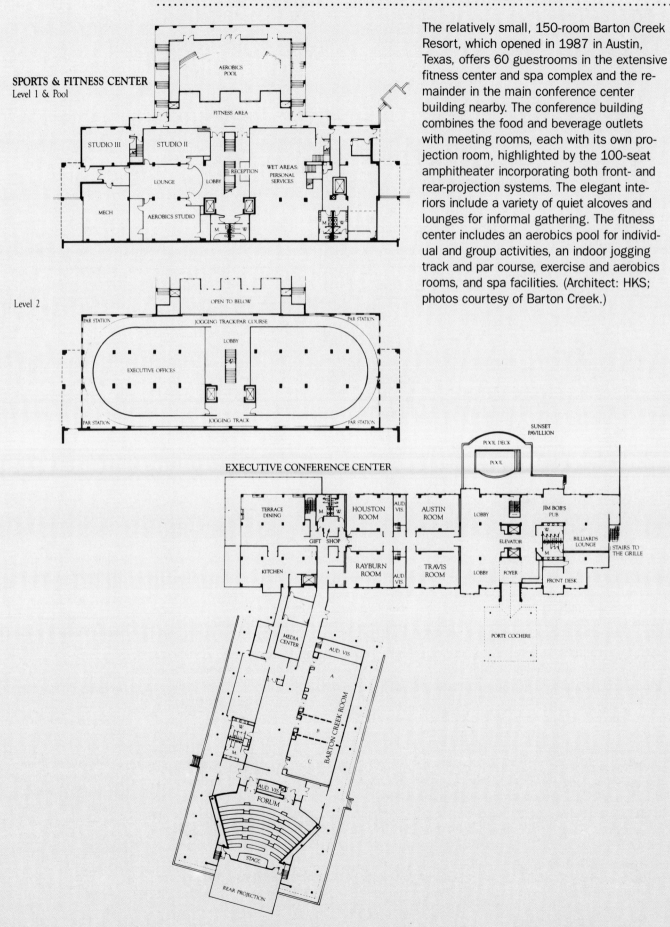

SPORTS & FITNESS CENTER
Level 1 & Pool

AEROBICS POOL

FITNESS AREA

STUDIO III

STUDIO II

LOUNGE

LOBBY

RECEPTION

WET AREAS: PERSONAL SERVICES

MECH

AEROBICS STUDIO

Level 2

OPEN TO BELOW

PAR STATION

JOGGING TRACK/PAR COURSE

PAR STATION

LOBBY

EXECUTIVE OFFICES

PAR STATION

JOGGING TRACK

PAR STATION

EXECUTIVE CONFERENCE CENTER

SUNSET PAVILLION

POOL DECK

POOL

TERRACE DINING

HOUSTON ROOM

AUD. VIS.

AUSTIN ROOM

LOBBY

JIM BOB'S PUB

GIFT SHOP

ELEVATOR

BILLIARDS LOUNGE

STAIRS TO THE GRILLE

KITCHEN

RAYBURN ROOM

AUD. VIS.

TRAVIS ROOM

LOBBY

FOYER

FRONT DESK

PORTE COCHERE

MEDIA CENTER

AUD VIS

A

BARTON CREEK ROOM

B

C

AUD VIS

FORUM

STAGE

REAR PROJECTION

The relatively small, 150-room Barton Creek Resort, which opened in 1987 in Austin, Texas, offers 60 guestrooms in the extensive fitness center and spa complex and the remainder in the main conference center building nearby. The conference building combines the food and beverage outlets with meeting rooms, each with its own projection room, highlighted by the 100-seat amphitheater incorporating both front- and rear-projection systems. The elegant interiors include a variety of quiet alcoves and lounges for informal gathering. The fitness center includes an aerobics pool for individual and group activities, an indoor jogging track and par course, exercise and aerobics rooms, and spa facilities. (Architect: HKS; photos courtesy of Barton Creek.)

ment does not hold true for most hotels, which are fairly compact, with public facilities closely grouped around the lobby or with restaurants and meeting rooms clustered around the kitchen and back-of-house areas; circulation issues and ease of access often determine the plan organization. With resorts, however, the building usually takes its form from the site. For example, Scanticon-Denver is a relatively narrow but long building, partly due to the site's configuration but, more importantly, because there are two primary views—one of the golf course to the east, the other of the Rocky Mountains to the west. Every guestroom has a dramatic view, and most of the restaurants, lounges, and banquet prefunction areas share similar visual contact with the outdoors.

A number of factors, including but not limited to the more extensive recreational facilities, influence the need for more floor area in resort conference centers when compared with executive properties—about 1,000 to 1,200 square feet (93 to 111.6 square meters) per room. In the residential wings, the individual guestroom units are somewhat larger, about 325 to 400 net square feet (30.2 to 37.2 net square meters) each; at some properties, the rooms are considerably larger, or there are more suites. For instance, at Barton Creek the typical room is 427 square feet (39.7 square meters), and at Squaw Creek, where half the units are suites, the most common plan is 622 square feet (57.8 square meters).

A second point of differentiation between resort and executive conference centers is the resort center's greater number and capacity of dining rooms and lounges. In many cases, these additional spaces are provided at the recreational centers, such as the golf or tennis club, and may be used largely by noncon-ference guests or club members. The main building at Kingsmill, for instance, contains only the conference dining room and an enter-tainment lounge; other outlets are available in

Landsdowne Confer-ence Resort, Leesburg, Virginia. Part of a 2,200-acre (890-hectare) mixed-use de-velopment, the 9-story, 310-room project, which opened in 1991, in-cludes 26 meeting rooms and a 135-seat amphitheater in one wing and an extensive fitness and sports club in the other. The lobby features an interior wa-terfall that leads guests to the dining rooms on the lower level. (Archi-tect: David Habib, Dew-berry & Davis; interiors: HKS; rendering courtesy of Lansdowne.)

the golf club and in the sports center, two separate buildings nearby. Squaw Creek has an informal café specifically for skiers; the Four Seasons in Irving, Texas, features a restaurant and lounge in the adjoining sports complex.

While resort centers' recreational facilities are generally larger as well, this is not always the case: At Squaw Creek, where the emphasis is on outdoor sports—skiing, skating, and swimming—the enclosed recreational component is less than 50 square feet (4.6 square meters) per room. However, the majority of the resort conference centers provide 50 to 200 square feet (18.6 square meters) per room in the swimming pool, racquet courts, aerobics and exercise rooms, health club or spa, and lockers. These amount to about 5 to 15 percent of the total project area. Indoor tennis, as provided at the Four Seasons and the executive Doubletree Hotel and Conference Center in St. Louis, raises the figure substantially.

The conference and meeting facilities usu-ally are somewhat smaller in the resort centers: about 125 to 200 square feet (11.6 to 18.6 square meters) per room, with at least 60 percent of this in salable space and the remainder in assembly and support areas. Many resorts include a ballroom, partly because of the focus toward marketing, sales, and incentive meetings, which are somewhat larger and feature special presentations and theme dinners. More resort conference centers also include an amphitheater, to further differentiate themselves from other resorts not fully equipped to serve the meetings market.

Other facilities are quite similar to executive centers. Although the food and beverage facilities may be more extensive, often the lobbies and other public facilities are smaller, primarily because most informal gatherings occur elsewhere. Administrative and back-of-house areas follow the normal rules of thumb. The space allocation for a sample group of resorts is illustrated in Table 3–2.

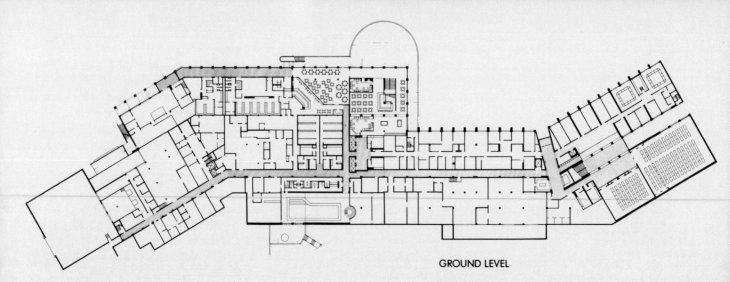

GROUND LEVEL

Located just south of Denver, Scanticon's third American property is its largest, with 301 rooms and 60,000 square feet (5,580 square meters) of conference space. Opened in 1989, with views of the Rockies on one side and the Inverness golf course on the other, the design of the resort conference center successfully separates the meeting, dining, banquet, and social functions from each other to help reduce the scale of the 367,000 square foot (34,131 square meter) project. The five-story lobby is flooded with daylight, with two skylit streets leading to the conference and banquet areas. The conference core features 33 meeting rooms, including 2 auditoriums, 8 conference rooms, 21 breakout rooms, and 2 boardrooms; several refreshment lounges are scattered throughout the area. Four restaurants and 4 lounges offer multiple dining options, with the conference and specialty restaurants featuring spectacular buffets. The top guestroom floor includes a club lounge and upgraded guestrooms and suites. (Architect: Friis Moltke Larson with RNL; interiors: Klenow Deichmann and Overbye; photos: Ron Solomon.)

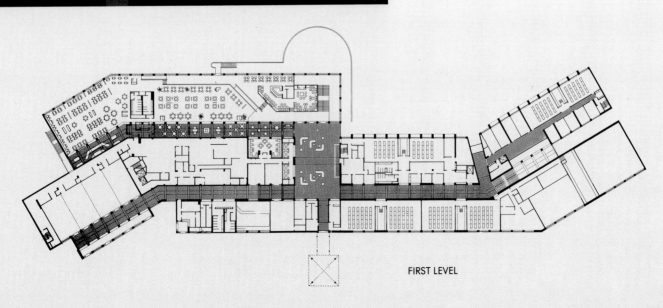

FIRST LEVEL

	Tega Cay[a] Charlotte, NC (267 guestrooms)	Doral Arrowwood Rye Brook, NY (276 guestrooms)	Scanticon Denver, CO (301 guestrooms)	Lansdowne Leesburg, VA (310 guestrooms)	Four Seasons Irving, TX (315 guestrooms)	Kingsmill Williamsburg, VA (361 guestrooms)
Guestrooms	129,200 (12,016)	152,300 (14,164)	152,900 (14,220)	163,500 (15,206)	208,700 (19,409)	202,500 (18,833)
Public areas	24,500 (2,279)	36,900 (3,432)	45,600 (4,241)	30,700 (2,855)	31,200 (2,902)	24,700 (2,297)
Conference areas	49,300 (4,585)	48,800 (4,538)	75,100 (6,984)	56,100 (5,217)	42,700 (3,971)	26,800 (2,492)
Administrative areas	6,300 (586)	5,700 (530)	9,300 (865)	7,000 (651)	10,200 (949)	8,400 (781)
Back-of-house areas	31,400 (2,920)	42,600 (3,962)	61,500 (5,720)	41,600 (3,869)	57,600 (5,357)	45,400 (4,222)
Recreation	13,700 (1,274)	12,800 (1,190)	23,600 (2,195)	29,700 (2,762)	121,000 (11,253)	29,600 (2,753)
Total	254,400 (23,659)	299,100 (27,816)	368,000 (34,224)	328,600 (30,560)	471,400 (43,840)	337,400 (31,378)
Average per room	953 (89)	1,084 (101)	1,223 (114)	1,060 (99)	1,497 (139)	935 (87)

[a]Schematic design.

DESIGN CONSIDERATIONS

The general conference center rule that the design of the individual areas reinforces the architectural concept and develops a consistency of product is especially true at the resort conference centers, where the design must reflect the physical setting in addition to carrying out the other planning goals. Scanticon-Denver, which continues the Scandinavian feel evident in their other properties, also incorporates western and Indian motifs and colors throughout the center. At that center, the local artist's boldly colored murals seemed out-of-place until a clear, prairie sunrise mirrored the orange hues.

Guestrooms. Resort conference center guestrooms are considerably different than those in other types of projects. First, the rooms often are remote from the public areas, either in separate low-rise buildings or in scattered condominium buildings. Thus, without the usual reliance on a double-loaded corridor or standard structural module, for example, the architect has the advantage of practically unlimited design opportunities. Individual units may take the form of condominium apartments, incorporating living and dining rooms and kitchenette in one expanded module, generally available under one rentable "key," with one or two adjoining typical guestrooms.

Resort rooms often are larger than those in other conference centers. This is due to several factors: higher double occupancy (both for conferences and nonmeeting resort busi-ness), higher multiple occupancy in the case of ski resorts, longer length of stay, and expanded storage needs. The individual units need to meet a number of design criteria more similar to those for recreational resorts than for executive or the more institutional types of conference centers. It is therefore more common to find a larger number of rooms furnished with two twin, double, or queen beds than in other projects. Work surface areas are somewhat reduced, while other elements—such as the seating, dining table area, and clothes storage capacity—become larger or more prominent. In the more upscale resort conference centers, the guest bathrooms are particularly more luxurious, often including a second sink, separate stall shower, or compartmentalized toilet. Many incorporate a wet bar, which, in the condominium developments, may grow to the status of a small kitchenette, not unlike extended-stay suite hotel units.

The resort setting can be enhanced by providing outdoor terraces or balconies for each room. These should be a large enough for the guests to use to full advantage, accommodating a dining table and at least two chairs or, in some resorts, one or two chaise lounges. Materials may vary: Warm-climate resort conference centers may continue hard flooring from the entry or bath, or from the balcony into a part of the room, creating a cooler, less hotel-like ambience.

Architects should seek out individual elements to make the resort experience unique. Mountain properties may incorporate fireplaces into condominium units or the upper-floor rooms, as has been done at Squaw Creek. Even at desert locations, the cool nights make a guestroom fireplace a welcome amenity. The Scottsdale Conference Resort and other southwest properties incorporate *casitas*, Spanish-style bungalows, for a portion of the guestrooms. More rural settings may feature dormers on the upper floors, enhancing the residential feel.

Public Areas. In resort conference centers, the designers have an unusual opportunity to combine a special or spectacular site and a building type with a strongly defined purpose. The task, then, is to pull these together to create a "sense of place" and a memorable experience. The lobby and the other public facilities are the places to first accomplish this.

The design challenge begins with the approach to the main entrance. The driveway might curve through the woods or along the edge of a ravine, offering glimpses of the building or other attractive views. Resort conference centers often draw meetings featuring group activities, such as trips to nearby attractions or off-site recreational facilities; as a result, the porte cochere must have sufficient height for buses, as well as queuing space for extra vans to transport guests to the condominiums, remote recreational facilities, and the airport.

Many resort lobbies are smaller than those in other types of conference centers, primarily because attendees can meet in other places, such as the several lounges, the outdoor terraces, the game room, the swimming pool, and other recreational outlets. Here the lobby is not the main assembly point. On the other hand, operational considerations influence the program. Resorts at golf and skiing destinations require additional space for the storage and handling of sports equipment; also, many resort properties include tour desks for local concessionaires to market tours and use as assembly points.

One of the essential distinctions of resort conference centers is the number and variety of food and beverage outlets. The dining operations are always important at any conference center, of course, but while most other properties have no more than two restaurants (and often only one), resort conference centers may have three or four, including some located at the recreational centers. In addition to the conference dining room, the dining alternatives usually include a specialty restaurant and a sports-oriented outlet, the latter associated

with the golf club, ski center, spa, or tennis complex. If there is a fourth operation, it is usually a gourmet dining room or a second recreational outlet. The Scanticon-Denver conference center has one of the most complete food and beverage programs:

☐ Conference dining room (buffet), 250 seats

☐ Specialty dining room (buffet), 180 seats

☐ Gourmet restaurant, 60 seats

☐ Golf club grille (adjoining the clubhouse), 140 seats

☐ Lobby lounge, 30 seats

☐ Specialty lounge (adjoining the lobby lounge), 56 seats

☐ Pub lounge (adjoining the game room), 90 seats

☐ Golf club lounge (adjoining the grille), 30 seats

The first four outlets on the list yield a total food capacity of 630 seats, or 2.1 seats per guestroom; the last four rooms give a total beverage capacity of 206 seats, or 0.7 seats per guestroom.

Resort dining and lounge operations are often oriented toward a view—perhaps the landscaped grounds, recreational features, or a more distant vista. To accommodate such views, many designers tier the seating areas, giving better sight opportunities for customers seated toward the rear. The steps or ramps must minimize any chance for falls or spillage, especially in conference dining areas, which usually feature buffets and self-service concepts. Seating should be provided in private or semiprivate alcoves to eliminate the sense of the large or institutional dining hall.

The several recreational outlet types have different food service needs. Golf and skiing centers, for example, need to offer quick service for guests trying to enjoy a maximum amount of recreation—a quick lunch after the front nine holes or between runs down the mountain, for example. These types of food operations must be carefully located within the project to offer easy customer access and must be designed to accommodate sports equipment, outerwear, and special footwear, such as golf spikes or ski boots. Often a simple snack bar, even at the most luxurious resorts, offers the guest the maximum practical advantage—the sports activity, not food quality, may be the priority. Wherever possible, opportunities for outdoor dining should be accommodated. (See also Chapter 10, Planning the Public Facilities.)

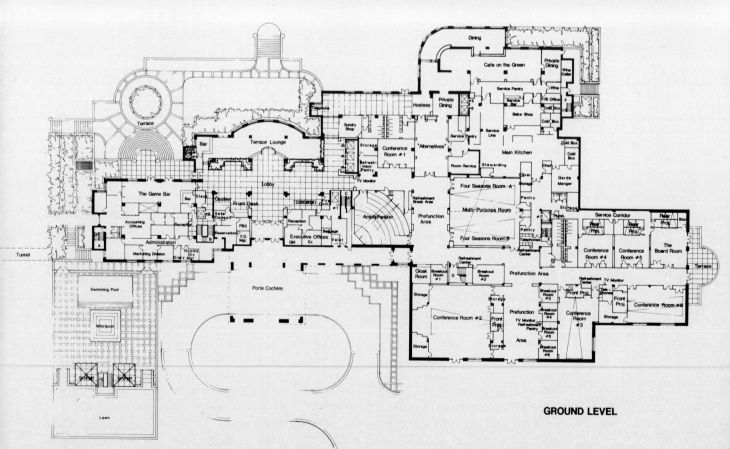

GROUND LEVEL

FOUR SEASONS HOTEL AND RESORT

Located on 400 acres (162 hectares) in Las Colinas near the Dallas—Fort Worth Airport in Irving, Texas, the Four Seasons combines 315 guestrooms and suites, 20,000 square feet (1,860 square meters) of salable meeting space, and a 175,000 square foot (16,275 square meter) sports complex into a *grande luxe* hotel with a sports and conference theme. The guestrooms are arranged on eight double-loaded floors, the length of the corridors visually reduced by the architectural massing into four offset structures. Each room features oversized bathrooms and step-out balconies. The 26 conference rooms are located on the first two floors, convenient to the lobby, restaurants, and numerous breakout terraces. The several restaurants and lounges are grouped around the lobby and at the sports center, most with views of the golf course. The sports club offers four indoor tennis courts (including a center-court stadium for 3,500 spectators), additional squash and racquetball courts, a 25-yard (23-meter) lap pool, a jogging track, and a complete European-style spa. (Architect: HKS; interiors: Wilson and Associates; exterior photo: Greg Hursley; interior photos: Jaime Ardiles-Arce.)

Cheyenne Mountain Conference Resort, Colorado Springs, Colorado. Cheyenne Mountain is organized so that the public spaces and guestroom lodges take full advantage of the hillside setting, with views of the Rocky Mountains. The dramatic lobby, with its massive fireplace, large beams, and overscale leather furniture, is the centerpiece, leading to the lounge and game room on one side, conference dining areas on another, and the meeting core on the lower level. (Architect: Richardson Nagy Martin; interiors: Wudtke Watson Associates; photos: Peter Vitale, courtesy of International Conference Resorts.)

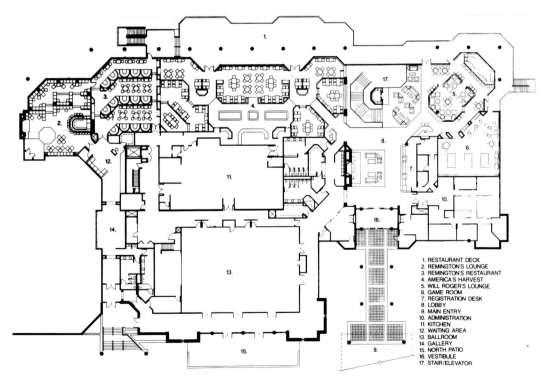

1. RESTAURANT DECK
2. REMINGTON'S LOUNGE
3. REMINGTON'S RESTAURANT
4. AMERICA'S HARVEST
5. WILL ROGER'S LOUNGE
6. GAME ROOM
7. REGISTRATION DESK
8. LOBBY
9. MAIN ENTRY
10. ADMINISTRATION
11. KITCHEN
12. WAITING AREA
13. BALLROOM
14. GALLERY
15. NORTH PATIO
16. VESTIBULE
17. STAIR/ELEVATOR

Conference Areas. Casualness is the order of the day at resort centers, and ambience and dress should be informal, no matter how high the level of business meeting. While the recreational activities may be relegated to the midafternoon or to a half day reserved for a complete break from the meetings, the surrounding recreational and sports-oriented atmosphere pervades the entire facility. The design of the conference areas should allow easy movement to the terraces and outdoor areas for coffee breaks, luncheon, and other informal gatherings, at least from the break areas if not from certain meeting rooms. The boardroom might include a private outdoor terrace, enclosed by landscaping, a berm, or a low wall.

The design of the meeting area in resort conference centers depends to a great extent on the property's market orientation and priorities. The true resort conference center should include meeting facilities similar to those of an executive conference center, emphasizing conference rooms of about 1,000 square feet (93 square meters) and smaller breakout rooms. Depending on its location, a resort center may have much less potential for social banquet business and if meetings of more than two hundred people are not anticipated, the resort may not need a large ballroom; instead, a large, multipurpose meeting–banquet room can provide flexibility for medium-sized groups and be used for both general sessions and functions. A few resorts, such as the Keystone Resort in Colorado, are situated where there is the need for large, multipurpose conference space; these centers need to be designed to offer maximum flexibility, with such features as multiple foyer and reception spaces, additional breakout rooms, and adequate support functions.

Many resort conference centers include an amphitheater—a tiered room incorporating built-in work surfaces, superior seating, and front- or rear-screen projection. Such rooms are expensive to build and maintain, in part because they are insufficiently flexible for different types of seating arrangements—groups that are the right size for the amphitheater still may not choose to use it because they prefer a different seating layout. In addition, the construction, furnishings, and equipment costs are high because of the varying floor levels and ceiling articulation, the millwork counters and railings, and the necessary audiovisual and computer connections.

But such special rooms may not be required. Although the amphitheater frequently

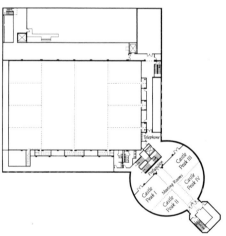

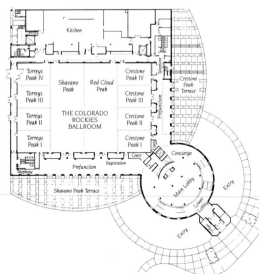

Keystone Resort, Keystone, Colorado. This dramatic conference center, opened in 1989 to complement the existing ski resort, offers a 16,000 square foot (1,488 square meter) ballroom capable of subdivision into ten smaller rooms, extensive prefunction and support areas, and even an outdoor terrace atop the rotunda. (Architect: Michael Barber; photos: Bob Winsett.)

is used as a marketing tool, the resort may, instead, use its setting and recreational facilities as the main attraction. No more than one boardroom is needed, and no special-purpose rooms (such as computer or teleconferencing) are required. Table 3–3 summarizes the conference rooms programmed at six resort conference centers.

There is some debate about the advisability of designing conference rooms with windows. At resort locations, however, windows are essential—the attendees are there not only for the meeting content but to enjoy the experience and the environment. Of course, drapes, blinds, or other window coverings are needed to control glare and darken the room for video or slide presentations.

The conference assembly areas must reflect the resort theme and ambience. The foyers and coffee break areas at resort properties must be light and airy, and should open onto terraces

and patios, even out to the swimming pool, although conflicts between meeting attendees and other resort users must be controlled. Because of the reliance on outdoor prefunction activity, The Resort at Squaw Creek includes gas connections for space heaters and food service equipment on the terraces, and the planning accommodates portable bar and food service stations.

The design and operations teams should consider what degree of service support is appropriate. For example, at more informal centers, the recreational users and meeting attendees both might expect and accept less sophisticated audiovisual and other systems. The more remote resort conference centers, however, might not have the advantage of off-site audiovisual vendors capable of meeting special or custom equipment requests, suggesting that perhaps more of the audiovisual systems might need to be built in.

TABLE 3-3. RESORT CONFERENCE CENTERS, CONFERENCE CORE SPACE PROGRAMS IN NET SQUARE FEET (NET SQUARE METERS)[a]

	Tega Cay[b] Charlotte, NC (267 guestrooms)	Doral Arrowwood Rye Brook, NY (276 guestrooms)	Scanticon Denver, CO (301 guestrooms)	Lansdowne Leesburg, VA (310 guestrooms)	Four Seasons Irving, TX (315 guestrooms)	Kingsmill Williamsburg, VA (361 guestrooms)
Ballroom	1 @ 8,700 (809)	1 @ 6,500 (605)	1 @ 5,500 (512)	1 @ 9,500 (605)	None	1 @ 4,000 (372)
Large conference[c]	1 @ 3,000 (279) 1 @ 1,900 (177) 1 @ 1,550 (144)	1 @ 1,800 (167) 1 @ 1,500 (140)	1 @ 5,100 (474) 1 @ 2,200 (205)	1 @ 2,700 (251) 3 @ 1,600 (149)	2 @ 3,000 (279)	1 @ 2,000 (186)
Medium conference[d]	3 @ 1,150 (107)	1 @ 1,425 (133)	4 @ 1,450 (135) 4 @ 1,150 (107)	None	1 @ 1,400 (130) 1 @ 1,250 (116)	None
Small conference[e]	None	2 @ 950 (88) 3 @ 725 (67) 2 @ 650 (60)	None	2 @ 925 (86)	8 @ 650 (60)	1 @ 900 (84) 2 @ 800 (74)
Breakout	6 @ 475 (44) 4 @ 400 (37)	4 @ 450 (42) 4 @ 300 (28) 11 @ 200 (19)	10 @ 350 (33) 11 @ 250 (23)	4 @ 450 (42) 4 @ 375 (35) 8 @ 300 (28)	3 @ 400 (37) 3 @ 300 (28) 5 @ 200 (19)	2 @ 375 (35)
Board room	1 @ 750 (70)	None	2 @ 750 (70)	1 @ 600 (56)	1 @ 850 (79)	1 @ 750 (70)
Amphitheater	1 @ 2,700 (251)	1 @ 3,100 (288)	None	1 @ 2,350 (219)	1 @ 2,025 (188)	None
Auditorium	None	None	None	None	None	None
Computer/special	None	None	None	None	None	None
Total conference	26,500 (2,465)	24,900 (2,316)	30,950 (2,878)	27,500 (2,558)	19,825 (1,844)	10,000 (930)
Total assembly	6,300 (586)	7,200 (670)	10,800 (1,004)	11,500 (1,070)	7,400 (688)	3,300 (307)
Total support	6,000 (558)	13,500 (1,256)	10,100 (939)	5,200 (484)	3,500 (326)	3,100 (288)

[a]Some program areas are rounded and averaged to simplify the presentation.
[b]Schematic design.
[c]Larger than 1,500 square feet (139 square meters).
[d]Between 1,000 and 1,500 square feet (93 and 139 square meters).
[e]Between 500 and 1,000 square feet (46 and 93 square meters).

Administration and Service Areas. Resort conference centers have special planning and design requirements in the back-of-house areas, too. The sales departments have extra staff to be accommodated, and at projects with condominium and second-home developments, these sales offices may be housed in the conference center building. The more remote resort conference centers, however, may establish their principal sales offices in a nearby metropolitan area; Squaw Creek, for example, has a large sales force in San Francisco.

Resort centers' expanded food and beverage operations greatly increase the design complexity of the back-of-house food service areas. The receiving area must be carefully positioned so as not to detract visually from the overall setting and views, which may necessitate placing it in a location somewhat remote from the main food and beverage storage and kitchen areas. The additional food outlets may require satellite kitchens, with a resulting increase in gross floor area and FF&E (furniture, fixtures, and equipment) costs. Each satellite kitchen, although possibly permitting slight decreases in the size of the main kitchen, will increase the total net area by at least 1,000 square feet (93 square meters).

Other operations will tend to be larger at resort conference centers. The laundry must be sized to accommodate both the increased volume of linen that will accompany the higher double occupancy in the guestrooms and the need for clean linen at the pools and health club; transportation systems must be available to move guests to outlying residential areas, requiring space for vehicles, additional staff, valet parking, and drivers; additional maintenance buildings are needed throughout the property; and storage areas are needed for outdoor and out-of-season furniture, awnings, and grounds equipment. Many of these can be at a remote location, such as the basement of one of the sports buildings, which is the usual location for golf carts. In a few locations, employee housing may be needed simply to attract staff and retain senior employees.

Recreation Facilities. At many resort conference centers, the recreational facilities set the tone for the entire experience. The spa at Barton Creek, the skiing at Squaw Creek, the golf at Kingsmill, and the tennis at The Woodlands—each dominates the other sports activities at its respective resort. The design team should decide how much visual emphasis the recreational component should have: Should it dominate the other parts of the project? Should it continue the same architectural theme or establish a new one? At Doral Arrowwood, the swimming pool is near the center of the project, visible on every trip to the guestrooms and close to the food, beverage, and entertainment areas. This establishes an important visual identity to the circulation space between the guestrooms and main building, and the design team should be alert for such possibilities.

THE KINGSMILL RESORT AND CONFERENCE CENTER

Part of the Anheuser-Busch holdings on 2,900 acres (1,174 hectares) overlooking the James River in Williamsburg, Virginia, Kingsmill offers an elegant central conference center building, detached golf and sports clubs, and 360 rooms situated in separate condominium structures. The main building has five levels, interconnected by a grand stair that itself serves as a frequent gathering area. Seven rooms, three with projection booths and all with full window walls, are conveniently clustered on one floor, with two coffee break lounges leading to outdoor terraces. The 4,000 square foot (372 square meter) ballroom is one floor below. The dining room adjoining the formal lobby offers the usual conference buffet, designed so that it can be closed off from the restaurant, and a separate dining area for private groups; a top-floor lounge is an active conferee meeting spot. (Architect: Bainbridge & Associates; interiors: Index The Design Firm; photos: Robert Miller.)

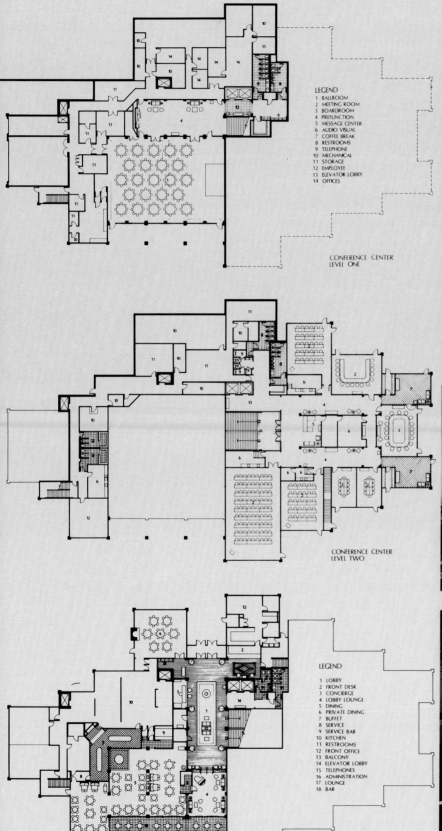

LEGEND
1 BALLROOM
2 MEETING ROOM
3 BOARDROOM
4 PREFUNCTION
5 MESSAGE CENTER
6 AUDIO VISUAL
7 COFFEE BREAK
8 RESTROOMS
9 TELEPHONE
10 MECHANICAL
11 STORAGE
12 EMPLOYEE
13 ELEVATOR LOBBY
14 OFFICES

CONFERENCE CENTER
LEVEL ONE

CONFERENCE CENTER
LEVEL TWO

LEGEND
1 LOBBY
2 FRONT DESK
3 CONCIERGE
4 LOBBY LOUNGE
5 DINING
6 PRIVATE DINING
7 BUFFET
8 SERVICE
9 SERVICE BAR
10 KITCHEN
11 RESTROOMS
12 FRONT OFFICE
13 BALCONY
14 ELEVATOR LOBBY
15 TELEPHONES
16 ADMINISTRATION
17 LOUNGE
18 BAR

CONFERENCE CENTER
LEVEL THREE

CHAPTER 4

Corporate Conference and Training Centers

Surprisingly, it is only relatively recently that American industry has realized the importance of training as a key factor in recruiting, motivating, and retaining staff. It took the growth of the service industries after World War II and, especially, in the 1980s, to fuel the expansion of corporate training and management development facilities. Corporate training centers are expanding into a variety of markets: Such industries as insurance, financial services, and telecommunications have the greatest number of training centers, with Bell Atlantic alone operating ten such centers in five states; Merrill Lynch, Peat Marwick Main, Arthur Andersen, and Shearson Lehman Brothers each has one or more centers at which corporate training is offered in specific settings appropriate to the company; IBM, in addition to its own employee training, operates training centers around the country for its customers.

The need for professional training centers is obvious. Concerns about increased domestic and international competition, employee productivity, and staff retention have encouraged companies to increase their training and human resources development budgets. Changing demographics has played a big role as well.

As the baby-boom generation matures and fewer young people enter the job market, some industries are anticipating a shortage of highly educated workers, making training and retraining increasingly important parts of the corporate agenda.

Such needs are being acted upon: A recent Carnegie Foundation study found that each year eight million employees participate in corporate training and development, beyond the usual on-the-job training. The American Society of Training and Development estimates that corporate education programs, in their many forms, cost over $40 billion each year. And according to the International Association of Conference Centers, American business spends about 2 percent of the gross national product on training.

SITE AND MARKET CONSIDERATIONS

The planners of corporate training or management development facilities are faced with a number of questions early in the feasibility or planning stages, many of which are summarized in Table 4–1. Certainly most critical is whether the company needs to have its own dedicated facility at all, or if it can instead satisfactorily house its programs within the

IBM Advanced Business Institute, Palisades, New York. This complex, one of the newest IBM facilities, opened in 1989. A series of ponds serves as the focal point for the three wings of the conference center, with a two-story enclosed bridge between the reception and residential blocks emphasizing the integration of the man-made and the natural. (Architect: Mitchell/Giurgola; photo: Mick Hales.)

TABLE 4-1. CORPORATE CONFERENCE CENTER FEASIBILITY CHECKLIST

Feasibility Issue	*Possible Determinants, Factors, or Solutions to be Considered*
Demand	☐ Demand generated from corporate headquarters
	☐ Demand generated from one or more divisions
	☐ New training or management development policy
	☐ Training currently occurring at local hotels
	☐ Training currently occurring at multiple locations
	☐ Corporation expanding into new industries or services
	☐ Corporation in high-tech field requiring constant reeducation
Location	☐ Within or adjoining corporate headquarters complex
	☐ Close to headquarters (within 30–45 minutes)
	☐ Remote from corporate headquarters
	☐ Close to other corporate demand (for additional revenue)
	☐ Accessible to participants
Public availability	☐ Available only for corporate education
	☐ Available for other corporate meetings and to subsidiary companies
	☐ Open to selected other corporations
	☐ Open to the public for day meetings or off-hours
	☐ Open to the public without restrictions
Schedule	☐ Open 365 days per year
	☐ Closed weekends and/or major holidays
	☐ Open only seasonally
Facilities and amenities	☐ Single building or separate structures
	☐ Residential accommodations
	☐ Food and beverage outlets
	☐ Dedicated or multipurpose meeting rooms
	☐ Amount of on-site recreation
	☐ Level of technology
	☐ Quality level throughout
Management	☐ Managed by corporate group
	☐ Managed by food service or other vendor
	☐ Managed by conference center manager
Future adaptability	☐ Anticipate growth and expansion
	☐ Plan to reconfigure classrooms easily
	☐ Plan to grow into office or other space
	☐ Plan to shed guestrooms or other portion(s) if uneconomical

corporate office, at commercial hotels, at non-dedicated conference centers, or on university campuses. Many planners have concluded that a dedicated facility is necessary to ensure control over the learning environment. Also, a corporate facility sends the message to employees that training and management education are priorities and that they are seen as a key asset. Such tangible evidence of concern and commitment tends to yield a greater training benefit from the program.

The size and character of the particular corporation is important. Highly centralized companies, for example, try to influence the training companywide from a single training department; more decentralized firms disperse this role throughout various divisions and even across the country. In any case, it is necessary to conduct a feasibility analysis to determine, for example, the expected number of meetings, number of attendee room nights or participant weeks, anticipated demand, projected revenues and expenses, and whether a dedicated in-house facility would offer any cost savings, improved training program quality, heightened corporate image or morale, or other substantial benefits. For example, the financial services giant Arthur Andersen, which has offered in-house education programs since 1940, operates its own Center for Professional Education in St. Charles, Illinois. With over 1,200 guestrooms, it is the largest corporate education center in the world. In 1989, over 53,000 people attended programs, totaling nearly 270,000 employee-days; various analyses showed that the company was able to provide high-quality, specially tailored programs at a cost 20 to 50 percent less than would be incurred by sending employees to comparable courses elsewhere in the country.

Once the decision is made to conduct in-house training, a group of interrelated questions must be answered. These focus on the following:

☐ Location, especially with respect to proximity to the corporate headquarters.

☐ The training schedule and its effect on the annual utilization of the facility.

☐ The relative availability of the facility to outside groups.

☐ The program for the proposed facility, including whether or not it is to be a residential center.

☐ The space requirements for conference, food and beverage, recreation, and necessary support spaces.

Many corporate training and education centers (and practically all of the nonresidential facilities) are located at the headquarters site, generally within the main administrative structure or in nearby buildings. Residential centers, which require considerably more land, may adjoin the headquarters at suburban sites (as done by Merrill Lynch and McDonald's), which then take on the character of a campus. Residential centers also may be self contained, usually within a short drive of the headquarters (as done by GTE, GE, and IBM). Either format permits day use by nearly every department and frequent presentations to the participants by the corporation's senior executives. The training centers, unlike management development facilities, and those for highly decentralized corporations, may be more remote from the headquarters, as there is less need for this synergism between the top administration and meeting participants.

Many companies expect to use their training and conference facilities exclusively for their own employees, a decision that requires careful analysis by the human resources and training professionals to estimate the program demand in order to determine the facility size and plan the appropriate training spaces. Some of these corporations find that their facilities do not support themselves and that their in-house training programs fall well short of full utilization, necessitating that the centers be opened to the public.

Other firms want to maintain exclusive use of the facility and are therefore willing to accept the financial burden of operating only five days a week and 45 to 50 weeks a year. The IBM Advanced Business Institute in Palisades, New York, operates from Sunday afternoon through Friday afternoon and then closes for the weekend. It is also closed for about six weeks per year when major holidays interrupt weeklong programs. GTE, hoping to increase the utilization of its GTE Management Development Center in Norwalk, Connecticut, which also closes during weekends, reached an agreement with nearby Champion to share the center. This arrangement provided GTE with additional income and Champion with a permanent relationship with a quality conference center for training. When such fortuitous arrangements do not develop, though, many centers are open to the public when not being used for corporate training.

Some companies have found other ways to increase utilization: frequently, corporate centers restricted to in-house use are made available for evening meetings to community organizations, such as the United Way, or to arts groups. In addition, some corporations allow employees and their families to use the lodging and recreation facilities for personal use during restricted dates and times. For example, the handsome McDonald's Lodge in Oak Brook, Illinois, used primarily for corporation training, is available to employees for weekend resort packages at extremely reasonable rates.

Further utilization occurs in the dining and recreation facilities: projects located near the headquarters often are used for executive dining, or as an alternative to the normal dining venue. Such centers also allow employee use of the recreation center. The GE Management Development Institute in Croton-on-Hudson, New York, restricts the recreation center to conference participants in the early morning and postmeeting periods but allows GE employees (as well as the Marriott operations staff) to use it at other hours.

Corporate training and conference facilities fall into several categories. One major type is the *training center*, intended for middle-level and new professional employees. Often more institutional in appearance, these centers feature a large number of specially designed classrooms, sometimes as many as fifty, and might be located anywhere in the country. A second category is the *management development center*, intended for middle- to upper-level management. These often are close to the corporate headquarters, have fewer guestrooms (usually between fifty and two hundred), and have a more corporate or commercial hotel feel. Other types include the *customer training and support center*, such as what IBM offers for major purchasers of its equipment, the *corporate guest house* or retreat, which may not feature conferences so much as encourage informal meetings, and *non-residential centers*, which usually have a heavy training component (see Chapter 6).

PROGRAM AND PLANNING CONSIDERATIONS

The decision for a corporation to establish its own training center is not made lightly. Company executives need to balance the tremendous costs against the advantages of being able to better plan and implement their training programs. It is therefore important to establish educational and corporate culture objectives early in the process to assist the team as it develops the conceptual requirements.

Many of these strategic questions were discussed earlier. Once the corporation has determined the desired type of facility, its location, and basic operating criteria, it must define the programmatic requirements. The group developing or reviewing the conceptual requirements should include the training and human resources executives, the trainers themselves, the architect and design consultants, and the management company. A broad overview of the conceptual considerations is provided in Table 4–2.

More specifically, the corporate developer needs to have a preliminary idea of the gross space requirements for a particular project; otherwise, it is difficult to assess what the capital and operating expenses will be. Of the several types of conference centers, corporate training centers have the greatest range in size for several reasons:

1. The question of residential or non-residential will have tremendous space implications.

2. Corporate centers range from over nine hundred rooms (Arthur Andersen and Xerox) to fewer than one hundred.

3. Companies place differing emphases on their training centers, from an efficient, schoollike facility of perhaps 800 square feet (74.4 square meters) per room to a luxury educational retreat, such as IBM constructed, with 2,000 square feet (186 square meters) per room.

In addition, each of the program elements can be variously increased or decreased in size to meet the requirements of a particular center: one may have no trainers in residence, others a whole department; one may include little recreation space, others a fitness center with an indoor pool or racquetball courts. It is important, then, to develop each corporate center individually, based on the educational objectives and the demand for programs (Table 4–3).

While day centers may encompass as little as 10,000 to 40,000 square feet (930 to 3,720 square meters) for 200 participants, residential training centers require at least 200,000 square feet (18,600 square meters) to accommodate the same population, assuming single occupancy. The normal range for full-service residential corporate training centers is 1,200 to 1,600 square feet (111.6 to 148.8 square meters) per room. This added capital investment discourages many corporate planners, but trainers point out that much more is accom-

TABLE 4-2. CORPORATE CONFERENCE CENTER CONCEPTUAL REQUIREMENTS

Project Aspect	Aims and Requirements
Siting	Establish low-rise, estatelike center on wooded suburban or rural site; provide separate structures, sometimes connected, for housing, conference, and public facilities; provide controlled views from guestrooms and public areas; hide parking; create landscape attraction
Guestrooms	Design rooms primarily for single-occupancy, except in entry-level training centers, where double rooms may be anticipated; rooms require moderate- to high-level furnishings and amenities; minimum per-room area of 250 square feet (23.2 square meters); provide commons areas among the guestrooms
Lobby	Create residential-scale space with the potential to establish image for the center; front desk should be understated; provide only limited seating, as most lounge and social spaces are elsewhere
Restaurants	Provide conference dining room for full capacity; consider a second restaurant if center has more than 300 rooms; provide social lounge, game room, library or reading room, and, if corporate policy permits, pub or entertainment lounge
Conference rooms	Provide auditorium or banquet room for full capacity; amphitheaters for management development centers should seat up to 100; provide multiple rear-projection conference rooms, breakouts; and specialized training to meet corporate requirements (computers, telecommunications, etc.)
Conference support	Provide relatively large prefunction, coffee break, and flow areas to promote corporate image and opportunities for informal interchange; provide high amounts of audio-visual support, including rear-screen projection; decide whether trainers will be housed at the property, which might add 5,000 square feet (465 square meters) or more
Recreation	Provide an indoor pool (outdoor if climate allows); racquetball courts, exercise, aerobics, game room and lounge; include team sports facilities such as a gym and softball field

plished in the same number of days at a residential center because the working or study sessions in the evenings and the informal interchange among participants extend and expand the learning experience, thereby reducing the length of programs.

Residential training centers must include a more complete conference room and training core, additional food and beverage outlets, lounges, game rooms, and full recreation centers. Programmers must understand the different methods and objectives of meetings, which might include role-playing exercises, team building, or case studies. Many corporations now incorporate wellness programs and emphasize health and fitness. In the back-of-house areas, residential centers require additional amounts of space for food service, housekeeping, engineering, and administration.

Corporate Training Centers. Corporate training originally was accomplished in a haphazard basis, generally by managers and departments who understood and appreciated its value. Slowly, personnel departments were renamed *human resources*, and in the 1980s, separate training and development departments were established to assist in educating employees at all levels. As training has grown in importance, its visibility has increased to the point where most major corporations operate some type of corporate training facility, although it may be simply part-time use of multipurpose space within existing corporate offices.

Among the most influential major training facilities was New England Telephone's Learning Center in Marlboro, Massachusetts, which opened in 1974 but was expanded by more

TABLE 4-3. CORPORATE CONFERENCE AND TRAINING CENTERS, SAMPLE PROGRAMS IN GROSS SQUARE FEET (GROSS SQUARE METERS)

	Training Centers			Management Development Centers		
	Eagle Lodge Lafayette Hill, PA (120 guestrooms)	Aberdeen Woods Peachtree City, GA (150 guestrooms)	IBM Thornwood, NY (250 guestrooms)	GTE Norwalk, CT (118 guestrooms)	IBM Palisades, NY (206 guestrooms)	Merrill Lynch Princeton, NJ (350 guestrooms)
Guestrooms	70,300 (6,538)	77,700 (7,226)	133,500 (12,415)	62,000 (5,766)	125,600 (11,680)	189,100 (17,586)
Public areas	21,500 (2,000)	15,200 (1,414)	14,200 (1,321)	27,500 (2,558)	33,500 (3,116)	40,800 (3,794)
Conference areas	36,900 (3,432)	79,000 (7,347)	101,900 (9,477)	37,900 (3,525)	123,200 (11,458)	101,300 (9,421)
Administrative areas	2,300 (214)	10,000 (930)	5,500 (512)	4,000 (372)	43,800 (4,074)	5,200 (484)
Back-of-house areas	19,000 (1,767)	34,800 (3,236)	23,400 (2,176)	38,000 (3,534)	66,500 (6,185)	44,900 (4,176)
Recreation	11,000 (1,023)	5,200 (484)	14,900 (1,386)	14,900 (1,386)	17,400 (1,618)	18,000 (1,674)
Total	161,100 (14,982)	221,900 (20,637)	293,400 (27,286)	184,300 (17,140)	410,000 (38,130)	399,300 (37,135)
Average per room	1,343 (125)	1,479 (138)	1,173 (109)	1,561 (145)	1,991 (185)	1,125 (105)

than 50 percent in 1990 to include 221 guestrooms, 51 meeting rooms, and 28 breakout rooms. In 1979, Mountain Bell constructed a 149-room training and conference center in Lakewood, Colorado, and later AT&T opened facilities near Princeton and outside Chicago.

Two AT&T projects illustrate alternate architectural approaches that remain options for any project. The Princeton campus, in Hopewell, New Jersey, midway between New York and Philadelphia, includes separate low-rise classroom and residential buildings, approximately 400 yards (365.6 meters) apart, on a 217-acre (87.8-hectare) site. The single-story education building features a 200-seat auditorium, 37 meeting and breakout rooms, and extensive office space for the trainers. The low-rise, 305-room lodging structure includes dining and recreation facilities. In 1982, in Lisle, Illinois, AT&T opened a large, three-tower, ten-floor complex, including 400 guestrooms, 27 conference rooms, and a central 150-seat amphitheater. Within the building is a separate executive conference center, which can accommodate up to 100 guests for special meetings. Both centers are open to non-AT&T groups.

AT&T's approach to constructing a number of different training and development centers around the country can be compared with those of organizations choosing to centralize the training in a single location. One of the largest complexes yet built as a dedicated training facility is the Xerox International Center for Training and Development, which

opened in 1974 in Leesburg, Virginia, about thirty-five miles northwest of Washington, D.C. The design of the Xerox project has focused discussion on the character of corporate education centers. The building—really two paired structures containing five similar program blocks and approximately one million square feet, includes over 900 guestrooms, close to 150 classrooms and breakout rooms, expansive dining and lounge areas, and a full-service fitness and recreation facility. When this center opened, Xerox closed eight regional education centers and thereby reduced total training costs by about 20 percent.

The reinforced concrete structure is designed as a series of interlocking terraces, each guestroom floor sheltering dining rooms, lounges, and commons areas beneath. The building form dominates the immediate site and creates grand interior spaces. In contrast to the building mass, the guestrooms are purposely small, less than 200 square feet (18.6 square meters), yet lounge areas are provided for every six rooms throughout the upper floors, encouraging participants to meet informally and network rather than retreat to their rooms. The classrooms are designed for specific, dedicated purposes and feature a well-designed audiovisual module that can be stored in each room or moved easily to other locations. Another dramatic feature is the recreation building, with high-ceilinged, laminated-timber–framed roofs enclosing tennis and basketball courts. Like the lounges, the sports center is conducive to group meetings,

New England Telephone Learning Center, Marlboro, Massachusetts. One of the most influential corporate training facilities when it opened in 1974, the Learning Center originally consisted of four interconnected buildings with the conference and dining areas oriented around an open courtyard. The expansion program, completed in 1990, added a third wing of guestrooms, a fitness center, and 38,000 square feet (3,534 square meters) of new office space. The courtyard was enclosed for increased dining use, and the former training offices were totally renovated into advanced meeting rooms. (Architect: Symmes Maini & McKee Associates.)

Hickory Ridge Conference Centre, Lisle, Illinois. Located on 26 acres (10.5 hectares) outside Chicago, this AT&T facility includes 400 guestrooms in three towers, including an executive conference area for special groups of up to 100, with its own bedrooms, conference rooms, and dining area. (Architect: Clark & Post; photo courtesy of Clark & Post.)

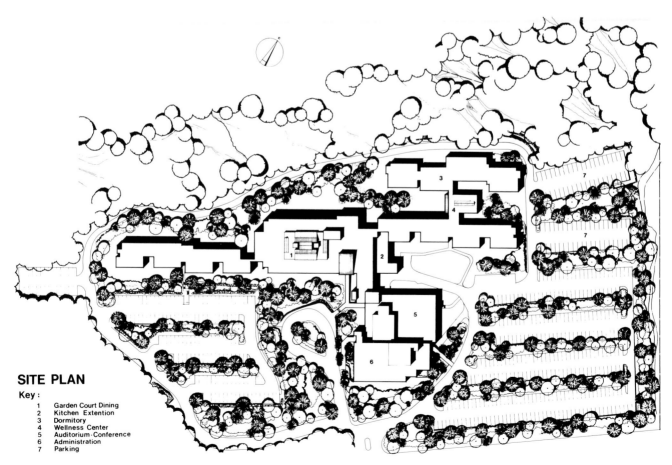

SITE PLAN

Key :

1 Garden Court Dining
2 Kitchen Extention
3 Dormitory
4 Wellness Center
5 Auditorium·Conference
6 Administration
7 Parking

allowing informal interaction among the participants and furthering Xerox's training goals.

More recent projects show a variety of different architectural, interior, and programming alternatives. Several corporations emphasize the campus feel by separating the functions. Aberdeen Woods, Pitney Bowes Corporation's national training center, opened in 1984 outside Atlanta with 150 guestrooms in one structure, forty-six classrooms and administration and training offices in another, and dining and recreation spaces in a third. The training campus, on thirty-six acres (14.5 hectares), is carefully sited to provide expansive views of landscaped grounds from the prefunction and dining spaces. The guestrooms, on the other hand, are tucked into a wooded glen, a short distance away.

At Aberdeen Woods a clear group of objectives were established: The separate buildings discourage guestroom use except in the evenings and emphasize the "going to work" aspect of training. The double rooms are designed for two participants, with double sinks, double closets and, in about half the rooms, wardrobe dividers to give each person some privacy. All meeting rooms are windowless interior spaces but are adjacent to a sunny, two-level prefunction and refreshment area. A large mezzanine overlooking the assembly areas provides office space for the trainers.

Another campus project is the McDonald's Corporation Office Campus, on an 81-acre site in Oak Brook, Illinois. The three principal elements, located in different buildings, are Hamburger University, a 109,000 square foot (10,137 square meter) training center, The Lodge, a 225-room hotel and conference center, and an office and research building. The campus is intended to encourage team building, reinforcing founder Ray Kroc's words, *None of us is as good as all of us.* The training building includes an auditorium and six tiered classrooms, each with rear projection and translation booths, as well as ten conference and seminar rooms, student laboratories, and office space for the trainers. The Lodge, including two restaurants and a ballroom, completed a major expansion phase in 1989 by adding guestrooms, conference rooms, and a full-service fitness center and indoor pool.

Corporate Management Development Centers. Corporate education needs are not based only in training. Many companies see the need to provide courses to managers, preparing them for additional responsibilities in

Xerox International Center for Training and Management Development, Leesburg, Virginia. The buildings at the Xerox center cover 40 acres (16.2 hectares) and contain about one million square feet (93,000 square meters) of space. Opened in 1974, the terraced structures include over 900 dormitory-style bedrooms and scores of meeting rooms, dining areas and lounges, and offices. Fitness facilities are in a separate building. (Architect: Vincent Kling Partnership; photo: Merrill Worthington.)

an ever-changing business environment and encouraging early-career associations and friendships that may later result in increased loyalty to the company.

Management development centers are usually near the corporate headquarters so that senior executives can address the participants and attendees can gain a feel for the corporate philosophy. Among the earliest management development facilities is the General Electric Management Development Institute in Croton-on-Hudson, New York, developed in 1954. Originally an estate, GE developed it into a campus facility, including separate guest-room and education buildings. In 1988 the company built a new residence building, including a major fitness center, dining rooms, and breakout rooms (the latter an important ingredient too often undersized in corporate education programs). At the same time, the original farmhouse was renovated to include a handsome reception area, a lounge, and game rooms for informal socializing.

One of the most influential projects is the GTE Management Development Center in Norwalk, Connecticut, completed in 1981. The 118 guestrooms are in one wing, connected by a bridge to the conference–dining building,

which features two amphitheaters, four conference rooms, six breakout rooms, and social lounges on the upper floor, and dining and banquet facilities on the lower floor. Recreational spaces are in a third interconnected structure. Intended for top management personnel, the three buildings, featuring brick exterior walls, wood-framed windows, and slate roofs, are comfortably sited on the wooded 66-acre (26.7-hectare) site.

A larger project is the Merrill Lynch Conference and Training Center, which is sited on the Merrill Lynch corporate campus in Princeton, New Jersey. This center not only meets the needs of training and management development programs, but is also used for corporate meetings and presentations on a space-available basis. The thirty soundproof meeting rooms are well configured for several commonly used seating arrangements and offer full audiovisual capability. The center includes 290 guestrooms in the main conference center; an additional fifty rooms are in a separate executive center wing, complete with its own entrance, dining, and conference rooms. This arrangement allows Merrill Lynch to offer special services and facilities on demand to small groups.

McDONALD'S LODGE AND TRAINING CENTER

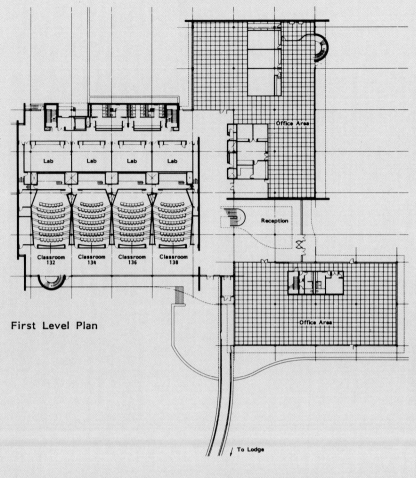

First Level Plan

Lab Lab Lab Lab

Classroom 132 Classroom 134 Classroom 136 Classroom 138

Office Area

Reception

Office Area

To Lodge

Second Level Plan

Office Area

Discussion Room 275

Seminar Room

Seminar Room

Classroom 222 Auditorium 224 Classroom 226

Seminar Room 247

Seminar Room 248 A

Seminar Room 248 B

Library 259

Conference Room 260

Seminar Room 263

Seminar Room 264 A

Seminar Room 264 B

The McDonald's office campus—consisting of the training center, Hamburger University, the 225-room Lodge, and an office/research building—share the 81-acre (32.8-hectare) site in Oak Brook, Illinois, near Chicago. The 110,000 square foot (10,230 square meter) training center was renovated in 1989 to convert office space into additional breakout and audiovisual rooms. The teaching facilities feature a 300-seat auditorium and six tiered amphitheaters, each seating 60 to 110 and featuring highly sophisticated student-response systems, infrared translation, closed-circuit television, and audio-visual systems, as well as more typical

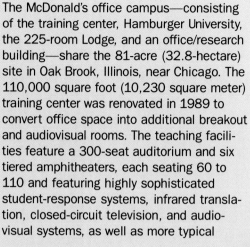

classrooms. The training center and the Lodge are connected by a winding covered walkway crossing one of the two lakes on the site. Also, the Lodge has been expanded with a new wing of 80 guestrooms and an adjoining health club and pool. The skylit area—designed for four simultaneous water volleyball games—also opens to a series of surrounding terraces with views across the site. In addition, the Lodge includes two restaurants, the informal hearth lounge, a 5,000 square foot (465 square meter) ballroom, and a magnificent 40-foot–high (12.2-meter–high) stone fireplace in the lobby. (Architect: Lohan Associates; photos: Ray Reiss.)

The new residential, dining, and recreation building offers a dramatic focus to this long-standing GE facility. Built atop a small knoll in Croton-on-Hudson, New York, the entrance leads to the three-story lobby and the peaked-roof dining hall at the rear. Internal zoning is effectively organized with the service level on the basement tieing together the kitchen and other back-of-house functions, while public access to the recreational facilities, dining, and guestrooms is on the lobby floor. The guestroom floors include pantries so that conferees can serve themselves snacks and light meals at any hour, day or night. The original house has been renovated into the Windrose Club, offering a variety of informal meeting rooms, a game room, and a lounge. The conference rooms are in a nearby structure connected to the training and program offices. (Architect: Shepley Bulfinch Richardson and Abbott; photos: Wheeler Photographics.)

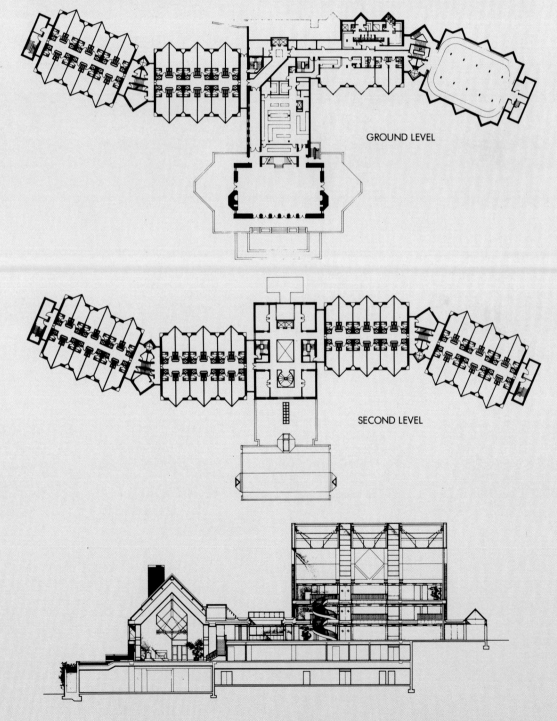

GROUND LEVEL

SECOND LEVEL

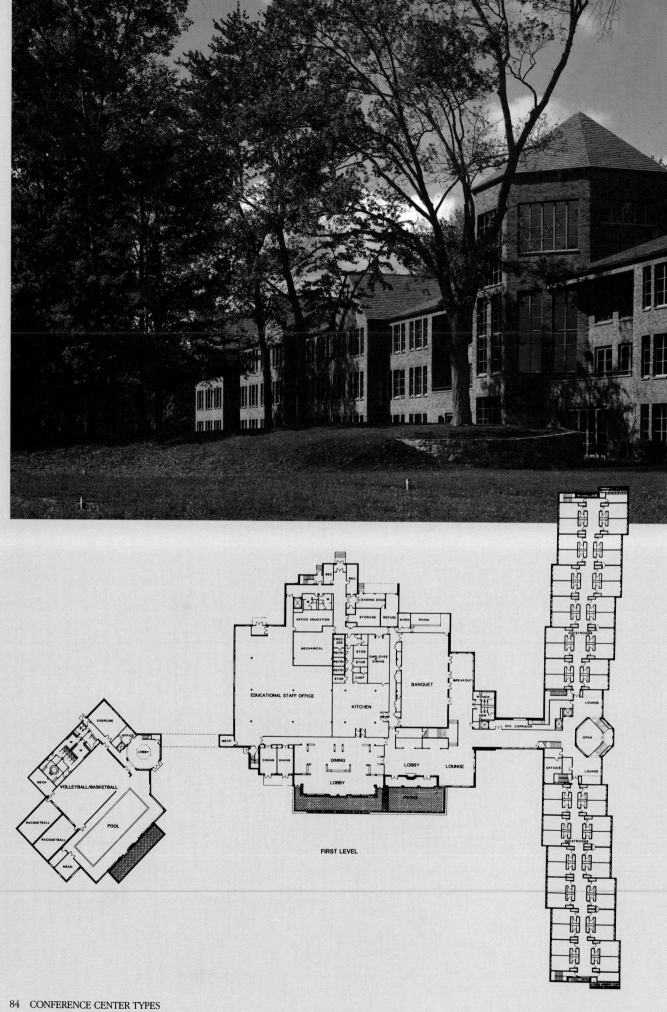

FIRST LEVEL

Located in Norwalk, Connecticut, only 15 minutes from the GTE world headquarters, yet set totally alone on a beautiful 66-acre (26.7-hectare) site, the 205,000 square foot (19,065 square meter) education center responds to the wooded character of the site. With allusions to old New England inns—slate roofs, copper detailing, and wood windows—the three interconnected buildings successfully establish a personal scale for the project. Guests enter into a three-story octagonal lobby, with bedrooms extending on either side. A grand stair leads visitors upstairs and across a bridge to the dining, lounge, and banquet areas; the conference core is located separately on a third level. A second bridge connects the public facilities to the fitness and sports complex. Two 60-person amphitheaters are positioned opposite four 35-seat conference rooms, with two coffee break lounges at either end of the hallway. Six breakout rooms and a group of lounge and game room spaces are close by. (Architect: Hellmuth, Obata & Kassabaum; interiors: Kovacs McElrath; photos: Martin Tornallyay.)

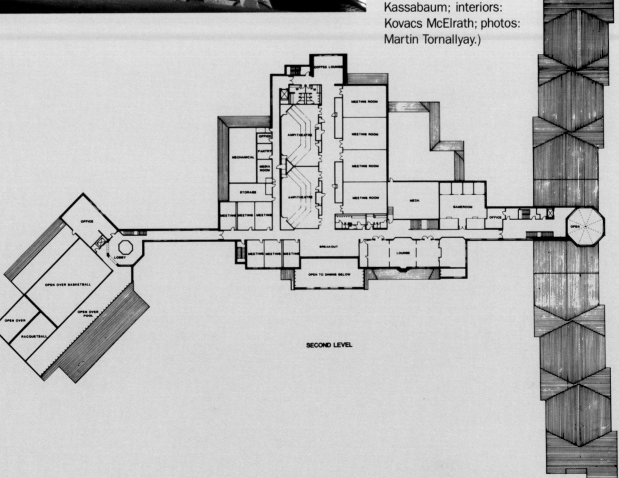

SECOND LEVEL

Part of Merrill Lynch's corporate office campus in Princeton, New Jersey, the 350-room center is designed not only for training but for in-house conferences and presentations as well. The main residential wings contain 290 rooms on five floors, extending out from the lobby and social center, including a pub, a game room, and recreational facilities. A bridge extends to the conference core, which also features the conference and informal dining rooms and a separate 60-room executive center with its own conference and dining areas. The 316-seat amphitheater includes the latest video and computer technology, such as an audience-response system, closed-circuit television, and teleconferencing (which is also available throughout the 30 soundproof meeting rooms). Five rooms are designed as telephone labs, which provide simulated and live training in telephone sales. Other rooms incorporate rear-screen projection, a multitude of built-in systems, and such amenities as in-room storage and oversized conference tables. (Architect: The Kling-Lindquist Partnership; interiors: Daroff Design; photos: Tom Crane.)

Customer Training and Support Centers.
A less common type of corporate center is the customer support center, which provides training to large corporate customers of such companies as IBM and Digital Equipment. As with other projects, the design and relative quality level of the training center sets a tone that reinforces the company's relationship with the facility's users—customers, rather than employees in this case. It is important here to carefully assess the operational program. These users are not company employees who can be told when to eat or where to gather. There should be a number of alternatives available to the users, including variety in the types of dining rooms, options for individual and team sports, and both indoor and outdoor areas for informal gathering.

IBM and DEC developed widely divergent plans for their customer centers. The DEC facility is designed to house both customer classes and employee training. Although the schematic plans include housing and recreational components for the employees, they clearly address the separate needs for the nonresidential customers. This includes demonstration classrooms, lounges, a separate dining room, and such support functions as storage and telephone areas. On the other hand, the IBM Advanced Business Institute in Palisades, New York, is intended only for corporate customers. Here the three conference functions are expressed architecturally with different building elements. The 206 guestrooms and fitness center are in one wing, the lobby, lounge, and dining in a central pavilion, and the conference and administrative functions in a third wing, all focused on a major pond. The expansive project, encompassing over 433,000 square feet (40,269 square meters) and designed to be further expanded if necessary, is beautifully integrated into the landscape and preserves the retreatlike woodland character of the site while establishing a memorable architectural presence.

Corporate Guest Houses. One of the most interesting types of corporate meeting centers is the guest house or corporate retreat, which can vary tremendously in intent as well as design. These luxurious corporate facilities are generally small (often having fewer than twenty rooms), personally scaled, and meticulously operated. Some of the most exciting are the remote mountain getaways, more often used for fishing trips than for corporate meetings.

IBM Management Development Center, Armonk, New York. The six-building management center, sited on 26 acres (10.5 hectares) of a larger corporate property, is placed on a ridge to take advantage of wooded views. The native field-stone buildings define small courtyards and are grouped to create an informal campus. The main two-level structure houses classrooms (the largest a 124-seat lecture room), a library, a dining room, an archive, and instructional and administrative offices. Three residence buildings provide 160 bedrooms and large lounges; a fourth 20-unit executive center includes its own classroom and dining area. Another building includes exercise space and a mechanical plant. (Architect and interiors: AG/ENA; photos: Norman McGrath.)

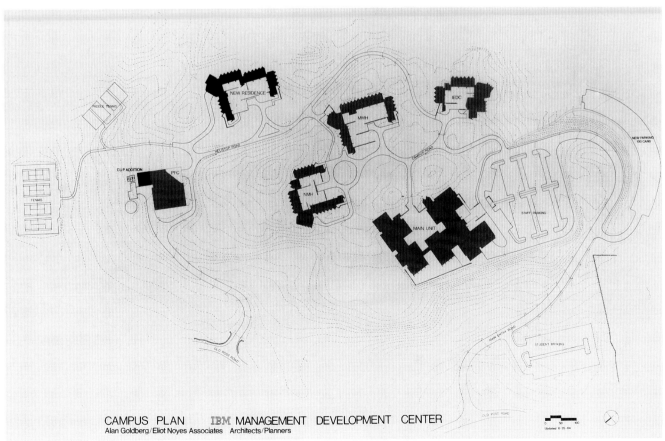

CAMPUS PLAN   IBM MANAGEMENT DEVELOPMENT CENTER
Alan Goldberg/Eliot Noyes Associates   Architects/Planners

IBM Technical Education Center, Thornwood, New York. This 285,000 square foot (26,505 square meter) training center consists of a group of interconnected white brick buildings organized around a central courtyard. The 250 rooms are located in three wings on one side; the educational spaces, including an auditorium, a library, several computer rooms, and scores of training offices, are placed on the opposite side; and the dining area and lobby close off the two ends. (Architect: RTKL; photos courtesy of RTKL.)

Generally the guest house is located within a few miles of the corporate headquarters so that it is convenient for senior executives and VIP guests. Often, the company will renovate an older property, sometimes the founder's home, and display a collection of corporate memorabilia. The Johnson Company in Racine, Wisconsin, spent six years developing The Council House, a guest house and 20-room executive conference center for corporate officials and company visitors, completed in 1979. Surrounding the atrium lobby are a group of public rooms: a conference room with closed-circuit television, rear-screen projection, and computer-operated communications; a board room specifically designed to accommodate the directors' quarterly meetings; and several distinctive lounge and dining areas.

More casual is Herman Miller's corporate educational and program center, completed in 1983. On the grounds of historic Marigold Lodge in western Michigan, the furniture manufacturer has rebuilt the former carriage house and boathouse, incorporating in the modified plan nine guestrooms and two small meeting rooms. As befits such small, personal retreats, the programs and designs for these small corporate centers are unique—no two are the same.

DESIGN CONSIDERATIONS

The corporate training and management development centers differ more as a group than does any other category: some companies separate entry-level employees from middle management; some wish to separate different classes within the center; others consciously attempt to integrate the different users so that they develop a single corporate identity and spirit. Accordingly, the design objectives are similarly diverse.

Guestrooms. Because of the relatively large amounts of space dedicated to the residential wings in corporate conference centers—generally slightly more than half the total gross area—the size of the standard guestroom unit is a key programming decision and one of the most highly discussed and debated aspects of corporate training facilities. A small room (200 net square feet, say) encourages participants to use the public areas, meet coworkers, and network, and it implies a serious, businesslike approach to training; a standard to large room suggests more concern for the attendees' comfort, a willingness to invest in their welfare.

Generally, corporations do not provide oversized rooms, partly because single occupancy makes them unnecessary, but some do provide near-luxurious furnishings and extra amenities. The IBM-Palisades project, for instance, includes handsome guest accommodations of about 280 net square feet (26 net square meters), featuring a carefully detailed built-in dresser and work surface, a computer, and an open millwork screen allowing natural light to reach the dressing area.

The program and design decisions are based on the level of the attendee, anticipated single or double occupancy, corporate intent, and, of course, budget. In any case, the rooms need to meet basic functional requirements and provide comfortable sleeping, work, and sitting areas, adequate clothes storage, good lighting, soundproofing, and so forth. The simpler rooms include twin beds against one wall, a built-in dresser–desk unit along the opposite wall, and wall-mounted fluorescent lighting, providing uninteresting but adequate and equivalent space for two occupants. The more luxurious rooms incorporate residential furnishings: a separate desk and dresser, comfortable lounge chairs, an armoire with television, and table lamps, for example.

The bathrooms are much like those in hotels. Training centers with high double occupancy should have at least one lavatory outside the bathroom. Nearly all centers include a combination tub-and-shower, although the GE Management Development Institute has large stall showers, each the size of a tub, that guests particularly enjoy. Corporate centers with relatively long programs—over two weeks, say—must consider additional space for clothes storage.

Corporate education centers have the most technologically sophisticated guestrooms. Many have computers as standard equipment, or are at least wired for their future addition. Most guestrooms receive closed-circuit television programs from the audiovisual control room. Two telephone lines, with call-waiting, voice mail, conference calling, and other typical features of office phone systems, are common. The GE center has an integrated office phone system throughout, including an outside line for each guestroom, allowing guests to make and receive calls directly, without going through the house operator.

Corporate facilities tend to include extra lounges within the residential zones, again to encourage informal contact. The character of these is similar to that of the guestrooms: the

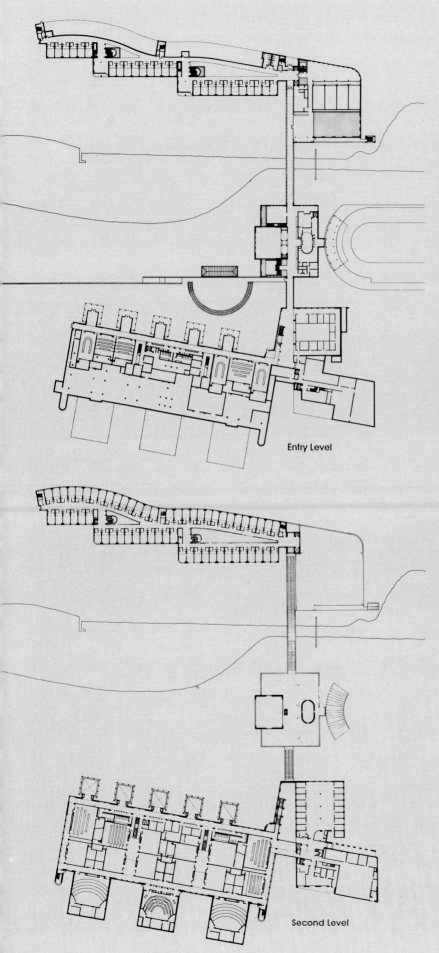

Entry Level

Second Level

IBM ADVANCED BUSINESS INSTITUTE
....

Among the newest IBM facilities, opened in 1989 in Palisades, New York, the customer education center surrounds a long pond on 106 acres (42.9 hectares) north of New York City. Sited to protect the local wooded character and take advantage of the terrain, the 206 guestrooms, organized along wide, multistory galleries, are in a serpentine structure, with the social and recreation center placed at one end. The elegant rooms feature a lattice divider between the bed area and the dressing room, as well as computer workstations. The three-story conference and administrative wing contains three large amphitheaters, 18 conference rooms, additional breakout rooms, and a floor of training and marketing offices. The educational spaces incorporate the newest computer and audiovisual technology. Refreshments are served in 10 pavilions, five on each floor, offering privacy and a more intimate scale to each individual class. Despite its great size—over 430,000 square feet (39,990 square meters)—the project is beautifully detailed, from the larger lobby, dining room, and teaching spaces to the smaller pavilions and guestrooms, with carefully selected finishes, furnishings, and artwork. (Architect and interiors: Mitchell/Giurgola; photos: Mick Hales.)

COUNCIL HOUSE

Johnson Wax built this 20-room guest house and conference retreat, six years in the planning and construction, near their corporate headquarters in Racine, Wisconsin. Housing an extensive international art collection, the project groups a number of public rooms around a central two-story lobby, with the guestrooms, including the four-room Chairman's Suite, upstairs. The public areas include a living room with a separate library area and a game room with a lower lounge area, both featuring large, native-stone fireplaces, as well as individual conference and boardrooms divided by audiovisual space, a dining room, and a small health club. Each of the rooms can be closed from the atrium and offers flexibility for receptions or private meetings. (Architect: Torke/Wirth/Pujara; interiors: Hague-Richards; photos: Hedrich Blessing.)

FIRST FLOOR PLAN

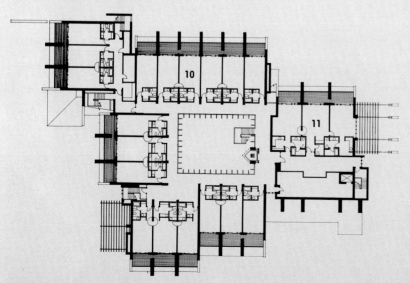

Legend
1. Entry lobby
2. Atrium
3. Living room
4. Game room
5. Health club facilities
6. Conference room
7. Boardroom
8. Dining room
9. Kitchen
10. Guestrooms
11. Director's office

SECOND FLOOR PLAN

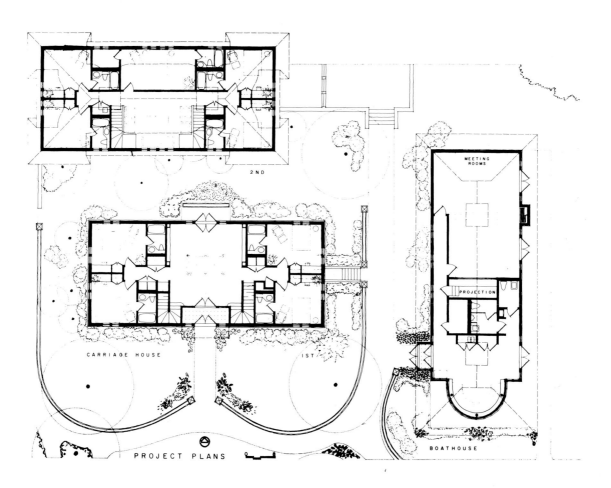

2ND

CARRIAGE HOUSE   1ST

MEETING
ROOMS

PROJECTION

PROJECT PLANS

BOATHOUSE

Marigold Lodge, Zeeland, Michigan.
The Herman Miller corporate guest and meeting facility is located on a former estate in southwestern Michigan. In addition to the restored 28-room Marigold mansion, the owners constructed a five-room learning center and rebuilt the carriage house and boathouse to provide further guestroom and meeting space. The boathouse offers a subdivisible meeting room and a comfortable lounge in a prowlike space, sheltered by low, overhanging roofs, as well as outdoor decks and terraces. (Architect: Nagle, Hartray & Associates; photos: Howard N. Kaplan, © HNK Architectural Photography.)

simpler, more spartan training facilities have dormitory-like lounges; the more luxurious, hotel-like center lounges include comfortable seating, group work areas, computers, and televisions. In some centers these lounges offer refreshments, at least a continental breakfast in the morning, and beverages and snacks in the afternoon and evening, further encouraging informal socializing.

Public Areas. For many corporations, the conference center provides a major opportunity to make a tangible indication of the importance of training. Public areas and lounges are especially important for conveying this message and, as a result, often are large or contain some special design element. At IBM-Palisades, the architects provided a great hall, a 30-foot-high space overlooking the immaculate grounds, featuring oversized leather seating and a fireplace. GTE architects designed a more personally scaled space, with a finely detailed oak stairway leading to the conference and residential spaces. The formal lobby, though, is little more than a piece of the entry sequence in corporate centers; most of the informal gathering occurs in other lounges, dining areas, or break spaces.

Like other types of conference centers, corporate facilities generally feature a three-meal conferee dining room with buffet or cafeteria service. This is one of the key spaces for enhancing the guest experience, and its interior layout, should provide an appropriate mix of tables, adequate privacy for conversation, discrete areas for the individual conference groups, proper orientation to attractive views, and opportunities for outdoor dining. Because of the importance of meal periods for informal conversations and learning, the dining rooms are generously sized and usually are flooded with natural light to make the room as comfortable and engaging as possible.

The design approach for breakfast varies widely at corporate centers. At IBM-Palisades, continental breakfast is available in the casual dining room and in two guest-floor lounges beginning at 5:30 A.M. for guests who are exercising or studying very early in the morning. In addition to recognizing the needs of early risers, this serves as an alternative to using the main dining room, which is some distance from the guestrooms and has a more formal dress code. At many facilities breakfast service ends at 8:00 or 8:30 because it is assumed that everyone is in class. The training department

or center management company should establish the final operational criteria.

Because meeting attendees are often captive for a week or longer, it is important to provide some alternative dining opportunities. These can be of several types: If the conferee dining room is formal, casual options are introduced; if the main dining room is more casual, a specialty restaurant offering a more formal meal is provided; or meals may be served or delivered in private dining rooms, lounges, or outdoor terraces, by prior arrangement.

Lounges—not the guest-area lounges discussed earlier, but in other areas—are important to the ambience and experience of attending a corporate conference or training center. A common feature is a somewhat formal game room located near the lobby (Merrill Lynch), a casual dining room (IBM-Palisades), or various pub-lounge spaces (GTE). Planners should note that some companies do not permit on-site alcoholic beverages, a stipulation requiring the design team to establish another focus for the lounge spaces.

Many corporate centers have found much more need for banquet space than they originally envisioned; several have added additional space or removed walls to double the size of private dining rooms. Banquet areas are more closely associated with the food and beverage outlets than with the meeting or function space. Such areas usually are located near the conference or specialty dining, with access to the same kitchen.

Conference and Training Areas. Obviously, careful consideration must go into planning and designing the conference and training areas—these are the reasons for the project in the first place. Each type of center has different needs for its largest conference space (Table 4–4). At corporate centers, this space generally is an auditorium or elegant amphitheater with 150 to 200 seats. Common uses include full-group lectures prior to breaking into instructional groups, panel discussions, and audiovisual presentations. If the center is near or adjoins the corporate headquarters, the auditorium may be used for major presentations or announcements by the corporate officers. Some programs have proposed a subdivisible auditorium seating arrangement, but this seldom works satisfactorily. Instead, the interior decor, acoustics, lighting, and possible inclusion of a balcony should make the room equally comfortable for small groups and the full capacity.

The meeting rooms must be carefully paired with the anticipated type of corporate meeting. Training centers generally emphasize rooms of 1,200 to 2,000 square feet (111.6 to 186 square meters), often set up classroom-style for 30 to 40 participants, while the higher-level meetings use rooms of about 1,000 square feet (93 square meters), conference-style, for groups of 20 to 25. The training centers generally have a greater number of identical windowless interior rooms.

Large and medium conference rooms must be sufficiently flexible to accommodate a variety of presentations, lectures, role-playing exercises, audiovisual presentations, and group-work sessions. While amphitheater setups are ideal for certain types of conferences, flat-floored rooms generally are preferable for their flexibility. Most corporate centers also install a large number of rear-projection rooms, often between two similar classrooms, with control from the lectern or front wall or by a wireless unit. *Every* conference room at Eagle Lodge and the IBM Advanced Business Institute incorporates rear-screen projection.

Breakout rooms are essential for most types of educational programs. While they can be provided in the form of subdivisible larger rooms, or in guestroom areas, it is short-sighted not to provide a substantial number of breakout rooms within the main conference core, each about 300 to 500 square feet (27.9 to 46.5 square meters). If the center anticipates groups of 10 to 12 people, the rooms need to be larger, about 400 to 650 square feet (37.2 to 60.4 square meters).

Assembly and break areas are usually in one or two major spaces rather than inside or immediately outside each classroom. This arrangement provides bright, airy lounge spaces, generally a welcome alternative to the often windowless interior rooms. At Aberdeen Woods, coffee and refreshments are served in small pantries, and participants carry their refreshments to the adjacent lounge; IBM features ten distinct coffee pavilions, each assigned to a different group. In any event, management must decide on a strategy for organizing these areas. For example, should there be fewer large spaces, or more small, discrete areas? Although there is usually very little sitting during the breaks, seating groupings help to soften the look of the space and make it suitable for other functions. In order to ensure hot coffee and a high level of service, it is important to have service areas immediately adjacent to the break areas.

Room Type	Training Centers			Management Development Centers		
	Eagle Lodge Lafayette Hill, PA (120 guestrooms)	Aberdeen Woods Peachtree City, GA (150 guestrooms)	IBM Thornwood, NY (250 guestrooms)	GTE Norwalk, CT (118 guestrooms)	IBM Palisades, NY (206 guestrooms)	Merrill Lynch Princeton, NJ (350 guestrooms)
Ballroom	None	None	None	1 @ 3,650 (339)	None	None
Large conference[b]	1 @ 2,900 (270)	1 @ 2,000 (186)	2 @ 1,800 (167) 4 @ 1,600 (149)	None	2 @ 2,000 (186) 3 @ 1,650 (153)	1 @ 2,800 (260) 4 @ 1,650 (153)
Medium conference[c]	None	3 @ 1,200 (112) 2 @ 1,100 (102) 26 @ 1,000 (93)	2 @ 1,400 (130) 2 @ 1,200 (112)	4 @ 1,100 (102)	8 @ 1,250 (116)	None
Small conference[d]	2 @ 775 (72) 9 @ 600 (56)	10 @ 500 (47)	2 @ 975 (91) 2 @ 600 (56)	None	4 @ 900 (84)	4 @ 850 (79) 1 @ 650 (60)
Breakout	12 @ 175 (16)	3 @ 325 (30)	3 @ 250 (23) 15 @ 150 (14)	6 @ 400 (37)	1 @ 350 (33) 17 @ 200 (19)	6 @ 375 (35) 2 @ 325 (30) 6 @ 250 (23)
Amphitheater	1 @ 1,250 (116)	None	None	2 @ 1,750 (163)	3 @ 2,300 (214)	1 @ 7,400 (688)
Auditorium	None	1 @ 1,600 (149)	1 @ 4,800 (446)	None	None	None
Computer/special	1 @ 5,000[e] (465[e])	None	1 @ 1,750[f] (163[f]) 5 @ 600 (56)	None	4 @ 1,100[f] (102[f])	5 @ 850[g] (79[g])
Total conference	18,200 (1,693)	41,375 (3,848)	30,900 (2,874)	13,950 (1,297)	37,600 (3,497)	29,500 (2,744)
Total assembly	5,200 (484)	9,300 (865)	10,600 (986)	3,400 (316)	15,800 (1,469)	16,400 (1,525)
Total support	6,300 (586)	14,500 (1,349)	32,400 (3,013)	12,300 (1,444)	33,100 (3,078)	34,300 (3,190)

[a]Some program areas are rounded and averaged to simplify the presentation.
[b]Larger than 1,500 square feet (139 square meters).
[c]Between 1,000 and 1,500 square feet (93 and 139 square meters).
[d]Between 500 and 1,000 square feet (46 and 93 square meters).
[e]Leased to a private client.
[f]Computer classroom.
[g]Telephone classroom.

Mount Washington Conference Center, Baltimore, Maryland. Constructed on part of the campus of a former women's college, the USF&G complex includes a massive data-processing and educational center. The 50-room conference facility includes a glass dining pavilion overlooking the grounds. (Architect: RTKL; photo courtesy of RTKL.)

Many corporate training centers report inadequate office space for the training staff. In many companies, executives are assigned to the training center to lead the educational programs for a period of six months to three years. These people need full-time office space, sometimes provided by landscape office partitions on a mezzanine or other area, as well as secretarial, copying, mail, and work areas, similar to those enjoyed by other teachers. In some leading corporate centers the office space devoted to trainers and program coordinators exceeds 50 percent of the actual classroom space.

Recreation Areas. When compared to other types of conference centers, corporate train-ing and conference centers generally show a rather restrained approach to fitness and recreational facilities, in part because such amenities are not necessary to help market the property. Most of these centers will feature an exercise room and game room, and many will also have outdoor tennis courts, but fewer than half of the residential centers have an indoor pool or racquetball courts. There is increased demand for team sports, such as softball, however, and more recently the trend has been to manage wellness and fitness by incorporating health-related programs into the class sessions. (Several of the corporate recreational facilities are illustrated later in Chapter 14, Planning the Recreational Facilities.)

CHAPTER 5

University Executive Education Centers

Executive and continuing education programs have been a major part of the university mission since the 1950s and in the late 1980s and early 1990s have become a growth area, representing a new profit center. In addition, they often symbolize the outreach objectives and the cooperative industry–education goals of many schools. Today, over fifty universities offer residential continuing education programs in nondormitory facilities; hundreds more develop summer courses to help utilize empty student housing.

The earliest indication of the change in university orientation from the elite universities of Oxford, Cambridge, and the American colleges of the eastern seaboard was the Morrill Act of 1862, which established land-grant universities whose mission was to combine liberal and practical (most notably agricultural) education. Before the turn of the century, the University of Wisconsin established a "system of extra-collegiate work," emphasizing the professional rather than scholastic needs of teachers and farmers who attended on-campus programs of two or more days. In addition, such private enterprises as the Chautauqua Institution in western New York (see Chapter 7),

provided summer programs combining a wide variety of humanities topics with recreational activities.

Recent studies of the makeup of continuing education programs show them to mirror the North American middle class. More than half of all adults, half of these between twenty-five and thirty-nine years old, attend some type of program. One-third of them have at least a bachelor's degree; half are professional people or managers.

The educational programs are established by a wide variety of public and private organizations. The colleges themselves, their cooperative extension units, professional associations, and corporations all sponsor educational programs held at university campuses. The American Management Association alone offers more than two thousand formal education programs each year, many at colleges. In 1989, the business schools at forty-four different American universities offered one or more general management programs at least one week in duration; additional schools offered other specialized courses.

The principal thrust for many of today's university programs originated with the efforts of the Kellogg Foundation, which supported a

Kellogg Center, Michigan State University, East Lansing, Michigan. The Kellogg Foundation's broad-ranging goals led to the construction of the Kellogg Center, which became a model for future university centers. (Interiors: DiLeonardo International; photo: Warren Jagger.)

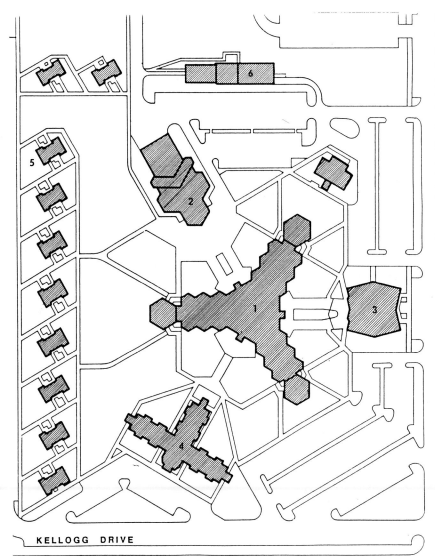

KELLOGG DRIVE

Kellogg Center, Michigan State University, East Lansing, Michigan
(facing page). First opened in 1951, the Kellogg Center has undergone several expansion and renovation projects, the most recent in 1989. The designers replanned many of the interior areas and created a unified theme through the consistent use of custom lighting and polished granite, rosewood, and other materials. (Interiors: DiLeonardo International; photos: Warren Jagger.)

Oklahoma Center for Continuing Education, Norman, Oklahoma
(above). Among the earliest Kellogg-funded projects, the Oklahoma Center is an adult learning community designed as a cluster of individual structures. The Forum Building includes an unusual amphitheater-in-the-round for 550 participants, smaller amphitheaters, and 15 conference rooms. (Plan courtesy of University of Oklahoma.)

Legend
1. Classrooms
2. Commons
3. Offices
4. Dormitory
5. Cottages
6. Maintenance

number of extracurricular educational endeavors. These programs were initially designed for rural youth, but expanded to include adult education. Among the earliest precedents to which the Foundation looked was the Center for Continuation Study at the University of Minnesota in the 1930s. Following this example, and after seven years of discussion and planning, the Foundation established its first residential continuing education center in 1951 at Michigan State University in East Lansing.

The Kellogg Center's immediate success soon meant that its facilities were inadequate. The high demand for conferences forced the school to teach larger classes, compromising the utility of the larger auditorium and conference rooms, exhausting the limited support equipment, and quickly outgrowing the administrative and education offices. Experience showed that the smaller rooms, originally intended for up to thirty people, were needed for breakout groups and committee meetings; in effect, they didn't serve to increase the capacity of the center. Two early additions added much-needed space, and the Kellogg Center, successful for nearly forty years, is still undergoing renovations today.

The second Kellogg-assisted program, established at the University of Georgia in 1956, similarly succeeded beyond its original concept, necessitating the addition of a subdivisible dining–banquet room and an informal cafeteria. The Georgia Center included over sixty private and semiprivate offices and twenty classrooms, most holding more than thirty people.

Two other Kellogg centers show interesting architectural solutions. In 1962 the University of Oklahoma developed a cluster of separate buildings, the Oklahoma Center for Continuing Education, described as "an adult learning community in miniature and the focal point for the continuing education and public service function of the university." The site plan includes conference rooms and a major auditorium in one building, dining and commons spaces in another, and administrative offices, hotel guestrooms, and small cottages in additional structures. In many ways, this approach is closer to that of resort conference centers, which require outdoor movement between functions and certain corporate training centers.

The other architecturally innovative design is architect Edward Durell Stone's 1962 concept for an urban continuing education facility

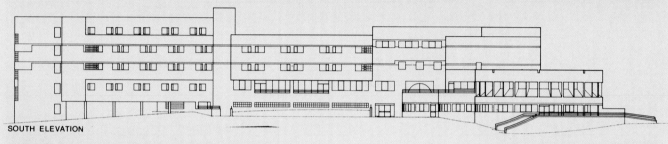

SOUTH ELEVATION

The American College in Bryn Mawr, Pennsylvania, offers certification and graduate degrees for the insurance and financial services industries on its 40-acre (16.2-hectare) campus outside Philadelphia. The Gregg Center contains 50 guestrooms, conference and meeting facilities, and dining for the entire college in three wings, joined by the lobby. The conference core features a formal 250-seat auditorium, six classrooms, breakout rooms, and faculty and program offices. Bilevel amphitheaters are constantly used for advanced management meetings requiring group interaction. The single-loaded residential wing is raised on pylons to allow uninterrupted movement and views under the building. The curved dining room overlooks the central campus, and the dining seating can be extended onto a terrace when the weather is good. (Architect and interiors: Mitchell/Giurgola; photos: Eric Mitchell.)

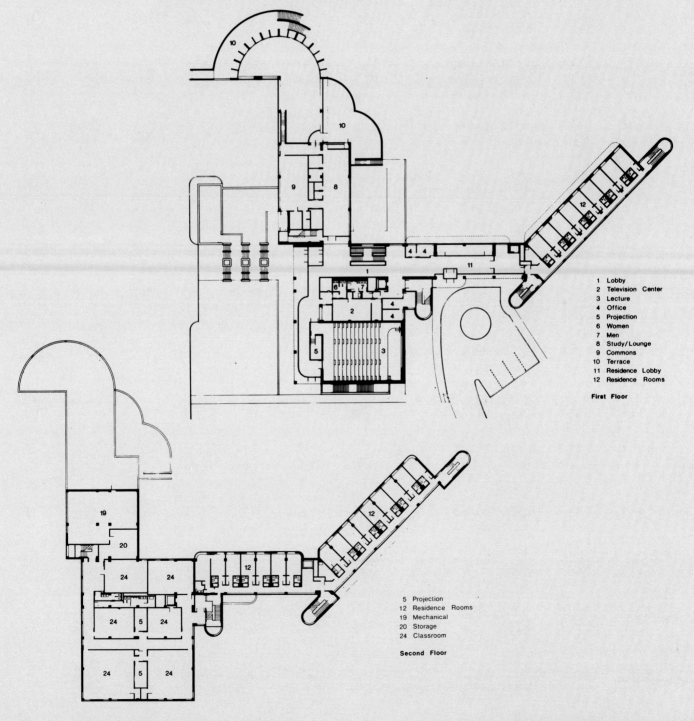

1 Lobby
2 Television Center
3 Lecture
4 Office
5 Projection
6 Women
7 Men
8 Study/Lounge
9 Commons
10 Terrace
11 Residence Lobby
12 Residence Rooms

First Floor

5 Projection
12 Residence Rooms
19 Mechanical
20 Storage
24 Classroom

Second Floor

at the University of Chicago, only recently converted to a graduate residence hall. The building consists of a monolithic three-story block raised above a podium containing service facilities and an auditorium. The 120-room center establishes a prominent and formal presence not unlike some of the architect's embassy designs of the same period.

Contrasting with the Oklahoma and Chicago facilities is the New England Center in Durham, New Hampshire, a group of interconnected hexagonal structures stretching through mature woods and in many ways the forerunner of some of today's executive conference centers, which often are sited in wooded suburban settings and feature a close relationship between the man-made and the natural. The New England Center has approximately doubled in size from when it opened in 1970, now offering 115 rooms following the completion of a second guestroom structure that duplicates the details of the original tower design. Each floor contains only ten rooms (both singles and doubles) and features a brightly daylit lounge opposite the elevator lobby. This commons area is a typical feature of many conference and executive education facilities, especially the more intensive business- or management-oriented programs, which expect the participants to undertake a large amount of evening study and discussion.

PROGRAM AND PLANNING CONSIDERATIONS

University conference centers gain immeasurable advantage from their campus location. Meeting participants welcome the opportunity to live and study in a college environment, with its proximity to the faculty, library, museum, and recreational opportunities. Indeed, many corporate conference and training centers try to establish just this sort of ambience. Often, the centers are part of a smaller campus belonging to the business school, as at Harvard, where the Graduate School of Management, including the 160-room executive facility, is across the Charles River from the Cambridge campus.

While it is beneficial to incorporate flexibility and adaptability into every project, the university projects often are closely modeled on a particular curricular design, such as when the business faculty establish a class size of fifty with very precise breakout needs. The guestroom floors at the Steinberg Center at Wharton, for example, feature one commons area for every seven guestrooms, the number

of students per group assigned to discuss and prepare business case studies. A university facility can be designed for this exact market, without the additional flexibility needed to attract a variety of business, management, association, or corporate groups. However, each project must consider to what degree the facility is open to the public. For example, does the conference center welcome corporate recruiters, prospective students or faculty, alumni, and parents, or is it restricted to the narrow but clearly definable educational conference?

As a result, there is an opportunity to provide conference facilities at colleges and universities in order to meet the growing demand from several segments. One type is the *executive education center*, usually affiliated with a graduate business or management school. Closely related are centers developed to sponsor or encourage new cooperative initiatives between business and education; these often are affiliated with business or medical schools. A second category is the *continuing education center*, generally associated with each state's land grant mission; the Oklahoma Center, for example, was intended to "facilitate the blending of occupational and special learnings with general and liberal education." Less closely imitative of generic conference facilities is the *university hotel and conference center*, which nonetheless features a much higher proportion of meeting space than similar non-campus properties. These hotels often house the business school executive programs as well as the full range of academic and research-oriented meetings. A last category is the *university retreat*, often remote from campus, and further discussed in Chapter 7. Conceptual requirements for university facilities are summarized in Table 5–1.

While most conference centers tend to establish a private, low-profile appearance, set among woods on suburban estates, the university center may be considerably more dominant architecturally. This is because the center serves as the primary public facility establishing the image of the university, especially when compared with most classroom, office, and research buildings. (Public relations officers have called the Statler Hotel at Cornell, for instance, "the gateway to the University.") Often this high-profile effect is accomplished in part because of tight site constraints requiring that the building be higher than it otherwise might be. In addition, the height offers views over the university campus, appealing to most visitors and especially to alumni.

TABLE 5-1. UNIVERSITY CONFERENCE CENTER CONCEPTUAL REQUIREMENTS

Project Aspect	Aims and Requirements
Siting	Select site convenient to business school; physically connect to academic buildings where possible; provide separate approach and porte cochere; establish views into private courtyards or across campus
Guestrooms	Provide designs for single occupancy (double occupancy at campus hotels and continuing education centers); rooms should be of average size; include case study discussion rooms on every floor
Lobby	Create special space to reinforce image of university; separate circulation to faculty club or other nonconference functions; provide seating area for informal gathering
Restaurants	Provide single conference dining room with buffet or servery design and with private dining alcoves; design discrete bar areas if required; include additional seating areas for spontaneous meeting
Conference rooms	Include 50-person capacity amphitheaters for case study curricula; provide additional generic classrooms and numerous breakout rooms; add computer classroom if required
Conference support	Provide single conference foyer convenient to all rooms; include additional seating; equip with standard audiovisual systems
Recreation	Provide small fitness center; other sports facilities are elsewhere on campus

Similar objectives lead to the development of grandly scaled interior spaces. The lobby may become a major meeting point on the campus, the dining room the home for entertaining official visitors, and the conference rooms the focus of prominent executive education programs. While larger hotels attempt to limit traffic by creating separate entrances to the function space, restaurants, and so on, the university facility may want to concentrate this activity to create a greater sense of energy.

University centers, usually ranging from 50 to 150 rooms, are smaller than their executive and corporate counterparts. The smallest focus on a wide variety of continuing education topics, the midsize often are associated with the executive programs, and the largest serve as the multipurpose hotel and conference centers now being added to many major research universities. On an urban campus, the best approach may be to build a nonresidential conference center near a commercial hotel, or to acquire a suburban property in order to establish an off-campus facility.

Frequently, university officials are challenged to use real estate that has been donated to the university. Although Temple and MIT operate such education centers, and Columbia University successfully converted the magnificent former Harriman estates into the mountaintop Arden House and Arden Homestead, urban townhouses, suburban estates, or rural farms are only occasionally appropriate for renovation as a university conference facility. These examples just cited are conducive to smaller meetings, their remote location assures that the participants remain together in the evenings, and there are none of the distractions that might be on the main campus, but the lack of proximity to the library, faculty, and university research and recreational facilities must be recognized.

Parking is a serious issue on all campuses, and the early planning of a university facility must consider appropriate and realistic solutions. Although visitors to an urban campus may not need or even have a car, conference guests to suburban and rural universities generally do; in addition, other guests, such as alumni, parents, and sports fans, are likely to arrive by car from the immediate region.

Executive Education Centers. Many major research universities have found that executive education programs continue to thrive as corporations compete for a dwindling pool of

THE STATLER HOTEL AND
MARRIOTT EXECUTIVE EDUCATION CENTER

Completed in 1989, the 150-room Statler Hotel at Cornell University in Ithaca, New York, replaced a smaller campus inn on the same site. The 10-story limestone and granite building houses the conference facilities, the university faculty club, and a teaching hotel for the School of Hotel Administration. Architectural and interior millwork details are carefully coordinated, repeating a low-arch shape at the entrances and throughout the public areas. The lobby level includes the 90-seat Marriott amphitheater and seven meeting rooms, as well as refreshment areas and a cocktail lounge. The hotel features two dining rooms, one serving faculty and conferees, the other a gourmet restaurant; a ballroom for 400; and five private dining rooms. Four of the guestroom floors include case study discussion lounges, which can also be used as suite living rooms. (Architect: The Architects Collaborative; interiors: Kenneth E. Hurd and Associates; exterior photo: Charles Harrington; interior photo: Ed Jacoby.)

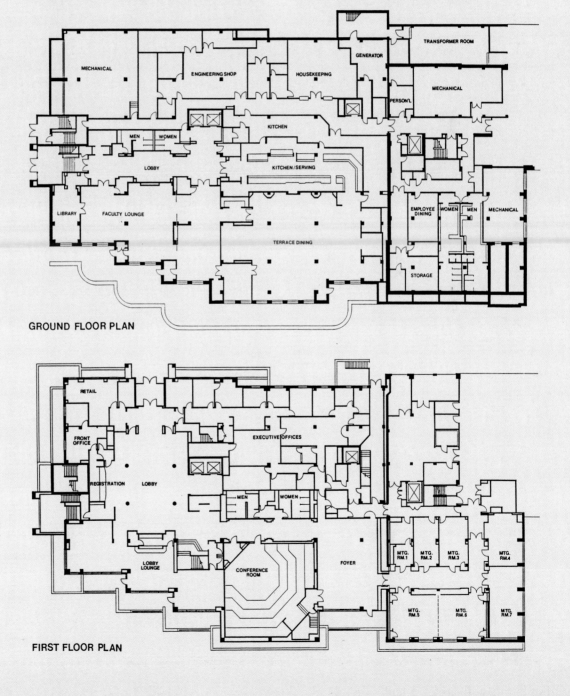

GROUND FLOOR PLAN

FIRST FLOOR PLAN

well-educated prospective employees. Ongoing changes in the global business and political community are likely to fuel further course development. Serving this need is the executive education center, the university meeting facility most similar to other conference centers, usually associated with the graduate business school. A 1988 report by the Graduate Management Business Council states there is "substantial growth in the demand for programs, stemming in part from the perceived challenges to management arising from increased international competition and the rapid development of new technology."

Most executive education centers are physically connected to the business or management schools they serve, although site-suitability issues force a few of them to be located a short distance away. The University of Michigan business school undertook a three-phase expansion program that included building, in sequence, a library, an office–conference structure, and the adjoining lodging–dining tower. And at both Duke and Wharton, the recently completed executive education centers are connected to the respective business schools. These projects, ideally, take the form of small executive conference centers, with conference rooms in dedicated wings or on separate floors, and other public facilities and guestrooms oriented around a courtyard, overlooking woods, or otherwise providing a respite from the academic rigors.

Of the principal conference center categories, university facilities require the least amount of area per room: about 800 to 1,000 gross square feet (74.4 to 93 square meters) (Table 5–2), although this provides only minimally sufficient space for sleeping and conference rooms. The residential areas tend to be slightly under half the total project area—about 45 to 50 percent. In most projects, the size of the individual guestroom is 250 to 275 square feet (23.2 to 25.5 square meters), although a few universities have constructed more dormitory-like housing with single rooms as small as 200 square feet (18.6 square meters), and schools with the potential for transient business hotel-like structures with rooms in the range of 300 to 325 square feet (27.9 to 30.2 square meters). These larger rooms are more likely to remain acceptable in the future to increasingly value-oriented customers; the smaller rooms, while adequate for basic sleep, study, and hygiene, are unsuitable for anything but single occupancy. Because of the immense amounts of group coursework in the evenings and weekends, it is particularly important for university executive education facilities to include large numbers of guest-room commons areas, case study rooms, or conference–living rooms convenient to or adjoining the sleeping rooms.

Lobby and dining areas average about 10 percent of the project area, although at centers with larger food and beverage operations, including faculty dining or catering operations, the figure may reach 15 percent. The confer-

Executive Residence, University of Michigan, Ann Arbor, Michigan. The residential and executive education conference buildings are part of a coordinated expansion of the business school facilities at Michigan. The dining and lounge areas look onto a courtyard defined by the new structures and connect directly into the two classroom levels, which include two amphitheaters and 10 other meeting and breakout rooms. (Architect: Luckenbach/ Ziegelman and Partners; photos: Christopher Lark.)

TABLE 5-2. UNIVERSITY EXECUTIVE EDUCATION CENTERS, SAMPLE PROGRAMS IN GROSS SQUARE FEET (GROSS SQUARE METERS)

	Executive Residence University of Michigan Ann Arbor, MI (96 guestrooms)	Steinberg Center University of Pennsylvania Philadelphia, PA (103 guestrooms)	Allen Center Northwestern University Evanston, IL (104 guestrooms)	Thomas Center Duke University Durham, NC (113 guestrooms)	Center for Executive Education Babson College Wellesley, MA (130 guestrooms)	Statler Hotel Cornell University Ithaca, NY (150 guestrooms)
Guestrooms	31,300 (2,911)	62,800 (5,840)	42,300 (3,934)	46,400 (4,315)	52,300 (4,864)	74,100 (6,891)
Public areas	10,600 (986)	10,200 (949)	12,300 (1,144)	12,300 (1,144)	11,100 (1,032)	28,500 (2,651)
Conference areas	27,000 (2,511)	29,100 (2,706)	26,700 (2,483)	19,500 (1,814)	29,600 (2,753)	21,700 (2,018)
Administrative areas	500 (47)	4,300 (400)	3,400 (316)	1,900 (177)	2,400 (223)	6,000 (558)
Back-of-house areas	7,000 (651)	9,900 (921)	8,300 (772)	21,800 (2,027)	13,500 (1,256)	29,100 (2,706)
Recreation	0	1,900 (177)	900 (84)	1,900 (177)	0	0
Total	76,400 (7,105)	118,200 (10,993)	93,900 (8,733)	103,800 (9,653)	108,900 (10,128)	159,400 (14,824)
Average per room	796 (74)	1,148 (107)	903 (84)	918 (85)	837 (78)	1,063 (99)

ence dining room often is integrated with the classrooms rather than being located in a separate wing. At both the Steinberg Center (which is part of the Wharton School at the University of Pennsylvania) and the Center for Executive Education at Babson College, for example, seminar participants, immersed in several weeklong classes, move smoothly from class to meals and back with little interruption, functioning as a single group or as a number of case study groups.

The conference dining room should be sized at between 25 and 35 square feet (2.3 and 3.2 square meters) per guestroom, which allows 1.2 to 1.5 seats per room—sufficient for the limited double-occupancy rate and to accommodate the teaching and senior executive education staff. Food and beverage service tends to be of a high standard, in keeping with the reputation of the educational programs.

The conference facilities, which comprise 25 to 35 percent of a university center, are distinguished by the careful programming of highly specific classrooms, usually tiered case study rooms. These amphitheaters total more than 30 percent of the total conference room area, and at the Steinberg Center, the three rooms—two identical rooms for forty and one for one hundred—total 75 percent of the teaching and breakout space. These are sharply curved into a horseshoe shape, providing easy eye contact and encouraging active participation among the attendees.

Some university projects include a dedicated computer room, which is used both for instruction and as a student resource room. Because of the difficulty in instructing more than twenty people at one time, the capacity should be sized at one-half or one-third of the principal classrooms' capacity.

University executive education centers, like corporate training facilities, may need large office suites for educational staff, including the program coordinators, case study writers, and teaching faculty. At the University of Michigan, these offices exceed the amount of classroom space. Also, many university centers house semi-autonomous research centers or institutes, which may require several thousand square feet (several hundred square meters) of office space and present a number of special planning requirements, possibly including a separate outside entrance.

Not surprisingly, university centers have very little or no recreational facilities—generally a small exercise or fitness room is all that is provided, which helps to reduce the

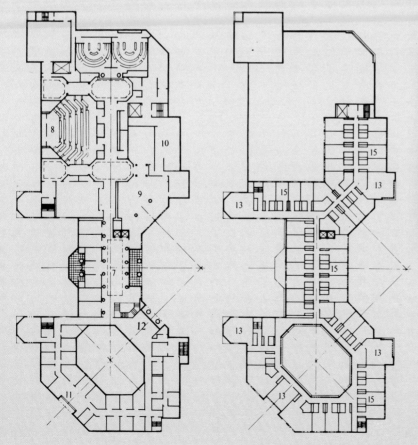

STEINBERG CENTER

Designed specifically for executive education programs at the University of Pennsylvania's Wharton School in Philadelphia, the Steinberg Center was completed in 1988. The five-story brick and limestone building establishes a major presence on the busy street side and includes a passageway to the quieter pedestrian campus behind. An entry courtyard leads to an elegant formal registration lobby. A grand stair rises to the teaching level that includes three amphitheaters, two classrooms, and seven breakout rooms, as well as extensive reception and support areas, the conference dining room, and administrative and faculty offices; the latter are contained in their own wing. The two 45-person tiered rooms are used almost continually and have been enthusiastically accepted by instructors and participants. The three upper floors house 103 guestrooms, arranged so that about seven rooms share a case discussion room furnished with a large seating area, conference table, stocked pantry, television, VCR, and computer. The fifth floor includes a cocktail lounge and small fitness facility. (Architect and interiors: The Hillier Group; exterior photo © 1988 Nathaniel Lieberman; interior photo © Mark Ross, 1988.)

Legend
1. Entry court
2. Lobby
3. Computing resource center
4. MBA reception
5. MBA social space
6. Parking
7. Reception
8. Instructional spaces
9. Dining
10. Kitchen
11. Administration
12. Lounge
13. Study and living space
14. Courtyard
15. Guestroom

project cost. Most guests who want more physical activity can use the athletic facilities elsewhere on campus, often including a university golf course. In fact, when the full campus facilities are considered, university centers offer practically unparalleled recreational opportunities at a moderate cost. Table 5–3 summarizes the mix of teaching spaces in several of the best-known university executive education facilities.

Continuing Education Centers. Many universities see their outreach mission not in terms of small, high-priced executive education courses but in larger continuing education programs for a wide range of departments and individual disciplines. Most land-grant universities, for example, serve as central information points for extension services throughout their respective states and, as a result, are host to scores of educational conferences annually. Other universities establish successful professional development or career development centers, offering noncredit programs on both open- and closed-enrollment bases. At these continuing education centers—which may be residential or nonresidential centers (some are developed in conjunction with an adjacent commercial hotel)—the majority of the area is devoted to conference space. For example, the Paul W. Bryant Conference Center at the University of Alabama includes a multipurpose auditorium for 1,000 people, a 400-seat assembly room, two 50-person tiered amphitheaters, and additional small conference and breakout rooms. Conference dining is available at the Sheraton Inn next door. The center also has state-of-the-art computer and video systems available, including teleconferencing, audio and video recording and dis-

TABLE 5-3. UNIVERSITY EXECUTIVE EDUCATION CENTERS, CONFERENCE CORE SPACE PROGRAMS IN NET SQUARE FEET (GROSS SQUARE FEET)[a]

	Executive Residence University of Michigan Ann Arbor, MI (96 guestrooms)	Steinberg Center University of Pennsylvania Philadelphia, PA (103 guestrooms)	Allen Center Northwestern Evanston, IL (104 guestrooms)	Thomas Center Duke University Durham, NC (113 guestrooms)	Executive Education Babson College Wellesley, MA (130 guestrooms)	Statler Hotel Cornell University Ithaca, NY (150 guestrooms)
Ballroom	None	None	None	None	1 @ 2,350 (219)	1 @ 4,200 (391)
Large conference[b]	1 @ 1,800 (167) 1 @ 1,650 (153)	None	1 @ 1,675 (156)	None	None	None
Medium conference[c]	None	2 @ 1,175 (109)	1 @ 1,250 (116)	1 @ 1,100 (102)	1 @ 1,025 (95)	1 @ 1,150 (107)
Small conference[d]	2 @ 900 (84)	None	1 @ 775 (72) 1 @ 600 (56) 4 @ 500 (47)	None	3 @ 950 (88) 2 @ 550 (51)	1 @ 625 (58)
Breakout	6 @ 125 (12)	1 @ 350 (33) 6 @ 225 (21)	2 @ 325 (30) 2 @ 250 (23)	15 @ 275 (26)	4 @ 450 (42)	3 @ 300 (28)
Boardroom	None	None	None	None	None	1 @ 475 (44)
Amphitheater	2 @ 1,400 (130)	1 @ 2,500 (233) 2 @ 1,175 (109)	1 @ 2,600 (242) 1 @ 2,150 (200) 1 @ 1,750 (163)	2 @ 1,450 (135)	1 @ 1,800 (167) 1 @ 1,100 (102)	1 @ 2,100 (195)
Auditorium	None	None	None	None	None	None
Computer/special	None	None	None	None	1 @ 950[e] (88[e])	None
Total conference	8,800 (818)	8,950 (832)	13,950 (1,297)	8,125 (756)	12,975 (1,207)	9,450 (879)
Total assembly	3,400 (316)	3,400 (316)	4,300 (400)	3,350 (312)	3,800 (353)	4,175 (388)
Total support	14,500 (1,349)	8,800 (818)	2,125 (198)	2,100 (195)	6,800 (632)	1,800 (167)

[a]Some program areas are rounded and averaged to simplify the presentation.
[b]Larger than 1,500 square feet (139 square meters).
[c]Between 1,000 and 1,500 square feet (93 and 139 square meters).
[d]Between 500 and 1,000 square feet (46 and 93 square meters).
[e]Computer classroom.

tribution, multi-image projection, and full internal cable networks. Technicians can prepare custom audiovisual programs, and the media technology rivals that of some of the finest executive conference centers.

Penn State University is developing a massive research park, to be completed by the year 2000, which will include a technology center and research laboratory, a new university conference center, and a commercial hotel. The educational center is expected to feature a ballroom–exhibit area with capacities ranging from 800 people for banquets to 1,400 for theater-style presentations. Other spaces include a 900-seat auditorium, a 200-seat amphitheater, a computer lab, and 37 additional meeting and breakout rooms.

The university continuing education department often needs to demonstrate the demand for a larger facility to the university trustees. To accomplish this, the director or dean needs to undertake or commission a market study, much as would be done for a new hotel or conference center, assessing demand and competition. The study should anticipate future competitive programs, establish prototype programs, and project the facility's guestroom occupancy, classroom utilization, and financial performance. Past experience and a nearby university's existing programs are useful for estimating the necessary number of programs, their length, the number of attendees, any potential for concurrent classes, seasonality factors, and so forth.

Sometimes municipal institutions can assist in the project. The University of Miami, Florida, in partnership with the city of Miami and private investors, developed a combined Hyatt Hotel, city convention center, and university conference center. The university portion includes a 5,000-seat convention auditorium, a second auditorium and amphitheater, and nine smaller meeting rooms; the hotel and convention facility offer additional and complementary spaces for overflow.

University Hotel and Conference Centers. The third type of university conference facility is the campus hotel, which more often includes a major meeting center, similar in many ways to the ancillary executive conference centers discussed in Chapter 2. Universities are generating increasing amounts of overnight lodging and meeting business, and it is natural to offer on-campus accommodations and facilities for this market. Cornell recently razed the former 50-room campus inn and replaced it with the 150-room Statler Hotel and Marriott Executive Education Center, housing the university faculty club on the lower level. The conference center, provided as a gift by the Marriott chain, is an integral part of the project and adjoins the hotel lobby. It includes a 97-seat amphitheater and seven meeting rooms; additional restaurants, lounges, a ballroom, and banquet rooms are in the hotel. Four two-bay conference case study rooms are provided on the upper floors for the executive education participants or for hospitality suites.

Similarly, Georgetown University recently opened the Leavey Center, a new conference center and guest house boasting 146 rooms. The facility is part of a mixed-use project incorporating the hotel, conference rooms, and ballroom with the university bookstore, student dining rooms, faculty club, student affairs offices, credit union, and other functions. Although the ballroom is designed to accommodate banquets for as many as 1,300 people, the conference rooms are best suited to small meetings of twenty-five to fifty.

Other universities are developing or seeking private proposals for hotel conference centers on land leased from the university. Emory University in Atlanta, for example, is pursuing a project intended to serve the needs of the campus and of the National Centers for Disease Control and the American Cancer Society. Both organizations offer scores of professional conferences and seminars and are headquartered on the university grounds. The schematic plans call for a hotel, a ballroom–banquet facility, and a small executive conference center, physically separated to assure the requisite high service level and limited amount of distractions.

These university hotel–conference centers typically include guestrooms of 300 to 325 square feet (27.9 to 30.2 square meters), similar in size to those of many hotels. Also included are conference dining, alternative dining rooms, and a variety of meeting rooms designed to match the unique needs of the local and university markets. These projects have somewhat less conference space than do executive conference centers—about 100 to 150 square feet (9.3 to 13.9 square meters) per room—but somewhat more than university executive education facilities oriented toward a limited enrollment. The university hotels also have less meeting space than the continuing education centers, which are primarily designed to meet the needs of the larger academic conferences.

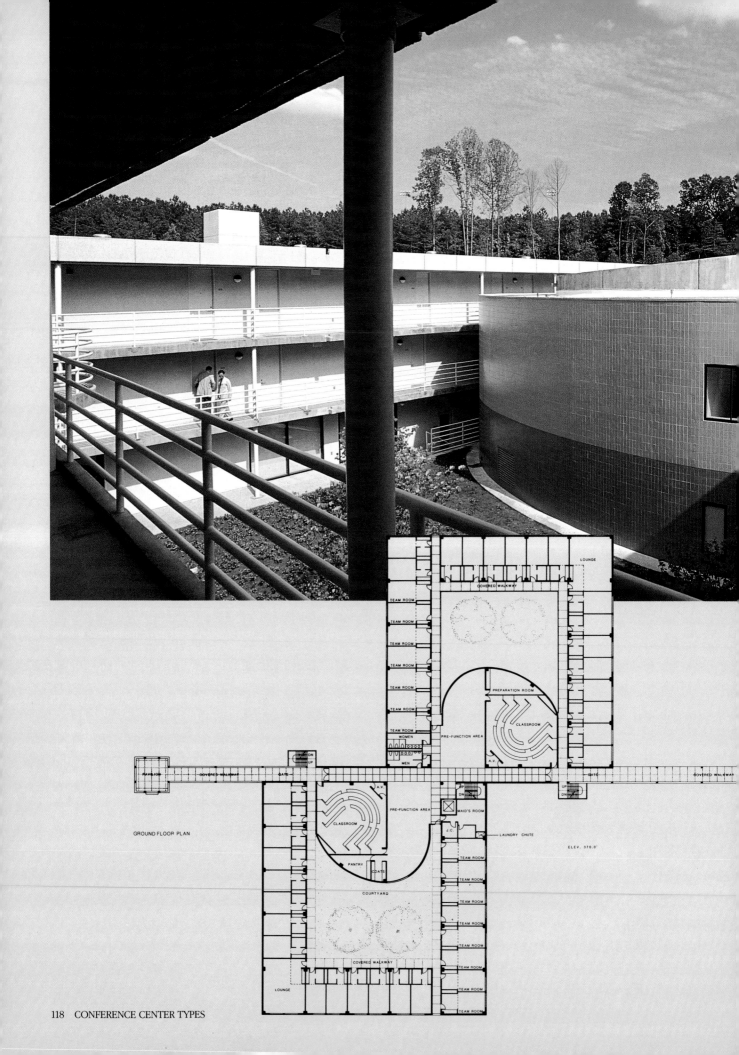

GROUND FLOOR PLAN

LOUNGE

COVERED WALKWAY

TEAM ROOM

TEAM ROOM

TEAM ROOM

TEAM ROOM

TEAM ROOM

TEAM ROOM

TEAM ROOM

WOMEN

MEN

PRE-FUNCTION AREA

PREPARATION ROOM

CLASSROOM

A.V.

PAVILION   COVERED WALKWAY   GATE   A.V.   GATE   COVERED WALKWAY

PRE-FUNCTION AREA

MAID'S ROOM

J.C.

LAUNDRY CHUTE

ELEV. 370.0'

CLASSROOM

PANTRY

COATS

TEAM ROOM

TEAM ROOM

COURTYARD

TEAM ROOM

TEAM ROOM

COVERED WALKWAY

LOUNGE

TEAM ROOM

THOMAS CENTER

Housing the executive programs at Duke University's Fuqua School in Durham, North Carolina, the Thomas Center spreads out over a sloping wooded site adjoining the main campus. The 120,000 square foot (11,160 square meter) center consists of two buildings: one contains the lobby, dining, lounge, and office areas; the other, connected by a covered bridge, includes classrooms and residential spaces in a double-courtyard configuration. The teaching spaces feature two 65-seat tiered amphitheaters, a flat-floored room, and 15 team rooms for group study and discussion. The adjoining 113 guestrooms, arranged along single-loaded exterior walkways, include personal computers; six lounges with kitchenettes are located nearby for informal work sessions. (Architect: Edward Larrabee Barnes/John M. Y. Lee & Partners; aerial photo: Robin Alexander; other photo courtesy of Duke University.)

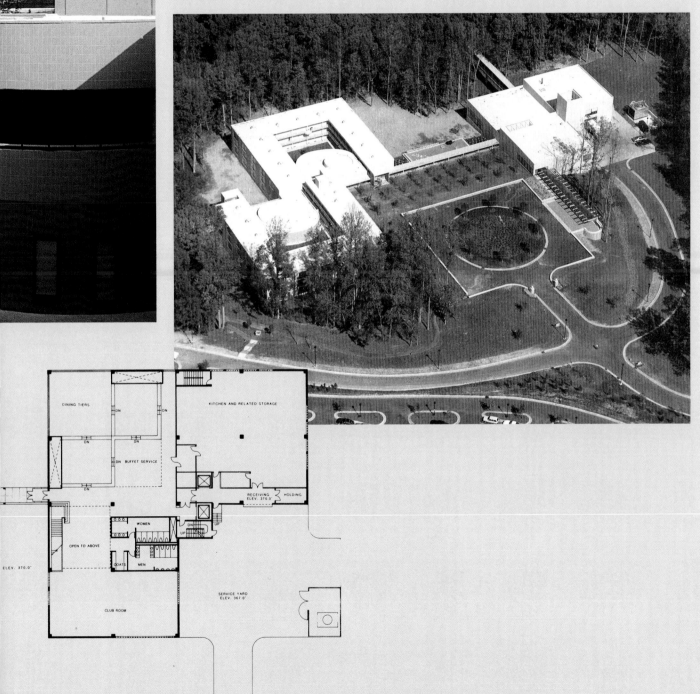

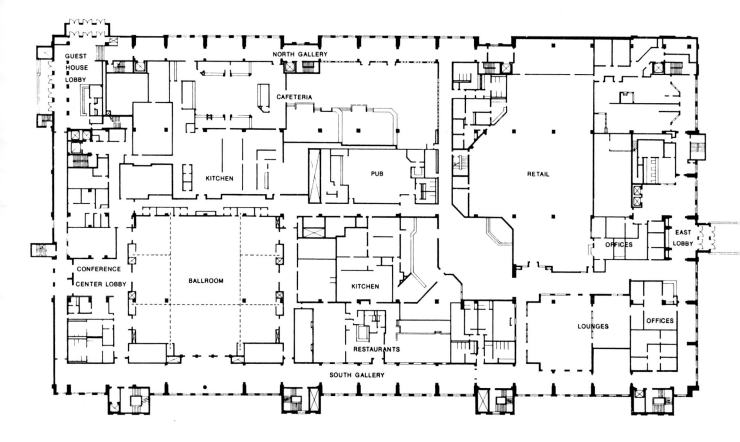

DESIGN CONSIDERATIONS

Among the many design challenges at university centers is to project the appropriate collegiate ambience without resorting to clichés. These centers can be thought of as constituting a continuum, from the upscale executive education center and hotel conference center to the continuing education facility and student union. For the former, designers need to develop a set of spaces that reinforces the sense of a campus while imparting the feeling of a business and educational facility; for the latter, the architects should select images that recall campus events or sports highlights, to appeal to both alumni and students. The different university facilities are intended for very different markets, which needs to be reflected in the design.

Guestrooms. Many meeting participants attending their first university conference may fear that they will be housed in dormitory accommodations. Given the broad base of potential guests—conference attendees, primarily, but also guest lecturers, alumni, trustees, corporate recruiters, parents and family, business visitors—the university guestroom must meet widely acceptable criteria for size and amenities. While student housing is heavily used for certain types of summer conferences, the newer continuing education and executive

education centers offer many of the luxuries of hotels. Older facilities may have small guestrooms, but those being constructed today are generally from 275 square feet (25.5 square meters) (single occupancy, queen bed) to over 325 square feet (30.2 square meters), very much within industry standards.

Most importantly, the room must meet the needs of the conference attendee. This necessitates a large desk, a well-placed television, room for a computer, and seating area for one or more fellow participants. Because some programs run for several weeks (Harvard's management development program has been *shortened* to twelve weeks), a spacious bathroom, large dresser and closet, and comfortable seating are essential.

While most conference centers host groups who are willing to pay for single occupancy, educational groups frequently expect their attendees to share rooms. This is especially true for the school, religious, labor, government, and state organizations, such as 4H and cooperative extension, who constitute large markets for many university continuing education programs, especially at the land-grant institutions. If single occupancy is anticipated, at least 60 percent of the rooms (and possibly as many as 70 to 80 percent) can be planned with queen beds, and the remainder with oversized twins; if large numbers of double occupancy is antici-

Leavey Center, Georgetown University, Washington, D.C. The Leavey Center combines lodging, conference, and multiple university services—student activities, bookstore, student dining, and faculty club—into one carefully zoned building. Separate from the student area are the 146-room university guest house and conference center, including an 850-seat multipurpose ballroom and six breakout rooms. (Architect: Mariani & Associates; plan courtesy of Mariani.)

pated, the majority should be double-double rooms. In both cases, the amount of nonconference business needs to be gauged and the room mix modified accordingly. For instance, the projected market segmentation at Cornell's Statler Hotel and Marriott Executive Education Center is as follows:

Conferences: 35% (90% single occupancy)
University business: 35% (95% single occupancy)
Parents: 10% (90% double occupancy)
Recruiters: 5% (100% single occupancy)
Guest speakers: 5% (80% single occupancy)
Alumni: 5% (85% double occupancy)
Other: 5% (60% double occupancy)

At the Steinberg Center at Wharton and the Thomas Center at Duke, both designed entirely for executive education programs, all the rooms are furnished with one queen bed. On the other hand, Miami University in Ohio built a 40-room campus conference center for the wider market and furnished all rooms with two double beds. Again, the different approaches reflect varying needs and anticipations.

The university conference centers generally provide three types of lounges or commons areas on the guestroom floors:

1. *An open lounge*, away from public circulation, similar to those in many corporate and executive centers.
2. *A rentable guestroom parlor*, furnished as a living room and available by request of the group sponsor. This solution provides the flexibility of additional revenue at peak periods such as graduation, when the floor lounges are not required for group work.
3. *A commons or case study area*, dedicated to a specified number of guestrooms. This essentially creates a suite, because it is dedicated to a specific group of participants.

Public Areas. The conference center has the potential to make a great contribution to the university's overall image and, as a result, often is designed to have a major presence on the campus. The lobby should provide just such a feeling, of course, but other public areas

122 CONFERENCE CENTER TYPES

should receive similar treatment. The Nassau Inn at Princeton University, which was recently remodeled and expanded, houses a fine group of old, antique-furnished, panel-walled lounges, dining rooms, and conference and banquet rooms, which complement the ambience of the old campus.

Through the 1980s, universities increasingly minimized the emphasis on alcoholic beverages at social functions. Many campus centers and hotels now downplay the traditional hotel bar or cocktail lounge, and the old college bars have given way to social centers offering a wide range of food, nonalcoholic beverages, and game activities. Campus conference centers have done much the same. At Wharton, the only bar is part of a residential floor lounge and game room next to a small fitness center; at Cornell, the Regent Lounge, adjoining the lobby but well screened visually, is intended to double as expanded lobby seating and as a conference lounge during the day.

Restaurants need to be sized for the projected conference business but also should anticipate the appropriate amount of prospective local business—many campus conference centers serve the university administration and faculty in the business school, for example. At the American College in Bryn Mawr, Pennsylvania, the 50-room conference center feeds several hundred at lunch, including a large number of day conferees and the entire administrative staff of the college. At Cornell and Georgetown, the university faculty club is housed in the same building as the conference center, increasing the need for food and beverage areas, lounges, administrative, and back-of-house areas. Private dining rooms (rather than a separate alternate dining room) may nonetheless be necessary for awards dinners or occasional school or campus functions.

Conference Rooms. The meeting rooms at university centers should be designed for the specific needs of the particular academic departments or the continuing education office. For example, at many business school executive education programs, only three types of teaching spaces are required: amphitheaters for the ideal class size (usually about forty to fifty), typical carpeted classrooms for the same number, and sufficient breakout rooms for groups of six to ten. If readily accessible, the commons areas located on the guestroom floors may function satisfactorily as breakout areas, reducing the need for multiple small rooms in the conference core. Because these

centers generally will host no more than two or three compatible groups at any one time, the conference assembly and coffee break areas can be combined in a single area.

Surprisingly, the technology needs at most campus centers are not particularly sophisticated. Business school faculty work primarily with overheads and chalk or markers; in fact, some professors are adamant about chalk rather than the newer markers and whiteboard. Management–human resources instructors favor easels, flip charts, and lots of tackable wall space. Only occasionally do professors insist on video projection and computer-generated images, although this can be expected to change as teachers become more comfortable with the instructional technology. Overall, however, most of the classroom design can follow traditional guidelines without becoming overly concerned with, for example, viewing angles.

The other side of the coin is that university faculty are notoriously demanding about room layout, and insist on rearranging tables and chairs for their own particular pedagogical needs. Although conference services staff should arrange the room furnishings, teachers often move from one teaching style to another several times within a program—a given room may need to be converted from straight rows to an open U to paired tables for group work. It is therefore important that the furnishings be sufficiently lightweight to allow quick and easy changes in the room configuration.

Administration and Back-of-House Areas. Administrative offices are similar in size and extent to those in other conference centers. However, the degree to which instructors are provided offices influences the programmatic requirements dramatically. At Wharton, approximately 180 square feet (16.7 square meters) is provided for each faculty member assigned to the executive education program, and the same is given to the management staff handling room reservations, food and beverage, housekeeping, and so forth. Many other centers provide no more than landscape office cubicles half that size.

Back-of-house or service requirements are also similar to those at most other conference and training centers. However, because the building is part of a larger institution, many functions, including the house laundry, maintenance shops, the food commissary, and central engineering services, may be located offsite, especially at urban universities.

CHAPTER 6

Nonresidential Conference Centers

I n addition to the several types of residential projects surveyed in the previous chapters, there is a substantial need for nonresidential conference centers to serve a wide variety of corporate and other users. Many major corporations and other potential developers of meeting and training facilities hesitate to move forward with residential centers because of the expense and risk involved in operating the lodging component of the property year-round. They reason, correctly, that the construction of guestrooms more than doubles the size and cost of the conference center. After studying the need for a conference or training center, these corporations and private developers eventually choose either to do nothing or to build smaller, nonresidential facilities.

Traditionally, most nonresidential centers have been corporate training facilities. Recently, however, a few independent developers have recognized the potential for small, dedicated day meeting centers positioned to attract specific industries for professional and technical conferences. Also, more institutions and organizations have begun to operate nonresidential centers; many medical schools, for example, create small meeting centers for their own conference and training needs, as well as for research symposia, medical association meetings, and conferences sponsored by health-related agencies and organizations. In addition, government agencies occasionally establish centralized meeting centers and hire outside management companies, rather than scattering their conference rooms throughout their office structure. Also, world trade centers include a conference center to complement their exhibit space.

The corporate nonresidential center is still the most prevalent type, however. The sites for these day training centers vary depending on the type of sponsoring organization, its relative centralization, and the location of its headquarters. Crowded downtown sites, for example, offer limited options for expansion; on the other hand, a suburban headquarters may provide the environment conducive to a learning center. For the most part, training centers are established in renovated space at existing office locations. Companies may take over one or more floors near the human resources department, be assigned to new space in nearby structures, or occupy a newly constructed wing.

The independent day meeting centers,

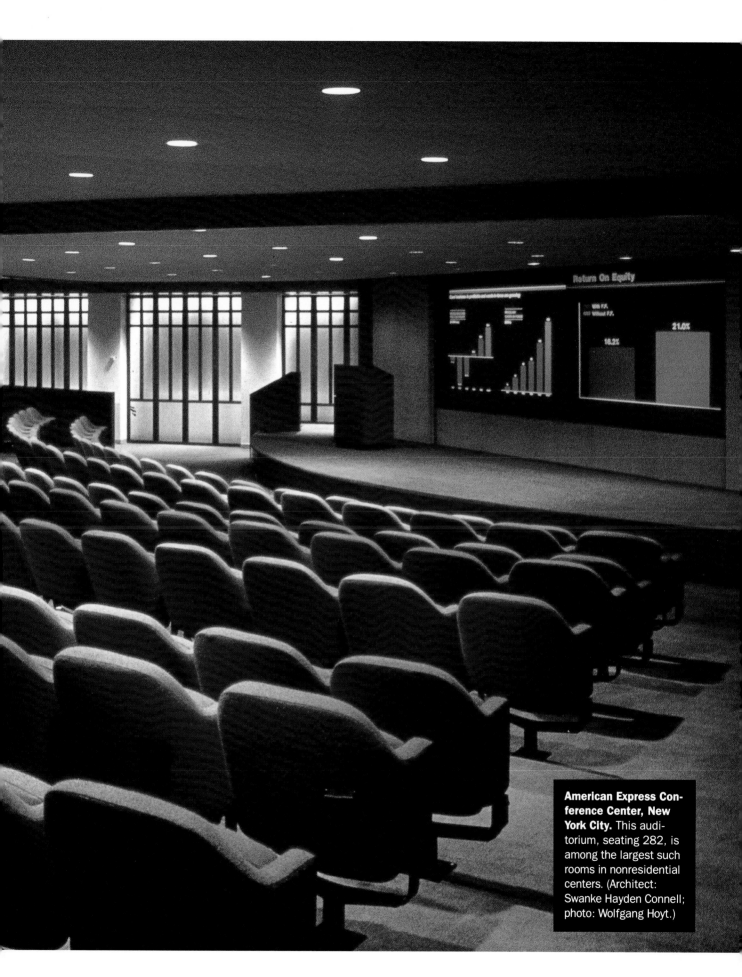

American Express Conference Center, New York City. This auditorium, seating 282, is among the largest such rooms in nonresidential centers. (Architect: Swanke Hayden Connell; photo: Wolfgang Hoyt.)

which are unprotected by corporate subsidies, face a greater risk. Day centers have relatively high start-up costs, including architectural modifications, furniture and equipment, and promotional expenses. Many do not provide food service, and therefore lose the potential revenues from luncheons and special functions. In addition, these centers have difficulty on weekends and off-peak weeks (such as those containing major holidays). For example, the Renaissance Meeting Center in Santa Clara, California, does almost half its business on two days—Wednesday and Thursday—and only 6 percent of its meetings on weekends. Other projects, at unique locations, may have more opportunities to fill the lean periods. Centers located at medical colleges, for example, attract a number of price-sensitive association and state health organizations, which are more willing to meet during low-demand periods.

PROGRAM AND PLANNING CONSIDERATIONS

The process for determining the feasibility of a nonresidential center is similar to that of other types of projects. First, the corporate training department—or an independent developer, medical school, or whatever—must establish the need for conference and training space and project its future growth. The anticipated number of training days or weeks is estimated. Since the project usually is part of a cost comparison between providing an in-house center and buying the space at hotels or other remote venues, the next task is to establish the cost projections for holding the training meetings at these outside locations. Then the development group must establish a development and operating budget for the proposed center, including all the project costs, operating expenses, and training outlays. Of course, hotel expenses must be added for the anticipated percentage of employees who are not local residents. It is also important to factor in the *qualitative* advantages of a company-operated center, including greater scheduling flexibility, better cost control, custom-designed training rooms, and better integration of the trainers with the conference space.

The feasibility determination begins with careful analysis of in-house training and management development needs. Each department should identify its expected number of training days, either per person or per class of thirty (or whatever size is established). Ultimately, the company must determine a realistic

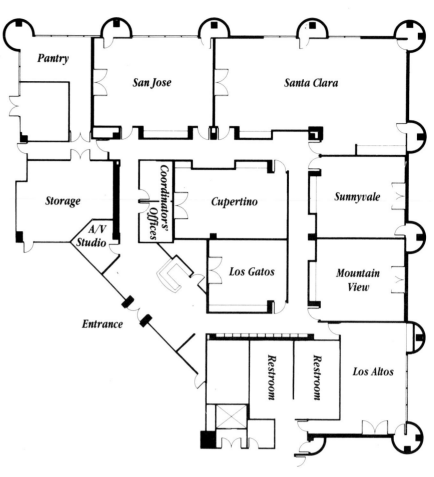

Renaissance Meeting Center, Santa Clara, California (above). Located in Techmart, the Silicon Valley computer-marketing center, this day meeting center focuses on providing high convenience and superior small meeting rooms. The seven first-floor rooms (with five more on an upper level) include basic audio-visuals and buffets for in-room refreshment service. (Courtesy of Renaissance Meeting Center.)

Shearson Lehman Brothers Conference and Training Center, New York City (facing page). Located on two upper floors of a Wall Street office building, the Shearson center contains 23,000 net square feet (2,139 net square meters) of dedicated conference space. Guests are greeted at a reception area on the lower floor and directed to one of 25 meeting rooms, including a 393-seat auditorium, four computer labs, and two rooms with rear-screen projection. Except for the computer rooms, all the conference and breakout spaces have windows with spectacular views of the harbor and lower Manhattan. Window coverings include three layers—drapes, blackout curtains, and a lighter sun screen—all electrically operated by the instructor. A small dining room is available for lunches and special receptions. (Architect: Skidmore, Owings Merrill; photo: Mark Ivins.)

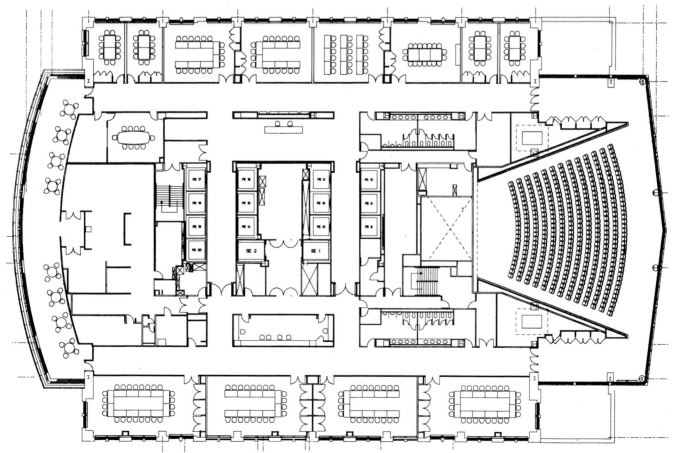

number of annual training days. After weekends and holiday weeks are subtracted, this number often totals less than two hundred. Dividing the total number of training days needed by the available days yields an estimate of the required number of rooms. The conference room program then must be expanded to include the conference foyer, lounges, breakout rooms, training and administrative offices, and support areas.

In the larger metropolitan areas, corporate nonresidential centers fill one or more floors in the high-rise headquarters buildings. In lower Manhattan, for example, Shearson Lehman Brothers recently opened a facility covering 70,000 square feet (6,510 square meters) on two floors. Nearby, the Chase Development Center is of similar size, filling three floors as well as a fourth level devoted to a resource library and cafeteria. In buildings such as these, of course, the program and design are highly dependent on the constraints of the structure—the number and location of elevators, column spacing, ceiling height, limitations on interconnecting floors, and so forth. These and other factors necessitate evaluating any high-rise building to determine the practicality of developing it as a training center.

The Renaissance Conference Company, a California-based developer of independent conference centers, approaches its projects by carefully scouting for, first, the right location and, second, an appropriate structure. Location criteria include:

☐ A high-image building

☐ Five hundred prospective clients in the immediate area

☐ Parking for 150 to 200 cars

☐ A nearby hotel for lodging and catering

More specifically, the building must offer:

☐ A minimum of 21,000 (and preferably 25,000) gross square feet (1,953 to 2,325 gross square meters) on the first two floors

☐ A separate entrance

☐ An owner willing to contribute substantial amounts toward tenant improvements

☐ Column spacing at least thirty feet (9.1 meters) wide (column-free space preferred)

☐ Ceilings at least ten (and preferably eleven) feet (3 meters) high

☐ Outside terraces for receptions and luncheons

Although the different types of nonresidential conference centers are quite similar in many

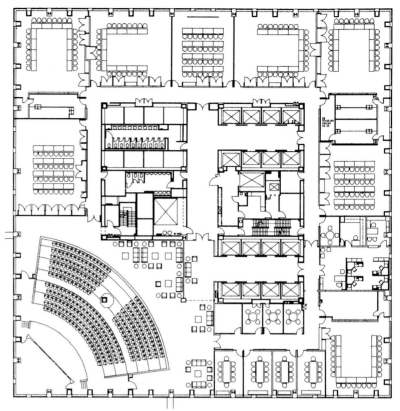

American Express Conference Center, New York City. Located on the twenty-sixth floor of American Express's lower-Manhattan offices, the meeting facility includes eight exterior meeting rooms, nine small breakout rooms, and an auditorium with carefully crafted acoustics and closed-circuit television connections to the neighboring training rooms. The foyer formed by the curved back wall is used for receptions and social events. (Architect: Swanke Hayden Connell; photos: Wolfgang Hoyt.)

respects, they do exhibit some variation in their program and plan organizations. Most centers fall between 20,000 and 70,000 gross square feet (1,860 and 6,510 gross square meters), representing a range of 10,000 to 40,000 net square feet (930 to 3,720 net square meters) of conference and meeting support space. Some comparative figures are included in Table 6–1. The larger centers, such as Chase Development and Shearson Lehman Brothers, contain about 24,000 net square feet (2,232 net square meters) of useable conference space (36,000 net square feet, or 3,348 net square meters, if the assembly and conference support areas are included) from about 70,000 gross square feet (6,510 gross square meters). This ratio of net to gross areas holds true for most of the nonresidential centers: The gross project area is about three times the net conference room area and approximately double the conference area, including assembly and support.

The majority of the nonresidential centers feature midsize conference rooms, about 900 to 1,300 square feet (83.7 to 120.9 square meters) each, and many breakout rooms. While these are intended principally for training, they may serve the corporate need for daily conferences as well. A few of the corporate facilities provide large auditoriums (the American Express and Shearson Lehman Brothers centers have auditorium capacities of 282 and 393, respectively), while the specialized centers, such as those at medical colleges or government facilities, utilize large, multipurpose rooms that can be flexibly arranged in several configurations.

In place of a hotel lobby, nonresidential centers include a conference foyer, which functions as a major reception space and incorporates the meeting registration and conference concierge functions. The guests arrive here, register, receive directions to the proper conference room, and return for messages. The architect must provide a foyer with sufficient seating, nearby office space, and such support functions as toilets, coat rooms, and telephones. From this point, circulation is organized much as it is in most conference cores. Conference rooms and break areas are arranged along the outside of a circular corridor, while the interior areas are devoted to win-

TABLE 6-1. NONRESIDENTIAL CONFERENCE CENTERS, CONFERENCE CORE SPACE PROGRAMS IN NET SQUARE FEET (NET SQUARE METERS)[a]

	American Express New York, NY	Shearson Lehman New York, NY	Chase Development New York, NY	Procter & Gamble Cincinnati, OH	CoreStates Philadelphia, PA
Ballroom	None	None	None	None	None
Large conference[b]	None	2 @ 1,800 (1,674)	None	1 @ 2,100 (195)	1 @ 1,500 (140)
Medium conference[c]	5 @ 1,350 (126) 3 @ 1,100 (102)	None	4 @ 1,300 (121)	6 @ 1,150 (107)	1 @ 1,100 (102)
Small conference[d]	None	11 @ 950 (88) 4 @ 650 (60)	11 @ 700 (65)	2 @ 800 (74)	2 @ 850 (79) 3 @ 725 (67) 2 @ 525 (49)
Breakout	4 @ 300 (28) 4 @ 150 (14)	2 @ 400 (37) 4 @ 300 (28)	5 @ 400 (37) 22 @ 200 (19)	3 @ 325 (30) 17 @ 275 (26)	2 @ 425 (40) 7 @ 200 (19)
Amphitheater	None	None	None	None	None
Auditorium	1 @ 2,950 (274)	1 @ 4,550 (423)	None	None	None
Computer/special	None	4 @ 900[e] (84[e])	None	None	None
Total conference	14,750 (1,372)	22,900 (2,130)	24,100 (2,241)	15,800 (1,469)	9,800 (911)
Total assembly	6,900 (642)	5,350 (498)	5,850 (544)	7,000 (651)	5,900 (549)
Total support	3,000 (279)	5,500 (512)	6,100 (567)	1,100 (102)	2,100 (195)

[a]Some program areas are rounded and averaged to simplify the presentation.
[b]Larger than 1,500 square feet (139 square meters).
[c]Between 1,000 and 1,500 square feet (93 and 139 square meters).
[d]Between 500 and 1,000 square feet (46 and 93 square meters).
[e]Computer classroom.

dowless amphitheaters, special-purpose classrooms, offices, or support functions.

If the center is part of a high-rise headquarters building, the planning solution is dictated by the column spacing. This is a change from the other types of conference centers, for which the structure may follow the dictates of the meeting space. The architect must configure the conference rooms to minimize the dimensional limitations caused by the structural bays. This results in a finite number of large conference rooms, few special-purpose rooms, relatively narrow corridors, and small prefunction and break areas. To lesson the effects of the narrow hallways, the design often includes a series of private daylit lounges, which the management assigns to each group as a dedicated gathering and break space.

If the center is part of a suburban headquarters—perhaps a new wing added to a building in the office campus—the planning issues are more similar to those of other corporate or executive centers. These projects frequently feature an auditorium, located near the main entrance, as well as a group of midsize conference rooms, breakout rooms, and larger assembly spaces. A cafeteria may be included, or attendees may find food services provided elsewhere in the campus. The plan usually accommodates offices for the conference coordinators within the learning center but houses the trainers themselves in another building or wing.

The programming and planning also must account for the different technology levels among the various nonresidential centers. These range from very limited audiovisual and computer support at the independent day centers, to moderately sophisticated levels at corporate training centers, where the level of technology can be closely paired to the training needs, to the most advanced computer and multimedia systems at corporate development centers. The relative sophistication of the training program and instructional methods, of course, influences the budget and establishes whether the project requires special audiovisual, graphics, communications, or technical support spaces.

DESIGN CONSIDERATIONS

The design of the nonresidential centers is much like that of corporate conference centers, often combining utility with a high level of design sophistication. The design team must fully understand the user criteria and development goals—some corporations may seek a

highly workable but relatively simple center with standard finishes and limited audiovisual equipment; other companies may attempt to build a luxurious facility that reinforces their commitment to training and the corporate identity. Either philosophy is acceptable, and the designers must recognize and respect the company's goals.

Conference Foyer. Because there is no hotel or residential lobby, day meeting centers must create a conference foyer to set the tone for the entire facility or perhaps reinforce the initial impressions gained from the ground floorlobby, elevators, or elevator lobby. If the designer cannot control the visual appearance of the approach route, the design of the foyer is especially critical. In addition to setting the ambience, it must accommodate a number of specific functions, including registration and information kiosks, seating areas, a meeting directory, and support functions.

Many meetings are only one day long or attract first-time visitors who are unfamiliar with the layout of the conference center. Therefore, the foyer design should accommodate these guests by incorporating monitors or display boards listing the meeting locations, maps or graphics indicating direction and circulation, and clear visual clues for locating toilets and support functions.

Conference and Training Rooms. The conference rooms differ little from those in other centers. While some corporate facilities may include specialized training rooms (Shearson has four computer labs furnished with carrels for individual training) and may feature front- or rear-screen projection, for the most part nonresidential centers have relatively typical rooms that can be used for a variety of conferences and meetings. The usual furnishings and special finishes include modular tables, executive chairs, writing boards, projection screens, tackable wall surfaces, acoustical tile ceilings, flexible lighting, and sufficient systems and power to provide mobile videotaping and playback. Many centers include coat closets at each conference room, providing a more secure place for overcoats than a central coat room.

Because these centers are located near the corporate headquarters, the conference center may be the site for major public presentations, stockholders' meetings, and media events. Larger centers with auditoriums therefore often incorporate additional audiovisual capa-

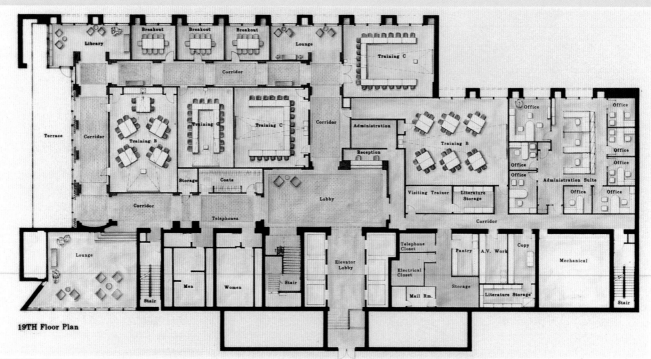

19TH Floor Plan

CORESTATES EMPLOYEE DEVELOPMENT CENTER

Completed and occupied in 1989 in downtown Philadelphia, this financial services training facility includes 11 classrooms and 28,000 square feet (2,604 square meters) on two floors. Employees enter a spacious reception area, from which they are directed to the appropriate rooms. Many of the smaller rooms and the refreshment lounges are located on the exterior, where they are exposed to natural light and panoramic views. The larger rooms, including the 90-seat main conference room on the upper floor (which features a control room, electrically operated systems, a 20-foot [6-meter] vaulted ceiling, and clerestory windows), are located on the interior of the block. (Architect and interiors: The Hillier Group; photos © Matt Wargo Photography.)

bility, including teleconferencing and complete audiovisual production studios, allowing the auditorium events to be videotaped and transmitted to overflow audiences in nearby rooms or remote locations. The Shearson Lehman Brothers facility goes so far as to include a separate room near the auditorium for the print and broadcast media.

Frequently, a majority of the conference rooms are located at outside walls, with windows dictated by the building design rather than the requirements of the conference rooms. And although most conference planners prefer rooms with windows (a minority strongly prefer distraction-free windowless interior rooms), the curtain-wall design of most office structures provides an excessive amount of glass. It is therefore common for these rooms to feature electrically operated drapes or blinds. The design criteria also must address the amount of tackable wall, writing, and projection surfaces, and the rooms' blackout capability.

Conference Assembly and Support.
Because of tight architectural and structural constraints, especially in high-rise office towers, many nonresidential centers have relatively narrow circulation areas, certainly inadequate for assembly and breaks. To compensate, these projects often feature a group of private lounges assigned to individual conference groups and offering such amenities as dedicated refreshment setups, comfortable seating areas, convenient message boards, and telephones. Often, these lounges also accommodate some of the breakout activity—small group discussions or role-playing exercises, for instance—in a comfortable setting. At the Chase Development Center, these lounges are located on each floor at outside walls with stunning views of lower Manhattan and the Hudson River.

In the larger conference centers, it often is necessary to direct guests to meeting rooms on other floors. In these projects, the connecting stairway should be prominently designed, perhaps as one of the visual organizing elements of the center. This may be difficult for projects located in high-rise office towers, because building codes often require the stairs to be enclosed; in any event, the designer must find a way to clearly show the interconnection between floors.

The more upscale centers may include a selection of corporate artwork, or display company products throughout the public circula-

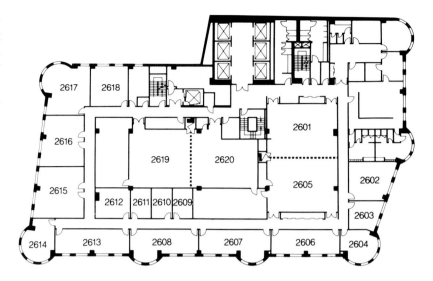

Chase Development Center, New York City (facing page). Located on three floors in lower Manhattan (plus a fourth level featuring the research library and cafeteria), the Chase center includes a large number of exterior lounges where groups can gather between sessions. Totaling 24,000 net square feet (2,232 net square meters) of conference space, many of the smaller meeting and breakout rooms feature windows with views of the skyline and Hudson River; all meeting rooms are equipped with hanging-rail systems for increased flexibility, and the larger interior rooms utilize sophisticated audiovisual systems. (Architect: Culimore Clark; photos courtesy of Chase Development Center.)

tion areas, helping to reinforce the desired identity, an especially effective measure if the corridors and lounges are interior spaces.

The support functions are similar to those at larger centers. Conference services usually are placed at the foyer, providing the amenities of a business center, including information, messages, fax transmission, copying, and light secretarial tasks. One or two private offices should adjoin the concierge desk. Other administrative offices, including those of the center manager and senior conference services staff, need to be nearby.

Most nonresidential centers need sufficient storage space and staff to handle the usual complement of audiovisual equipment. Some centers, as already touched upon, feature a higher level of service; others may provide almost no equipment, instead renting it from outside vendors as required.

If the training department is located off-site, it is important to provide a work space for assembling course handouts and other materials. Such a room requires storage cabinets, tables or built-in counters, and the necessary equipment for copying, collating, and binding training manuals.

Conference Dining. The conference dining operation is cooperatively established by the developer and operator. Most nonresidential centers provide only lunch (plus midmorning and afternoon breaks), although breakfast meetings or afternoon receptions are occasionally on the agenda. The dining room

should be large enough to accommodate the full conference-room population (excluding breakouts) plus about 10 percent more capacity for staff and visitors. Most nonresidential centers feature a buffet located near a pantry, which reduces staff requirements and can be closed off to make the dining room more practical for receptions and other public functions.

The dining room ambience varies. Many centers simply have a highly practical employee lunchroom, a single open room with resilient tile floors, fluorescent lighting, and laminate-surfaced tables; in other centers, however, the space is upgraded substantially, with semiprivate seating areas separated by millwork or plants, carpeted floors, table linen, and armchairs. Most corporate planners believe the meal functions are important to continuing the training or conference sessions, and therefore try to make the dining room as comfortable as possible. The staff eat in the dining room daily, the trainees need to feel they are valued by the company, and, if the center tries to attract outside business, these customers may demand an upscale dining room.

The dining room is supported by a small pantry or off-site commissary. If the menu does not include hot entrées and the center utilizes only paper plates and plastic utensils, the pantry can be quite small; hot dishes and china, on the other hand, add substantially to the kitchen requirements but greatly enhance the dining program. Alcohol usually is not available except at receptions.

YWCA of the U.S.A. Leadership Development Center, Phoenix, Arizona (right). A national center for the training of religious workers, the YWCA facility incorporates a large multipurpose room, large and small conference rooms, breakout rooms, and a variety of special facilities, all built around a series of skylit public atriums. The one-story building offers opportunities to move outside in the winter and introduces natural light into the interior spaces. (Architect: Clark/Van Voorhis; plan courtesy of YWCA.)

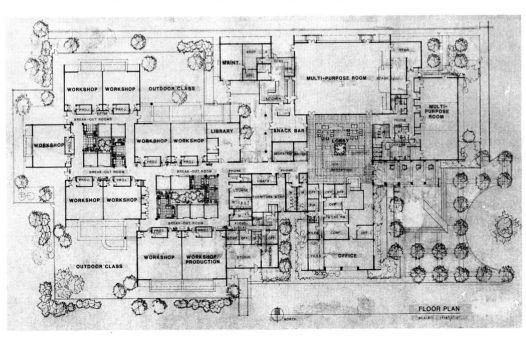

FLOOR PLAN

CHAPTER 7

Not-for-Profit Conference Centers

A mong the first conference centers, dating back to the late 1800s, were those established for educational and religious purposes by such organizations as the Grange, the YMCA, and individual religious denominations. Many of these centers were built around campgrounds, where people of average means could stay relatively inexpensively for a week or longer. The best-known of these is the Chautauqua Institution, now over one hundred years old, which was founded in western New York state to foster the arts, education, religion, and recreation. Chautauqua, originally established for the training of Sunday school teachers, continues to operate a successful seven-week summer program with lectures, concerts, drama, and far-reaching recreational offerings.

The YMCA has facilities with much the same history. Having held encampments in the Rockies since the 1890s, the organization decided to establish a permanent training center for religious workers and purchased a site at Estes Park, Colorado, in 1909. The records show that only men were invited to the first meeting; women and children were housed in nearby cabins because they were thought to be distractions. Since then, the Estes Park Center

has been greatly expanded and the facilities improved to the level of a year-round conference center open to the public.

Also dating from the early 1900s, and notable for its grand scale and individual architecture, is Asilomar, on California's Monterey Peninsula. The project was conceived by the mother of newspaper publisher William Randolph Hearst, and commissioned in 1913 the influential architect Julia Morgan (who also designed Hearst's estate, San Simeon) to design a building complex including a chapel, lodge, and main hall. The property originally was dedicated to the YWCA, but the state of California purchased it in the mid-1950s, expanded and modernized portions, and converted the facility to a conference center oriented toward nonprofit groups of all kinds, including youth organizations, artists, humanitarians, scientists, educators, religious workers, and medical groups. Furthermore, Asilomar (which translates to *refuge by the sea*) houses the country's only training center for state park rangers.

Today, many not-for-profit conference centers are operated by colleges and universities, both on campus and at remote sites. Other such centers are operated by not-for-profit cor-

Asilomar Conference Center, Monterey Peninsula, California. Sited on 105 acres (42.5 hectares) of forest and dunes overlooking the Pacific Ocean, Asilomar includes 11 buildings designed by noted architect Julia Morgan. Merrill Hall, the last of her buildings, dates to 1928 and was designed in the Arts and Crafts style with local materials—redwood shingles and shakes, stone, and pine. It serves as the main meeting space for up to 850 conferees. (Architect: Julia Morgan; photo: Ken Roberts, courtesy of Asilomar.)

porations (the Educational Testing Service, for instance) or research centers (Battelle), associations (American Chemical Society) and foundations (Wingspread, Johnson Wax), YMCA/YWCA, the Scouts, and the multitude of private organizations established to foster particular ideals. Some of these centers are elegant, others simple, but practically all are designed to appeal to a specific audience. For this reason, they are unusually successful in terms of design.

SITE AND MARKET CONDITIONS

The variety of types of not-for-profit conference centers leads to a similarly wide diversity in the choice of a site, influenced in part by relative proximity to urban areas, interstate highways, and major airports. While some projects start with the site (which in some cases is donated to the organization) and then develop a suitable program for it, more often an organization or foundation establishes a mission statement, creates a conceptual blueprint for its implementation, and searches for the appropriate setting. The Arbor Day Foundation, for instance, is developing a 140-room education and conference center, modeled after an Adirondack lodge, on a rural hillside site adjoining a working orchard outside Omaha, Nebraska. Intended partly for the organization's use, the facility also will be available to such conservation-related groups as the National Park Service, the National Audubon Society, and local environmental organizations. The beautiful site was chosen to complement the group's organizational purpose. More established organizations with a major presence in a particular community, such as Battelle in Seattle or the Educational Testing Service in Princeton, create projects not unlike many executive or corporate centers: a wooded campus seemingly removed from the congestion and bustle of the surrounding city.

Many not-for-profit centers focus on a regional market, drawing from a 150- to 200-mile (241- to 321-kilometer) radius. These centers can be more remote, with no close proximity to a major airport, for example. Syracuse University's Minnowbrook Lodge is deep in the Adirondack Mountains on the shore of Blue Mountain Lake, remote from major population centers. While such seclusion is an option, some organizations prefer their facilities to have a wider presence, establishing a national or even international identity. For these projects, the same site criteria apply as for other types of centers: proximity to highways and

airports, retreatlike setting, ambience reinforcing the educational focus, and so on. The Aspen Institute at Wye Plantation in Maryland is located ninety minutes from Washington and Baltimore on Chesapeake Bay, yet it has hosted a meeting of the NATO foreign ministers and is a favorite retreat site for dozens of government agencies. The Institute also organizes a long series of seminar and policy programs, which bring together senior corporate management personnel and people from academia, government, media, and the arts.

When not running their own programs, not-for-profit conference centers generally give first priority to organizations with similar interests and goals. The Rensselaerville Institute in upstate New York sponsors a variety of programs for people concerned with community and organizational development; the Nature Place, located on six thousand acres (2,428 hectares) high among the Rocky Mountains west of Colorado Springs, offers programs in national history and is designated a "natural environmental study area" by the National Park Service.

The market for the not-for-profit centers varies as widely as do the locations and architectural character of the projects. But these centers have one key advantage: because their mission is to offer inexpensive lodging, dining, and conference space to price-sensitive and, generally, noncorporate customers, they have a greater opportunity to attract off-season and weekend business. As a result, with careful scheduling of dedicated programs and aggressive public marketing, many operate effectively at high occupancies year-round.

PROGRAM AND PLANNING CONSIDERATIONS

There is no single prototypical model for the not-for-profit centers. A few of the more urban facilities have no lodging, the suburban centers are composed of low-rise guestroom wings, and the more remote rural projects often feature a number of separate residential lodges. In general, the not-for-profit facilities tend to be smaller than other categories of conference centers. The larger projects often are part of comprehensive developments; most of the YMCA conference centers, for example, are part of larger campground and education centers.

The facilities program must reflect the needs of the type of not-for-profit center. A research organization or wealthy foundation may be able to afford larger public spaces,

Battelle Seattle Conference Center, Seattle, Washington. The Battelle project combines a research–seminar building with office, apartment, and dining structures on a wooded 18-acre (7.3-hectare) site adjoining the University of Washington campus. The residentially scaled buildings, landscaped grounds, and pond provide a secluded environment ideal for productive conferences. (Architect: NBBJ Group; photo courtesy of Battelle.)

better-equipped conference rooms, and high quality finishes. They may subsidize the construction of a large multipurpose meeting room or an auditorium, even to meet a limited need. The more rural centers, established to further an environmental mission or humanitarian philosophy, might best be planned as a series of independent elements, to be built and expanded as the market matures. Often, the owners will purchase small properties (or one is donated) and add individual buildings for lodging, conference rooms, dining, or recreational purposes.

Many of the more urban properties follow a similar model of locating the several functions in different structures. Battelle Seattle is a complex of four lodging buildings, a conference center, a dining facility, and administration and office buildings. The design for the new headquarters and conference center for the Howard Hughes Medical Institute, scheduled to open in 1992 outside Washington, features four individual two-story houses containing about half of the residential units, with the remainder in the main complex.

A great many of the not-for-profit conference centers have been adapted from other uses; some were campgrounds or rural farms, for example. As with the earliest executive conference centers, a few also are converted private residences. The Johnson Foundation established an educational conference center in Wingspread, the residence Frank Lloyd Wright designed for Herbert F. Johnson in the late 1930s. Attendees have the unusual opportunity of meeting in the former bedrooms or attend-

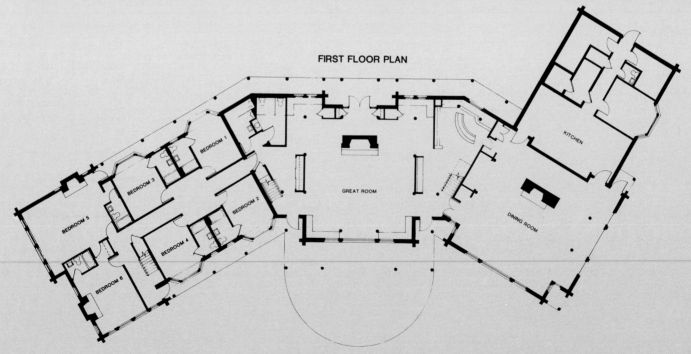

FIRST FLOOR PLAN

BEDROOM 1

BEDROOM 3

BEDROOM 5

BEDROOM 2

BEDROOM 4

BEDROOM 6

GREAT ROOM

KITCHEN

DINING ROOM

MINNOWBROOK LODGE

The Adirondack lodge structure in Blue Mountain Lake, New York, is a replacement for the original turn-of-the-century camp, which burned in 1988. The 8,800 square foot (818 square meter) lodge is larger than the original, increasing the dining room's capacity and providing additional guestrooms. The design duplicates the spirit of the original Great Camp building yet meets current building and energy codes. Artisans and craftsmen from throughout the northeast laid the logs, rebuilt the four granite fireplaces, and recreated Adirondack furnishings. The main lodge contains 10 guestrooms (23 more are in outlying buildings), the Great Room, with its 24-foot (7.3-meter) log-truss ceiling, and a dining room for 70 guests. (Architect: Schleicher-Soper; photos: Harvey H. Kaiser.)

SECOND FLOOR PLAN

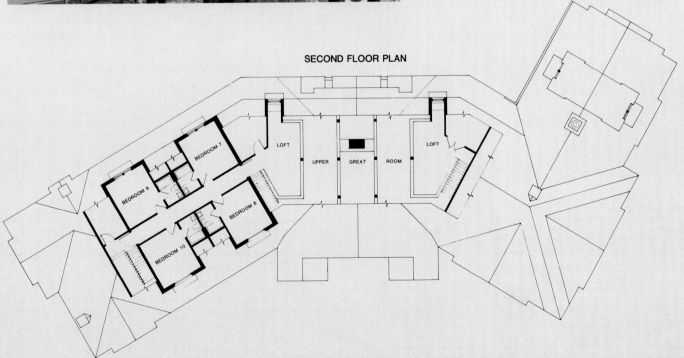

Ground Floor

1. Headquarters entrance
2. Library
3. Conservatory
4. East court
5. West court
6. Service
7. Dining
8. Dining terrace
9. Terraced garden
10. Main hall
11. Living room
12. Auditorium
13. Meeting room
14. Conference center entrance
15. House

Second Floor

1. Library
2. Open to below
3. President's office
4. Trustee's room
5. Bedrooms
6. Lounge
7. House

CONFERENCE CENTER ENTRY

DINING TERRACE

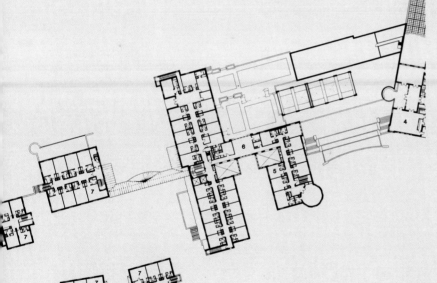

Ground Floor

HOWARD HUGHES
MEDICAL INSTITUTE

This new headquarters and conference center, to be completed in 1992, is located on 22 acres (8.9 hectares) in a residential area in Chevy Chase, Maryland, outside Washington, D.C. Adjoining the office building is the conference facility, which will be used for Institute-sponsored meetings (generally workshops and seminars for 10 to 25 people). The program includes an auditorium, five meeting rooms, numerous lounge and reception rooms, dining (shared with the office personnel), a small fitness center, and 75 guestrooms, located both in the main building and in four separate guest houses. Terraces for informal gathering and social functions surround the complex. The siting of the buildings was planned to create a secluded campus, preserve existing trees, incorporate a functional storm-retention pond, and buffer the project from local traffic. The two-story buildings are faced with brick and stone and feature wood-framed openings to help establish a quiet, residential atmosphere. The landscape plan calls for the planting of thousands of trees and shrubs, including a group of cherry trees ringing the central pond. (Architect: The Hillier Group; photo © Wolfgang Hoyt.)

Second Floor

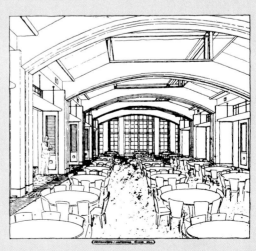

Wingspread, Racine, Wisconsin. One of Frank
Lloyd Wright's last great prairie houses, Wingspread served for 20 years as the home of the
Johnson family before being transformed into an
educational center. The house spreads elegantly
over its 30-acre (12.1-hectare) site and rises to a
domelike structure enclosing the living room—
Wright compared it to a wigwam. The 2,400
square foot (223 square meter) living room
serves as the main reception space, bedrooms
were converted into meeting rooms and offices,
and additional conference space was created
next door. (Architect: Frank Lloyd Wright; photo
courtesy of the Johnson Foundation.)

ing a reception in the handsome living room, the latter architecturally unchanged from when the Johnson family lived there.

The facilities program varies with the type and quality level of the conference center. Most not-for-profit properties include double rooms, about 300 square feet (27.9 square meters) each, one dining room sized to accommodate full capacity, and a small number of meeting rooms designed for between twenty and one hundred people and offering the usual conference services and audiovisual amenities; few centers can accommodate larger groups. Recreational amenities often are little more than a game room or exercise room and such outdoor facilities as swimming—often in a pond or lake—hiking, boating, and volleyball. The total project area may be in the range of 600 to 800 square feet (55.8 to 74.4 square meters) per room but can vary depending on individual conditions. At Battelle Seattle, for instance, the thirty-seven guestrooms and six conference rooms are overshadowed by the larger complex, which includes two floors of offices for researchers.

DESIGN CONSIDERATIONS
The design of not-for-profit conference centers illustrates a broad range of somewhat rustic, less formal building types. Some, including Asilomar and Wingspread, are located in national Historic Landmark structures. Others are housed in collections of small buildings, often added over a lengthy period as the center owners or sponsors gained funds and land to expand.

Because the not-for-profit centers tend to have fewer dedicated spaces—only one dining room and six to eight meeting rooms—each room must serve multiple functions. It is not unusual for the lobby or foyer to be used for a reception, or the living room for a private dinner. Although such arrangements may seem makeshift, much of the success of the not-for-profit centers comes from their less formal character. This is enhanced when architects and designers incorporate traditional native materials and design in the local idiom or tradition. Many projects feature fieldstone fireplaces and timber-beamed ceilings; centers

housed in old estates or farms maintain and replicate the eighteenth century decor.

The majority of not-for-profit centers anticipate a high rate of double occupancy, which fosters heightened exchange between participants outside the designated meeting periods. The rooms offer few of the amenities of more cosmopolitan properties: Clock-radios suffice for modern technology; televisions and even telephones are unusual, except in the urban and suburban locations. Yet the balconies or terraces overlooking lakes and hills offer a visual and psychological amenity that deluxe furnishings and services cannot approach.

Some not-for-profit conference centers favor large, sometimes monumental dining rooms, which usually serve buffet or cafeteria-style breakfasts and lunches and banquet-style dinners. The architect should consider approaches to reducing the scale in the larger, impersonal spaces, providing some flexible means of separation. Other critical issues include acoustics, lighting, and natural ventilation. Furniture storage must be considered for the frequent times when the dining room will be used for receptions or other public functions. Rensselaerville and the Wye Plantation, which are, in part, collections of older residential buildings, locate the conference dining in individual private rooms for twenty to thirty people.

This group of conference centers offers somewhat more limited types of meeting rooms, which often are constructed in existing spaces with uncompromising architectural irregularities. Still, the properties furnish and fully equip the rooms for professional meetings: comfortable chairs, oversized tables, portable equipment, good lighting, and audiovisual support. A few centers have audiovisual technicians on the premises. Although the levels of service and support may not quite measure up to those found in corporate or executive centers, groups should keep in mind that the spectacular settings of many of these centers offer vistas unparalleled in more sophisticated meeting facilities. When the goal is a distraction-free conference in an environment that promotes relaxation and recreation, these properties have much to offer.

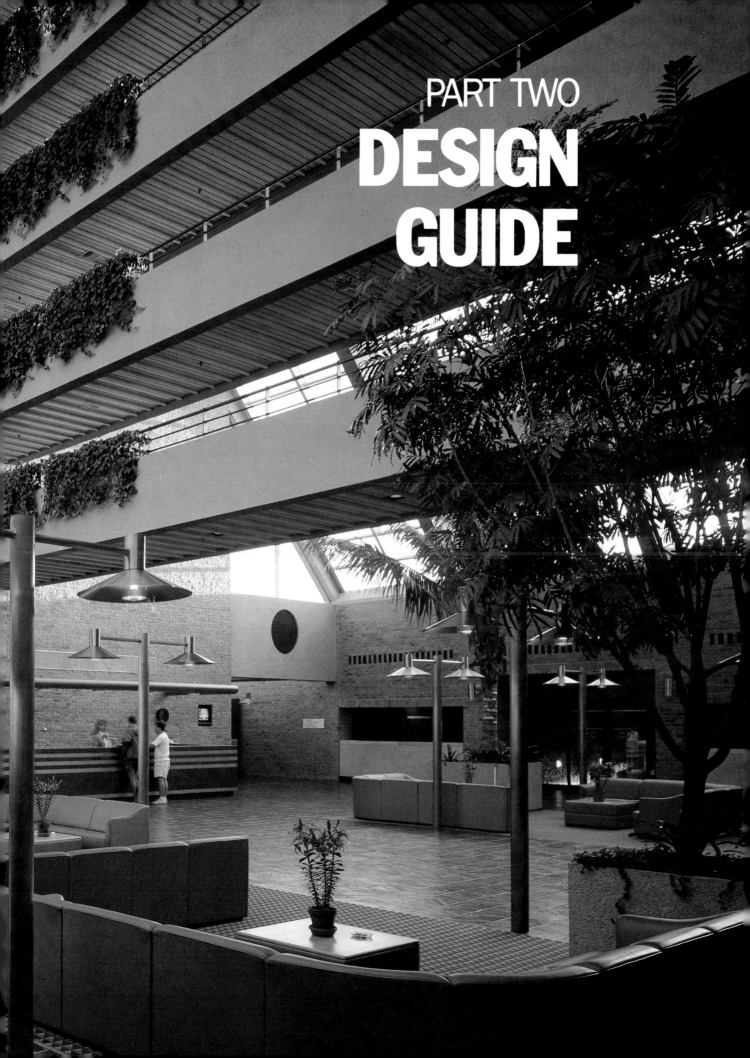

PART TWO
DESIGN GUIDE

CHAPTER 8

Program and Conceptual Design

Experienced conference center developers have learned that scores of early decisions are critical to a project's success. Most of these decisions occur well ahead of the schematic design phase and relate to the organization of the development effort and the clear definition of key objectives. Careful consideration of these issues is especially important when one considers that developing a new conference center easily can take four years or more: roughly one year for the predesign steps (acquiring the land, establishing feasibility, assembling the team, defining objectives, securing financing, preparing the program, and so forth); a second year for design and approvals; and two more years for construction and opening. It is during the first year, however, that most of the essential decisions are made.

These predesign decisions include establishing the financial or investment objectives of the developer, the operational objectives of the management group, and the initial architectural and interiors concepts of the design team. Other decisions include site selection, accurate assessment of demand against existing and anticipated competition, and assembly of a development and design team that can work harmoniously toward a single goal.

Consider how these decisions would vary for the conference center types described in the previous chapters. The corporate training goals, for instance, are substantially different if a company establishes a 300-room conference center instead of renovating headquarters office space for a nonresidential facility. Similarly, university goals (and corresponding site and facilities programs) differ for an upscale executive education center and a midprice continuing education center. The resort conference center may be constructed to enhance the value of a larger mixed-use recreational and residential development, or the executive center may be the keystone of a suburban office park. The development team must recognize and respond to the conference center's ultimate *raison d'etre* and establish an operational and architectural program accordingly. Table 8–1 identifies the types of architectural and operational decisions the development team must make during the initial predesign phase.

Obviously, the site, architectural program, financial resources, budget and schedule pressures, and team makeup will vary drastically. This chapter describes these elements, and subsequent chapters will explore the variety of planning and design opportunities.

Hershey Medical Center, Hershey, Pennsylvania. A unit of the state university, the proposed Hershey complex shows clear zoning between conference "villages" and the auditorium, dining, and support spaces. The low-rise scheme was designed to blend into the rural landscape and allow easy expansion of additional meeting clusters. (Architect: Curtis Cox Kennerly; plan courtesy of Curtis Cox Kennerly.)

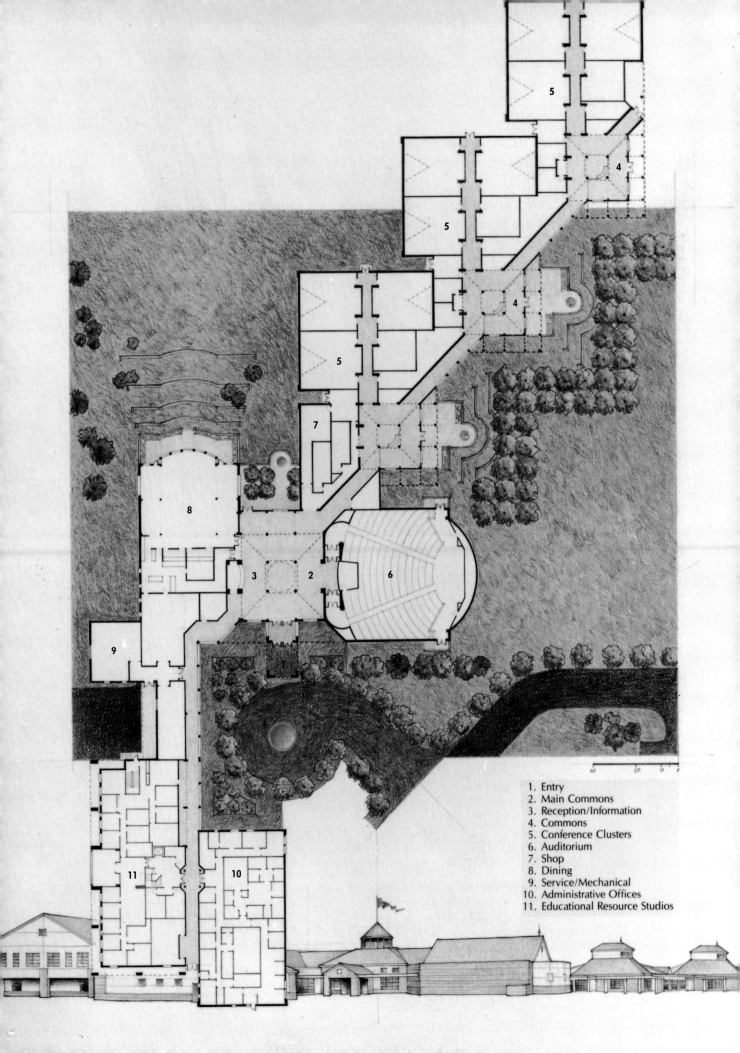

1. Entry
2. Main Commons
3. Reception/Information
4. Commons
5. Conference Clusters
6. Auditorium
7. Shop
8. Dining
9. Service/Mechanical
10. Administrative Offices
11. Educational Resource Studios

TABLE 8-1. ARCHITECTURAL AND OPERATIONAL CHECKLIST

Project Aspect	Decisions to Be Made
Project definition	☐ Determine principal and secondary markets ☐ Identify type of center ☐ Select potential sites ☐ Determine required size (number of rooms, amount of meeting space, etc.) ☐ Create detailed facilities list ☐ Determine service levels ☐ Determine quality level ☐ Establish need for phasing ☐ Prepare project budget and capital requirements
Architectural program	☐ Prepare general objectives ☐ Consider site requirements ☐ Determine basis for size criteria ☐ Prepare detailed net area allocations ☐ Calculate gross area requirements ☐ Establish functional criteria ☐ Establish functional relationships ☐ Establish future adaptability and phasing
Operational program	☐ Develop front-office procedures ☐ Establish security requirements ☐ Determine communications and data requirements ☐ Prepare food and beverage concepts ☐ Establish recreational program ☐ Develop conference services policies ☐ Prepare back-of-house procedures ☐ Research solid-waste handling alternatives
Budget	☐ Establish land costs ☐ Establish construction and site-development costs ☐ Establish furniture, fixtures, and equipment costs ☐ Establish development expenses (fees, taxes, insurance, etc.) ☐ Account for financing during construction ☐ Consider preopening costs, working capital, and a reserve against operating shortfall
Conceptual design	☐ Confirm architectural program ☐ Identify site opportunities and constraints ☐ Establish ideal arrangement of functional elements ☐ Develop architectural massing ☐ Determine outline specifications ☐ Verify project budget

DEFINING THE CONFERENCE CENTER PROJECT

Among the first steps is conducting a feasibility study. The project team hires a consulting firm, such as Horwath Consulting or Pannell Kerr Forster, to prepare the report and establish projections of guestroom and meeting activity for different market segments, further detailed by variations from weekday to weekend and broken down by month. The demand estimates should be further refined by comparing them with those at existing competitive properties. Consultants then identify the future competition, assess the anticipated market penetration, and project the average daily rate and occupancy. The financial projections should also consider the influences of the complete meeting package pricing, day meetings, and the further revenues that may be generated by local food and beverage sales and recreational use.

For most hotel projects, the feasibility study is prepared for a single site, under the control of the owner. For conference centers, however, a development company often establishes the need for a property in a specific region or metropolitan area and only then turns its attention to potential sites. Then follows a site evaluation phase—assessing highway access, proximity to the airport, proximity to concentrations of office, residential, and shopping areas, and the physical suitability of the site. (See Chapter 2 for more detail.)

The completed feasibility study should propose a conference center type, identify principal and secondary markets, list the necessary number of rooms and key facilities (number and capacity of restaurants, number and capacity of conference space, recreational amenities), and project revenues and expenses. The actual definition of the project, though, depends on confirmation and approval of these recommendations by the owner or developer, and further study may be necessary to define precisely the project type and scope. For example, a private developer who controls a suburban site may modify the scope of a planned executive or resort conference center based upon a market assessment and the size and character of the site. And corporations go through a much lengthier process, carefully analyzing their employment and training projections and considering, for example, the relative merits of establishing a centralized training center, or the benefits of a residential versus nonresidential facility.

One shortcoming of some feasibility studies is their emphasis on market and financial information, sometimes at the expense of sufficiently defining the proposed facilities. As a result, a prospective management company may be retained to help prepare the detailed program information needed to begin conceptual design. Because the gross area fluctuates tremendously among the types of conference centers (only suburban executive conference centers follow a fairly predictable program model), this professional help is critical; preliminary estimates *must* be determined rationally. It is therefore essential that the developer and future operator establish their objectives together and mutually agree upon a space program document.

In addition, the project definition should include some detail on the quality and service levels of the proposed conference center. This commentary will influence the schematic planning decisions, determine certain details of the project budget, define the necessary abilities of the design team, affect the construction schedule, and help motivate interest from prospective lenders. A clear operational program should detail such food and beverage operations as the restaurant concepts, catering, and room service, and should also describe the lodging, conference services, recreation, parking, and other elements.

The comprehensive definition of the project scope allows the developer to establish a preliminary project budget that pulls together the cost of land, construction, site development, FF&E, development fees, financing, and other expenses. While costs vary among the types of centers, construction should total only 50 to 60 percent of the total project costs, excluding land. Once the preliminary project budget is completed, developers must immediately compare it with the financial projections to test the project's economic feasibility in light of their particular objectives.

It may be possible to consider phasing of the conference center project by, for example, building a first wing of guestrooms and later adding more as the market matures. The initial concept, however, should envision the larger project and provide for its orderly expansion at a later date. In order to be fully competitive, the developer must not attempt to reduce costs by, for example, deferring the recreation complex or postponing the installation of appropriate audiovisual systems. More often, a project is scaled down slightly at all its parts and levels, and the schematic design is geared to permit orderly expansion later.

In fact, this potential for expansion should be an overriding planning goal whether or not the project faces budgetary pressure. Each project should have a concept for orderly additions from the outset. Such expansion capability can prove critical later: New England Telephone's original 1974 complex successfully met the firm's corporate training needs for fifteen years, yet was not so large that the utility had to open the facility to the public to make the operation financially viable. As utilization increased, the firm initiated plans to expand the facility and in 1990 completed the addition of 80 guestrooms, 200 more dining seats, 32 additional meeting and breakout rooms, expanded kitchen and back-of-house services, and enlarged corporate training offices.

ESTABLISHING THE SPACE PROGRAM

While early rules of thumb may be used to obtain estimates for the gross building area or the total project budget, these should be refined at the earliest opportunity. The detailed program is usually prepared by the prospective operator or an experienced architect or consultant. Hotel rules of thumb may be applied quite accurately to the back-of-house areas, but the public spaces (conference and dining rooms, especially), guestrooms, administrative spaces and recreational facilities all differ from those at transient or convention hotels. Careful cooperation among the team is therefore essential.

Because some members of the team may not be completely familiar with the conference concept, and because there are real differences among the several center categories, it is advisable to prepare a comprehensive written program at the outset. An architect may be retained to prepare a fuller program document, establishing technical and systems requirements, reviewing environmental and code criteria, and proposing interior design

TABLE 8-2. SCHEMATIC DESIGN PROGRAM BY CONFERENCE CENTER TYPE

	Executive Centers	Resort Centers	Corporate Centers	University Centers
Guestrooms				
Number of rooms	225–300	150–400	125–400	50–150
Typical room in net square feet (net square meters)	300–350 (28–33)	325–375 (30–35)	275–325 (26–30)	250–300 (23–28)
Gross square feet (gross square meters) per room	470–525 (44–49)	525–625 (49–58)	450–550 (42–51)	400–525 (37–49)
% of total	50–53	45–55	35–45	40–53
Public areas				
Number of restaurants	2	3	1–2	1
Number of lounges	2	2–3	1	0–1
Gross square feet (gross square meters) per room	90–125 (8–12)	90–125 (8–12)	60–200 (6–19)	85–115 (8–11)
% of total	8–12	8–12	7–12	9–14
Conference				
Number of ballrooms	1	2	0	0
Number of auditoriums/amphitheaters	0–1	1	1–4	2–3
Number of meeting rooms	10–20	6–15	6–40	3–10
Number of breakout rooms	6–20	4–8	4–20	6–15
Gross square feet (gross square meters) per room	175–225 (16–21)	125–190 (12–18)	250–400 (23–37)	175–300 (16–28)
% of total	16–22	8–20	20–35	20–35
Recreation				
Gross square feet (gross square meters) per room	15–50 (1–5)	50–200 (5–19)	35–90 (3–8)	0–20 (0–2)
% of total	2–6	4–15	3–5	0–2
Administrative/service				
Gross square feet (gross square meters) per room	125–175 (12–16)	140–190 (13–18)	200–300 (19–28)	125–200 (12–19)
% of total	13–18	14–17	15–25	12–15
Total gross square feet (gross square meters) per room	950–1,100 (88–102)	1,050–1,200 (98–112)	1,150–1,500 (107–140)	800–1,100 (74–102)

standards. (Alternatively, these issues might be discussed and resolved by the entire project team during schematic design.)

Actual space requirements vary tremendously. Table 8–2 provides area ranges and approximate percentages for each conference center type; these can be used to gain a preliminary quantitative understanding of the principal differences. Note, for example, that the conference and training spaces for executive and university projects are almost identical in terms of program area per guestroom, but the university centers' substantially smaller guestrooms and relative lack of recreational space serve to increase the university conference space to 20 or even 35 percent of the total project. Table 8–3 describes these differences in more qualitative terms. An overall understanding of this program variation is especially useful in early discussions among the development team. Table 8–4 illustrates representative architectural programs for conference centers

of the several types. One obvious caveat is critical: these typical program numbers can be used only as guidelines and must be modified for each project to meet the specific demands and opportunities of the market, site, owner, and operator.

ESTABLISHING THE OPERATIONAL PROGRAM

While the architectural program is being prepared, the future operator should prepare a description of the operations to help establish the functional relationships, including their priorities and staffing needs. This operational program is essential as a tool for the architect as he explores alternative planning solutions to the lodging registration, food and beverage, conference, recreation, and building services areas. The operational program not only describes the hospitality concepts and their procedures, but it establishes to a large degree the space program requirements. For example,

TABLE 8-3. PROGRAM COMPARISON BY CONFERENCE CENTER TYPES

	Executive Centers	Resort Centers	Corporate Centers	University Centers	Nonresidential Centers
Guestrooms	Average to large guestrooms, few suites; occasional dialogue centers; club floor	Large to very large rooms, 5–10% suites; occasional commons area	Small to average rooms, few or no suites; commons area on each floor	Small to average rooms, few or no suites; case study or commons areas on each floor or for cluster of rooms	None
Public areas	Large lobby with lobby lounge; conference dining and specialty restaurant; entertainment lounge; game room	Average lobby with view over grounds; conference dining, specialty restaurant, and recreation dining; entertainment lounge	Lobby size highly variable, with lobby lounge if corporate policy permits; conference dining and private dining; game room	Small to average lobby; reading room or quiet lounge; conference dining and private dining; cocktail lounge	Small reception area; conference dining or cafeteria; no lounge
Conference and training areas	Ballroom; large variety of conference rooms and many breakout rooms; boardroom	Large ballroom; moderate number of meeting and breakout rooms; amphitheater	Auditorium; large number of similar classrooms; computer or special-purpose rooms; offices for trainers	For executive education programs: amphitheaters, breakouts, and faculty offices; for continuing education programs: auditorium and many classrooms	Auditorium; many midsize rooms; breakout rooms; computer labs
Recreation	Swimming pool; racquet courts; exercise and health club	Many outdoor facilities; pool; exercise and health club	Gym or pool; racquet courts; exercise and health club	None	None

	Executive Centers	Resort Centers	Corporate Centers	University Centers
Guestrooms				
Number of guestrooms and suites	250	300	200	100
Number of suites	10	30	0	0
Typical room size	325 (30)	350 (33)	300 (28)	275 (26)
Commons areas	1,000 (93)	0	3,000 (279)	4,500 (419)
Total net area[a]	87,125 (8,103)	120,750 (11,230)	63,000 (5,859)	32,000 (2,976)
Total gross area (+ 45%)	126,300 (11,476)	175,100 (16,284)	91,350 (8,496)	46,400 (4,315)
Public areas				
Main lobby	4,000 (372)	4,500 (419)	3,000 (279)	2,500 (233)
Retail	500 (47)	1,000 (93)	300 (28)	0
Support	500 (47)	750 (70)	500 (47)	300 (28)
Total net area	5,000 (465)	6,250 (581)	3,800 (353)	2,800 (260)
Conference dining room	4,500 (419)	6,000 (558)	5,000 (465)	3,000 (279)
Specialty restaurant	3,000 (279)	2,000 (186)	1,500 (140)	0
Other food outlet	0	3,000 (279)	0	0
Private dining	800 (74)	1,000 (93)	1,000 (93)	0
Lobby lounge	1,200 (112)	2,000 (186)	0	1,600 (149)
Pub	1,500 (140)	2,500 (233)	2,500 (233)	0
Game room	1,500 (140)	1,500 (140)	1,800 (167)	0
Library or reading room	0	0	0	500 (47)
Support areas	500 (47)	1,000 (93)	400 (37)	200 (19)
Total net area	13,000 (1,209)	19,000 (1,767)	12,200 (1,135)	5,300 (493)
Total gross area (+40%)	25,200 (2,344)	35,350 (3,288)	22,400 (2,083)	11,350 (1,056)
Conference and training				
Ballroom	5,000 (465)	8,000 (744)	0	0
Large conference rooms[b]	4,000 (372)	6,000 (558)	9,000 (837)	0
Medium conference rooms[c]	4,000 (372)	3,000 (279)	6,000 (558)	2,400 (223)
Small conference rooms[d]	4,000 (372)	4,000 (372)	3,000 (279)	3,000 (279)
Breakout rooms	3,000 (279)	3,000 (279)	3,500 (326)	1,500 (140)
Boardroom	700 (65)	700 (65)	0	0
Amphitheater	0	2,500 (233)	0	3,000 (279)
Auditorium	0	0	5,000 (465)	0
Computer/special	0	0	4,000 (372)	800 (74)
Total net area	20,700 (1,925)	27,200 (2,530)	30,500 (2,837)	10,700 (995)
Assembly and break areas	8,000 (744)	8,000 (744)	8,000 (744)	2,500 (233)
Support areas	1,200 (112)	2,500 (233)	1,500 (140)	700 (65)
Total net area	9,200 (856)	10,500 (977)	9,500 (884)	3,200 (298)

(Continued)

TABLE 8-4. CONTINUED

	Executive Centers	Resort Centers	Corporate Centers	University Centers
Conference services	1,000 (93)	500 (47)	1,000 (93)	500 (47)
Projection rooms	1,600 (149)	1,500 (140)	1,500 (140)	300 (28)
Audiovisual and graphics	1,200 (112)	500 (47)	2,000 (186)	1,000 (93)
Storage	1,500 (140)	2,000 (186)	3,000 (279)	500 (47)
Pantry	200 (19)	400 (37)	400 (37)	200 (19)
Training offices	0	0	12,000 (1,116)	5,000 (465)
Total net area	5,500 (512)	4,900 (456)	19,900 (1,851)	7,500 (698)
Total gross area (+30%)	46,000 (4,278)	55,400 (5,152)	77,200 (7,180)	27,800 (2,585)
Recreation				
Swimming pool	3,000 (279)	3,500 (326)	4,500 (419)	0
Racquetball courts	1,600 (149)	1,600 (149)	1,600 (149)	0
Exercise room	1,000 (93)	1,000 (93)	800 (74)	800 (74)
Aerobics room	800 (74)	800 (74)	0	0
Lockers and toilets	1,500 (140)	3,000 (279)	1,500 (140)	400 (37)
Reception or snack bar	800 (74)	1,000 (93)	500 (47)	0
Gym, golf, or tennis club	0	7,000 (651)	7,000 (651)	0
Total net area	8,700 (809)	17,900 (1,665)	15,900 (1,479)	1,200 (112)
Total gross area (+30%)	11,300 (1,051)	23,300 (2,167)	20,700 (193)	1,550 (144)
Administration				
Front office	1,000 (93)	1,200 (112)	600 (56)	400 (37)
Executive office	1,200 (112)	1,500 (140)	800 (74)	800 (74)
Sales and conference planning	1,800 (167)	2,000 (186)	500 (47)	0
Accounting	1,200 (112)	1,000 (93)	1,000 (93)	1,000 (93)
Total net area	5,200 (484)	5,700 (530)	2,900 (270)	2,200 (205)
Total gross area (+40%)	7,300 (679)	8,000 (744)	4,050 (377)	3,100 (288)
Back-of-house area				
Kitchen and food and beverage storage	7,500 (698)	9,000 (837)	7,000 (651)	3,000 (279)
Receiving and storage	3,500 (326)	4,000 (372)	6,000 (558)	1,000 (93)
Employee areas	3,500 (326)	4,000 (372)	2,000 (186)	1,000 (93)
Laundry and housekeeping	3,500 (326)	4,000 (372)	2,400 (223)	1,500 (140)
Maintenance and engineering	8,000 (744)	10,000 (930)	10,000 (930)	4,000 (372)
Total net area	26,000 (2,418)	31,000 (2,883)	27,400 (2,548)	10,500 (977)
Total gross area (+40%)	36,400 (3,385)	43,400 (4,036)	38,400 (3,571)	14,700 (1,367)
Project gross area	252,500 (23,483)	340,550 (31,671)	254,100 (23,631)	104,900 (9,756)
Square feet per room	1,010 (94)	1,135 (106)	1,270 (118)	1,049 (98)

[a]Based on suites equal to 2.5 typical rooms.
[b]Larger than 1,500 square feet (139 square meters).
[c]Between 1,000 and 1,500 square feet (93 and 139 square meters).
[d]Between 500 and 1,000 square feet (46 and 93 square meters).

will the conference dining operation feature a servery or a buffet setup? The answer will influence the size of the kitchen and dining room, the design of the public entrance to these areas and the transition between them, the ventilation and fire protection requirements, and the equipment and interiors budgets. These operational concepts, which are discussed fully in each of the next chapters, must be developed and approved before schematic design begins or during its earliest stages.

Lodging and Related Services. The concept for the conference center lobby is very similar to that for a hotel; the architectural plans must accommodate the checkin–checkout functions supported by administrative offices, seating and assembly areas, phones and similar support functions, and access to guestrooms and other public areas. The lobby generally is associated with the residential component, but in a few corporate facilities the registration area is located at the center of the conference core or near other public facilities, providing certain advantages but necessitating careful development of the registration and luggage functions.

The priority of the lobby functions can vary, however. In corporate and university centers, at which the average stay is relatively lengthy, and may even exceed three weeks, the registration activity is reduced and other residential services (such as mail, messages, guest laundry, and a cashier or cash machine) are more critical. Corporate centers may establish a security function near the lobby, checking guest identification badges and carefully controlling access to the property.

In addition, the design team should make early decisions concerning guestroom services, including bellman service, housekeeping frequency, room service, and such systems as telephone, computer, and fire alarm. Many corporate and some university centers plan future enhancements in the communications systems, such as two or three phone lines, sophisticated message systems, and data networks; resort and executive centers may consider minibars and even club or hospitality floors; corporate facilities occasionally provide central snack pantries on the guestroom floors; and centers anticipating long-stay programs may include coin-operated guest laundry facilities. (See Chapter 9, Guestroom Design, and Chapter 10, Planning Public Facilities, for more discussion of these issues.)

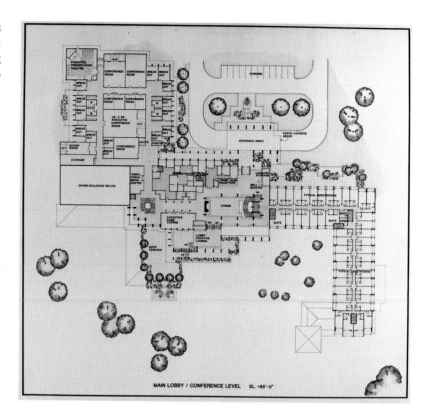

MAIN LOBBY / CONFERENCE LEVEL   EL. +95'-0"

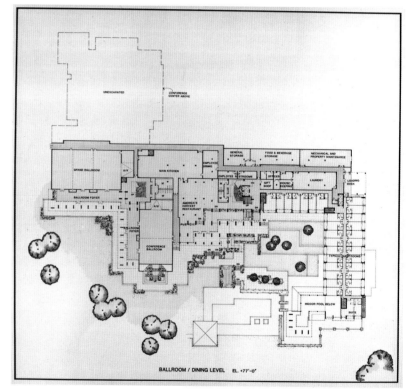

BALLROOM / DINING LEVEL   EL. +77'-0"

Proposed conference center, Annapolis, Maryland (facing page). The schematic plans show the clear separation of functions: conference core to one side; lounges and game room off the lobby; banquet and dining areas on the lower level, with direct access from the kitchen and back-of-house areas; guest elevators convenient to the front desk and entrance; and recreational facilities at the end of the residential block. One-third of the guestrooms encircle a mid-rise lobby atrium. (Architect: Rabun Hatch & Associates; plans courtesy of Rouse & Associates.)

Peachtree Executive Conference Center, Peachtree City, Georgia (right). The conference core plan shows a typical one-story arrangement with conference services offices and the larger ballroom and amphitheater closer to the entrance and hotel lobby; a block of small meeting and breakout rooms in the center; and additional conference rooms, boardrooms, and assembly spaces, many with private outdoor terraces, around the perimeter. Current Peachtree expansion plans call for the addition of about 50 percent more useable space. (Architect: Rabun Hatch & Associates; plan courtesy of Rabun Hatch.)

Food and Beverage Concepts. The operational concepts of the restaurants and lounges contribute substantially to the conference center's success. The team must develop the concept for each restaurant and lounge, including the capacity, service style, operational hours, menu, and so on. In addition, they need to define comprehensively the several related operations: conference area refreshment breaks, banquets and private dining, recreation-area dining or snack bar, office snack service (in the case of corporate training departments), and employee dining. Other operational considerations must be addressed at the outset; for example, many centers have traditionally used disposable cups and plates at refreshment areas, but the increasing costs of solid-waste disposal, as well the poor environmental image associated with using throwaways have caused many operators to convert to permanent-ware service, necessitating additional pantry space. (For further discussion, see Chapter 10, Planning Public Facilities.)

Conference and Training Program. Central to the entire conference facility is an understanding of the meeting objectives of the prospective attendees. Corporate and university centers, at which the operators also control the educational content of the sessions, are the easiest to program, assuming the company or institution has developed a comprehensive analysis of its needs or potential markets. Many such groups develop very focused facilities to meet those specific learning objectives. For example, a university center may have two case study rooms for forty students, sixteen breakout rooms for groups of five, and little else; this would indicate the university anticipates operating very limited types of advanced business and management programs. A corporation may also provide specialized computer laboratories specifically designed for its employees and customers.

On the other hand, executive and resort conference centers need to provide a broader mix of conference areas in order to attract a variety of groups at peak and off-peak periods. As a result, larger banquet spaces and such specialized rooms as amphitheaters and boardrooms may be required.

Universities also are developing and expanding their continuing education facilities, designed for larger, more price-sensitive groups. For these centers, the programmatic requirements are considerably different, including a 1,000-seat main auditorium and many large meeting rooms for fifty or more participants. There is little need for the small breakout rooms. Guestrooms are often occupied by two guests.

Recreational Program. The developer, in consultation with the operator, must determine the scope of the recreational facilities. Most executive and corporate centers include an indoor pool, a weight room or universal gym, an aerobics room, and locker facilities; many add racquetball courts and such outdoor facilities as a pool and tennis courts. Some

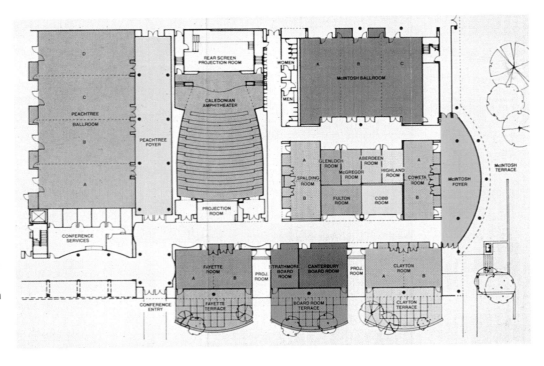

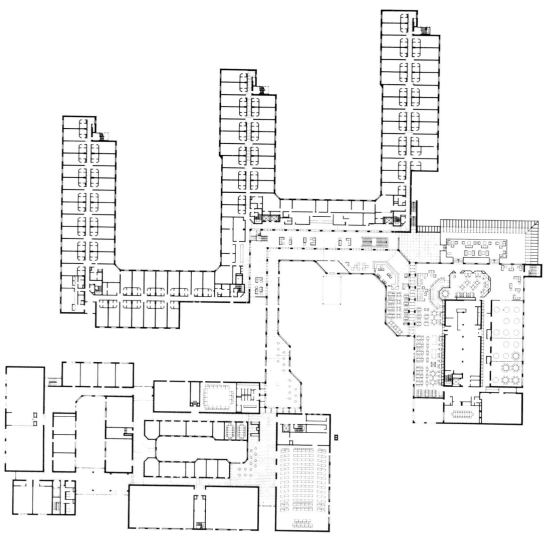

Scanticon-Princeton, Princeton, New Jersey (left). The one-story layout includes a large, multipurpose, flat-floored auditorium, eight conference rooms with front-projection booths between each pair, and oversized breakout rooms. Many of the original 150 square foot (14 square meter) rooms located around a courtyard have been combined for greater utility. The recent expansion added two conference rooms, two boardrooms, and seven breakout rooms around a second courtyard. (Architect: Friis and Molkte with Warner Burns Toan and Lunde; plan courtesy of Scanticon.)

Proposed conference center, Lewisboro, New York (facing page). Many developers have proposed a *pod* concept, in which several companies would group dedicated conference and training areas around a single public facility. The Lewisboro plan proposes five distinct meeting centers, creating the sense of a village, each with two large conference rooms, four breakout rooms, training offices, and 50 guestrooms, and a common public—support wing, including a 250-seat ballroom or multipurpose meeting room, dining and lounge areas, fitness center, and support functions. (Architect: Hellmuth, Obata & Kassabaum; plan courtesy of HOK.)

corporations specifically omit the pool but add a gymnasium or softball field with the intention of encouraging team-building activities. Resort conference centers may include golf, skiing, and large tennis complexes, depending on their location and the expectations of their nonconference markets. The operator needs to determine appropriate staffing levels and, in conjunction with the program director, decide how fitness and recreational program can be used to enhance the conference sessions. (See Chapter 14, Recreational Facilities.)

Administration and Service Functions. In addition to the visible lodging, foodservice, conference, and recreation programs, many back-of-house functions should be defined at the outset. These include the administrative offices housing the operating staff and such issues as the organization of the kitchen and food production areas (for example, their relative centralization), receiving and trash handling, laundry and housekeeping (does the

center include an on-site laundry?), maintenance operations (are repairs and major maintenance performed by center staff or outside contractors?), landscape maintenance, and relative computerization. Each of these functions or systems has an associated capital cost, equipment expense, staffing requirement, control level, and, to varying degrees, an impact on the overall guest experience.

ESTABLISHING THE PROJECT BUDGET
Conference and training centers are costly. Compared with hotels, they often are sited on larger land parcels (to ensure seclusion), require more floor area per room, have higher equipment costs, need larger staffs, and may struggle to achieve high occupancies for weekends and holiday periods. It is therefore essential that the preliminary project budget identifies the extent of the development costs and enables the developer and operator to plan effectively. The developer must realize that construction may represent only half the total

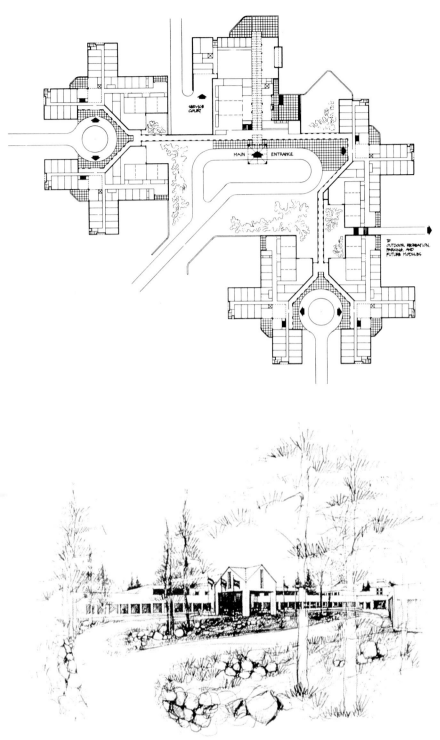

SERVICE
COURT

MAIN ENTRANCE

TO
OUTDOOR RECREATION,
PARKING, AND
FUTURE MODULES

ENTRY COURT

project costs, and that the other expenses (equipment, architectural and engineering fees, financing costs, operating supplies, pre-opening activities, training, landscaping, operating reserves, and so on) must be projected in order for the conference center to operate and compete effectively.

DEVELOPING THE CONCEPTUAL DESIGN

Among the first architectural tasks is developing an initial conceptual design for the conference center. Architects often are called upon to prepare a schematic design *before* the developer completes the program or establishes the operational criteria, in part to test the site capacity, generate preliminary construction estimates, and add credibility to a lender's package (used to solicit interest in financing). While these conceptual studies may occur early in the project schedule, they do make and follow some preliminary assumptions about the number of guestrooms, amount of conference space, relative emphasis on recreational amenities, operational procedures, and so forth.

The most common conceptual organization calls for three main clusters: one with the lobby, food and beverage outlets, banquet facilities, and back-of-house areas; another with the conference core; and a third with the guestrooms. The recreational amenities usually are grouped with the lodging, or may be located near the food and beverage areas, with the lounges, terraces, and game room close by. The public areas are grouped together, streamlining circulation, simplifying the location of the dining and banquet areas, and reducing service traffic (which, to a large degree, is foodservice-related). The conference areas are separated, articulating a businesslike character and reducing the chance for distractions from the hotel lobby, lounges, and recreation.

Also, this arrangement gives the architect more control over the ceiling heights, structural bays, and acoustics of the conference areas. These rooms can be designed to meet precise performance standards required for the conference areas, without compromises from other functional areas. And the guestrooms, more often in a low-rise wing than in a mid- or high-rise tower, are positioned conveniently to the lobby and dining outlets but sited to take full advantage of scenic views. (See the ground-floor plans for Scanticon-Minneapolis, Chapter 2, and Scanticon-Princeton, Chapter 8.)

Resort conference centers may exhibit

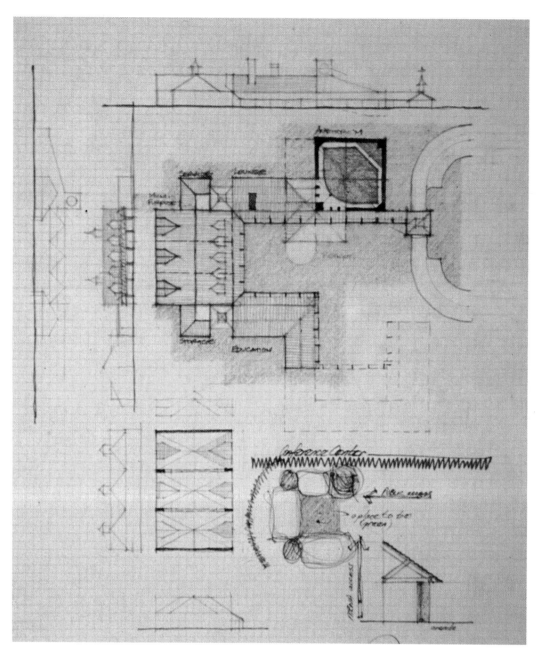

Proposed corporate training center, Eastern Seaboard. The proposal for a nonresidential training center for a financial services company illustrates a simple parti: the auditorium, multipurpose meeting room, and smaller training spaces and offices are conceived as four interconnected structures that define and enclose a landscaped courtyard. (Architect: Curtis Cox Kennerly; plans courtesy of Curtis Cox Kennerly.)

slightly different relationships among the functional areas. The recreational facilities, because of their increased emphasis, often are located within the main public building (see Doral Arrowwood, Chapter 3) rather than in a more remote location at the end of the guest-room structure. Also, many resort centers incorporate separate residential buildings (often condominium units), which are highly attractive to guests on golf or skiing vacations. In such projects as Kingsmill and Cheyenne Mountain (see Chapter 3), the public facilities, conference core, and service areas are organized in the main building, the recreational component is one or more additional structures, and guestrooms are in many smaller buildings scattered over a relatively large site,

often nestled among the golf, tennis, or other recreational amenities.

Corporate training and management development centers, which tend to be somewhat larger, frequently are conceived as a campus, either with separate buildings (Aberdeen Woods has a separate lobby, administration, and conference building, a dining and recreation building, and a residential building) or with two or more interconnected structures, providing weather protection while retaining a sense of separate functional components. In these projects, it is important that the corporate officers, the senior human resources, training, and architecture executives, and even the CEO agree on a conceptual strategy. The two most common options are to fully separate

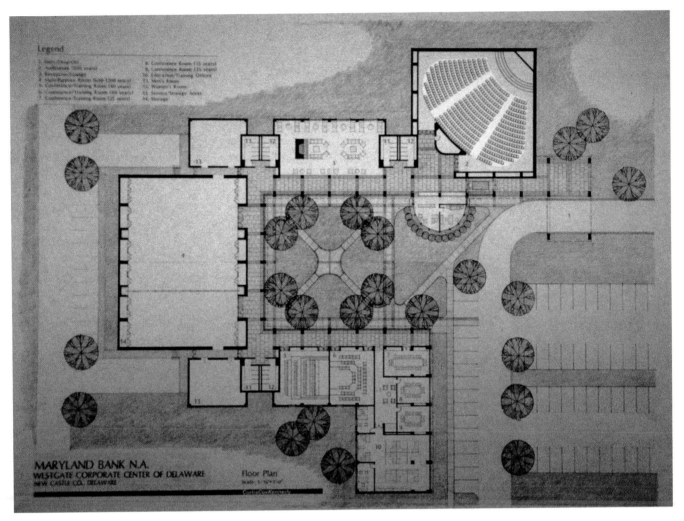

MARYLAND BANK N.A.
WESTGATE CORPORATE CENTER OF DELAWARE
NEW CASTLE CO., DELAWARE   Floor Plan

either the guestroom structure or the conference core from the remainder of the training center; much less common is to house the lobby and guestrooms in one building and the conference and food and beverage components in the other.

University facilities follow no one or two principal organizational models, partly because they tend to be located on fairly tight sites at the center of the campus, forcing the design team to respond to site rather than to the operational considerations. Many are closer to hotels, with the guestrooms on upper floors and the public and conference areas configured in a podium, which works quite well to encourage involvement among the participants as they move from seminars to breaks and meals, then back to afternoon sessions.

These centers often show less separation between the conference and dining or lounge areas. The program developers may consider combining the classroom and residential elements, facilitating continued study and discussion during the evenings (see Thomas Center, Duke University, Chapter 5).

Nonresidential centers, because they contain many fewer functional elements, are simpler to envision. For the most part they include a small reception lobby, an auditorium, a large number of meeting and breakout rooms, and a limited-menu cafeteria or dining room. The corporate nonresidential centers may contain a library or other resource center, computer rooms, and training offices. Design options tend to be highly limited, since the constraints of the building or site usually determine the schematic plan. It is not uncommon for the proposed training department program to be tested against the available space, followed by a negotiation period while the program is scaled back and the tentative site or available office floor is increased.

CHAPTER 9

Guestroom Design

Improving guestroom design will be the next facilities issue aggressively dealt with by conference center developers and managers. Although many hotel operators believe that guestroom design offers a valuable opportunity for influencing guest satisfaction and creating a memorable and positive experience, few conference center operators or designers have given it careful enough thought. Aside from the aesthetics and practical functions of the room itself (actually an interior design exercise), the long-term financial success of an entire project can rest on the efficient architectural planning of the residential wings or floors.

Guestrooms usually represent the largest amount of space in the conference center, about 35 to 55 percent of the total floor area (although this is considerably less than the 65 to 80 percent that is normal for other types of hotels). Therefore, they are a key part of creating an efficient building, especially if the gross project area or the furnishings and equipment costs are high: saving as little as 5 percent in planning the guestroom section—not with a smaller room but through *a more efficient floor arrangement*—can save as much as $750,000 in construction and FF&E expenses for a midsize conference center.

The architect and other members of the team should consider the future adaptability of the lodging areas as well. The conference center concept is still relatively young, and guestrooms may need to accommodate considerable changes as the industry and market matures. Some early corporate centers, for example, were constructed with extremely small guestrooms—under 200 square feet (18.6 square meters); now that these facilities are trying to attract noncompany executive meetings, they find their small rooms are an almost insurmountable obstacle. Similarly, the executive centers adapting to attract the weekend resort market are finding that the standard guest bathrooms, suitable for one person, are unpopular with the upscale weekend vacationer. It is impossible to anticipate the future precisely, of course, but new centers should be built with future adaptability in mind.

ESTABLISHING THE GUESTROOM PROGRAM

During programming and conceptual design, developers must first determine the number of guestrooms and the size of the basic guestroom unit. While midprice and first-class hotels usually have rooms in the 300 to 350 square foot (27.9 to 32.5 square meter) range,

The Statler Hotel and Marriott Executive Education Center, Cornell University, Ithaca, New York. The typical rooms, predominantly queen-bedded, feature cherry casepieces that recall the colors and details of the public space furnishings. Oversized desks and comfortable lounge seating is designed for the conference guest. (Architect: The Architects Collaborative; interiors: Kenneth E. Hurd and Associates; photo: Ed Jacoby.)

major conference and training centers being developed today may have rooms as small as 200 square feet (18.6 square meters) or as large as 400 square feet (37.2 square meters). Given this wide range, it is imperative that the designer accurately project the market expectations and financial capability of the developer, company, or institution. Unfortunately, the designer often is under pressure to reduce the size of the guestroom unit to compensate for the additional floor area required for the conference and training facilities; however, overly small guestrooms will result in a conference center that is obsolete as soon as it opens, with no flexibility for later adaptation to attract other market segments.

Therefore, the conference center guestroom should have dimensions similar to those of hotel rooms: 12 to 13 feet (3.6 to 3.9 meters) wide and 16 to 20 feet (4.8 to 6 meters) long, measuring from bathroom to exterior wall (or 24 to 30 feet, 7.3 to 9.1 meters, long including the bath and entry zone). Comfortable rooms for the university and corporate markets, anticipating single occupancy, would be at the low end of this range (288 square feet, or 26.7 square meters), and slightly larger if a high double-occupancy percentage is expected; for the executive and resort centers, where double occupancy is projected for nonmeeting business, the room size should be near the middle or at the upper end (325 to 390 square feet, or 30.2 to 36.3 square meters). Table 9–1 proposes guestroom dimensions for each type of conference center.

The *smallest* basic guestroom, which might be used in highly price-sensitive university or corporate training centers, should be no narrower than 12 feet (3.6 meters) and no shorter than 13 feet (3.9 meters) (measured from bath-

room to exterior wall). These rooms, intended for single occupancy, should be furnished with a long double bed, a single lounge chair, a large work area with a comfortable desk chair, and a television—spartan, at best. The minimal acceptable layout for the bathroom, closet, and entry vestibule adds another six feet to the length, resulting in a *minimum* guestroom area of 228 square feet (21.2 square meters). The utility of a small bathroom may be improved by providing only a stall shower, although the developer must be certain that omitting a bathtub is acceptable to the target markets. The most important problem, however, is that these small guestrooms are unsuitable for double occupancy, and therefore not adaptable for more upscale business that might be attracted in the future.

The guestroom program should address other issues, of course. The design team needs to consider a broad range of program decisions, including the following:

The number of guestrooms

The number of suites

Typical room size

Suite size and configuration

The number of interconnecting rooms

The number of handicapped rooms

Bathroom requirements

Provision of balconies or terraces

Acoustic requirements

Computer capability

Communications systems

Provision of commons areas

Provision of case study room(s)

Snack area/pantry

To some extent, each type of conference

	Living Area in Feet (Meters)	Bathroom in Feet (Meters)	Net Guestroom Area in Square Feet (Square Meters)
TABLE 9-1. PROPOSED GUESTROOM DIMENSIONS			
Conference Center Type			
University and corporate (with single occupancy)	12 × 16 (3.7 × 4.9)	5 × 8 (1.5 × 2.4)	288 (27)
University and corporate (with double occupancy)	12 × 18 (3.7 × 5.5)	5 × 8 (1.5 × 2.4)	312 (29)
Executive (with secondary transient market)	12½ × 18 (3.8 × 5.5)	5½ × 8 (1.7 × 2.4)	325 (30)
Executive (with secondary weekend resort market)	13 × 18 (4 × 5.5)	5½ × 8½ (1.7 × 2.6)	345 (32)
Resort	13 × 20 (4 × 6.1)	6 × 10 (1.8 × 3)	390 (36)

center includes similar guestroom-related features and amenities. For example, most conference centers have very few suites. In fact, in executive and resort centers, suites generally account for fewer than 5 percent of the rooms; in corporate and university centers, suites usually amount to fewer than 2 percent (often none). Exceptions include the resort conference centers, which consist of condominium units, frequently combining a living room with two adjoining bedrooms; these should be designed to be rented separately to three different guests.

Similarly, the club floors common in upscale hotels, featuring a hospitality lounge and upgraded furnishings and amenities, are rare, only available in conference centers with a high percentage of transient business. Instead of a club lounge, however, university centers in particular may offer commons areas on the guestroom floors, allowing easy collaboration among students in advanced courses. These may be in a format of one per floor or, as works well at Wharton and Harvard, as one case study room for each seven or eight guestrooms. The case study room at Wharton's Steinberg Center is a combination living room–conference room–kitchenette/pantry, and also features a computer, a television, and a VCR. At Duke's Thomas Center, the class breakout rooms are organized along guestroom corridors, convenient during the class day as well as in the evening for group work.

GUESTROOM AREA PLANNING

Following the definition of the guestroom program, the design effort starts in two directions: the layout of the standard residential unit and the planning of the lodging wing. The first establishes the structural module (which often influences the public and conference areas on the lower floors), while the second creates the typical floor configuration and architectural massing.

Efficiently planned guestroom wings offer the potential for great cost savings. This is especially true in executive centers, where the guestrooms constitute 50 to 55 percent of the total project area. The architect's first task is to conceive an organizational and architectural solution appropriate to the setting, site, and market orientation. But once the approach is determined, the schematic must be developed into an efficient plan that provides the maximum benefit to the guestrooms and minimizes nonsalable space (unless it offers substantial amenities, as do adding commons areas, atrium lounges, and other public spaces in the residential structure).

Architects and developers should test the practicality of a design, just as they do financial feasibility; if the project doesn't measure up to a certain objective standard, it needs to be reshaped or remolded, and the analysis repeated, until an economically feasible architectural plan is reached. The following are general objectives to assure more efficient planning of the guestroom areas.

Plan Configuration. Since the rooms can represent as much as half of the total project area, any planning efficiencies on one floor or one wing are multiplied manyfold. The key determinant of efficient planning is the early choice of a double- or single-loaded design and the arrangement of guestrooms in a relatively long, low building, high-rise tower, or atrium scheme. Double-loaded slab configurations require an addition of 40 to 45 percent to the net area (for corridors, vertical

TABLE 9-2. VARIATION IN GROSS ROOM AREA BY PLANNING CONFIGURATION

Planning Configuration	Guestroom Percent[a]	Gross Factor	Net Area in Square Feet (Square Meters)	Gross Area in Square Feet (Square Meters)
Double-loaded slab	70	+0.42	325 (30)	461 (43)
Circular tower	67	+0.50	325 (30)	484 (45)
Single-loaded slab	65	+0.54	325 (30)	500 (47)
Rectangular tower	65	+0.54	325 (30)	500 (47)
Atrium	62	+0.61	325 (30)	523 (49)

[a]Total of net guestroom areas as a percentage of the gross floor area.

Source: Rutes, Walter A., and Richard H. Penner (1985). *Hotel Planning and Design*. New York: Whitney Library of Design.

circulation, storage, walls, and so on), while towers, in which the guestrooms are grouped around a central vertical core, exhibit a gross factor of 50 to 55 percent, and atrium designs require 60 percent or more.

An analysis conducted at Cornell University in the early 1980s found that each planning configuration of rooms has a corresponding gross factor that represents, under normal conditions, the percentage of the net floor area that must be added to reach the gross area. The figures in Table 9–2 show how the *gross* area for a normal 325 square foot (30.2 square meter) guestroom varies substantially depending on the configuration of the plan. Well-planned projects exhibit a lower gross factor, but current analysis of forty conference and training centers shows that many facilities fail to meet these planning goals.

Vertical Circulation Arrangement. A second factor in the efficient planning of guestroom areas is the economical arrangement of the public and service elevators, stairs, and support functions. Grouping these areas together generally reduces the amount of floor area required. Also, the more guestrooms per floor in a project, the lower the percentage of space that must be dedicated to nonsalable vertical circulation. In urban projects, where public areas may be spread over two or three floors, an open stair between the public levels may allow the architect to provide one less elevator, a solution that has a corresponding savings in more efficient plans for the upper guestroom floors.

Guestroom Size. Obviously, the dimensions of the individual guestrooms greatly influence the project cost and potential profitability of a marginal conference center. However, unlike practically every other part of the project, an increase in guestroom size—simply adding length to the room—provides immediate payback in increased guest satisfaction and requires no corresponding additional investment in associated gross area. That is, corridors, stairs, linen storage, and so on need not be increased to match longer guestrooms.

Therefore, the projects with the smallest guestrooms—the university and corporate centers—are the least efficient. In these projects, the architect may need to provide an additional 80 percent to increase the net guestroom area to a gross figure. That is, a scheme with small, 200 square foot (18.6 square meter) guestrooms may require 360 gross square feet

(33.4 gross square meters) per room in the residential sections of the building (an increase of 160 square feet [14.8 square meters], or 80 percent); an alternative project with much larger, 320 square foot (29.7 square meter) guestrooms may be constructed for about 480 gross square feet (44.6 gross square meters) (an increase of 160 square feet [14.8 square meters], or 50 percent), all of the difference in gross area going to the guestroom itself.

Suite Configuration. Resort and some executive centers are the only conference centers that may have a relatively high number of suites; for example, The Resort at Squaw Creek has 180 suites out of four-hundred total units, and the Northland Inn is an all-suite property. The development team must assess the relative need for suites and, when they are deemed essential to the room mix, determine what size and features are essential.

The most common suites are achieved by interconnecting two standard rooms and furnishing one as a parlor or living room, which, with a convertible sofa and a full bathroom, can be rented occasionally as a sleeping room. But when suites are formed, the living room and bedrooms can be somewhat smaller—the bedroom need not have the normal amount of work or lounge space, and the living room can dispense with a bed or a full bathroom.

Recognizing this, Embassy Suites developed a prototype room in the early 1980s, positioning the bedroom and living room end-to-end rather than side-by-side. In addition to reducing the total suite area to about 450 square feet (41.8 square meters), this arrangement needs less corridor and exterior wall space, both representing cost savings. But one space in the suite, generally the living room, will not have outside windows.

The third common suite layout incorporates two slightly narrow spaces side-by-side into a similar 450 square foot (41.8 square meter) area. Many of the hotel operating companies have developed prototype suites of this genre, each with slight variations of the entryway, bathroom, closet, furniture layout, and the opening between the living room and bedroom.

Commons Areas. One distinguishing characteristic of conference centers is the guests' need to gather when not in meetings, both formally and informally, to continue discussions and work. Instead of expecting the par-

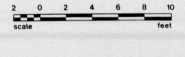

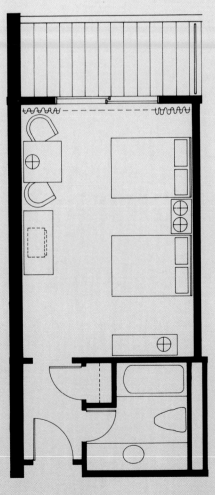

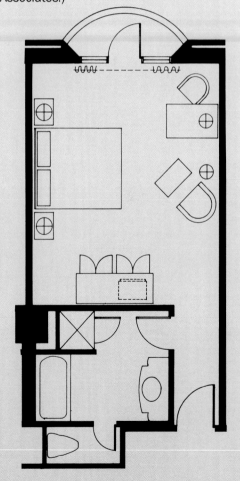

GUESTROOM LAYOUTS

At the executive Residence, University of Michigan (top left), guestrooms are efficiently planned with several functional elements organized into a single built-in module. (Design: Luckenback/Ziegelman and Partners.)

Aberdeen Woods (top right) features several different layouts, all with double closets, a compartmentalized bathroom, and two sinks, including one scheme with study carrels to provide increased privacy for the two trainees. (Design: Thompson Hancock Witte.)

Eagle Lodge (bottom left) completed a total guestroom renovation in 1991, enlarging the bathrooms and replacing the more institutional built-in work areas and fluorescent lighting with an executive—resort design concept. (Design: The Hillier Group.)

The Four Seasons Hotel and Resort (bottom right) offers large rooms with balconies and elegant oversized bathrooms to meet the needs and high expectations of the resort clientele. (Design: Wilson and Associates.)

2 0 2 4 6 8 10
scale   feet

ticipants to meet either in the restaurants and cocktail lounges or in someone's bedroom, many centers make a positive feature of lounges, commons areas, or case study rooms on the guestroom floors. These should be carefully programmed at the outset—it is not acceptable for poorly planned or otherwise unusable space to end up being designated as a guestroom floor lounge by default. The character of these areas may change substantially, depending on whether they are intended principally as social lounges or as informal work areas.

Various centers have taken their own approaches to the lounge issue: At the New England Center in Durham, New Hampshire, lounges are provided opposite the elevator foyer on each floor to add natural light and create sunny meeting places. Scanticon-Denver has two lounges on each floor, at the center of the guestroom wings. Given that the guests will have spectacular views from their bedrooms of either the golf course or the Rocky Mountains, the lounges offer guests an opportunity to experience the "other" view. Off the wide guestroom circulation spaces at the IBM Advanced Business Institute, two comfortable lounges overlook the central pond, each one furnished with newspapers, television, and, in the early morning, continental breakfast. Developers and the management team should brainstorm to find similar ways of making commons areas functional and useful to the guests.

Among the most convenient informal meeting spaces are case study lounges, such as those at the Steinberg Center at Penn. Positioned to serve about seven guestrooms each, the lounges combine such functions and roles as living room, conference room, pantry, and computer terminal. The Statler at Cornell offers four case study rooms (which otherwise function as hospitality suites or suite living rooms) with a computer work area in a locked alcove.

Upscale Club Floors. As conference centers become more competitive and seek out alternative markets, they are adopting some of the amenities of first-class hotels. One of these is the "club" or "tower" floor, a guestroom section with such upgraded services as concierge service, complimentary cocktails, continental breakfast, and a selection of morning newspapers. The club floor features a private lounge, usually the space equivalent of two to four guestrooms, incorporating several

lounge groupings, television, bar, pantry, and concierge area. Executive conference centers with a higher complement of suites generally locate them on the club floors. Some properties don't go this far but instead improve the quality of the guestroom furnishings or supply additional room and bathroom amenities.

GUESTROOM LAYOUT AND DESIGN

Before the team completes the architectural planning of the guestroom areas, the members must agree completely on the design of the individual units. If planning and budgeting proceed too far without the owner's and operator's approval of the room design, pressure may grow to approve a less desirable deign or accept time delays while the room design (or perhaps even the dimensions of the structural module) is changed.

The importance of the guestroom design and its features cannot be overestimated. While the meeting rooms are critical to the success of the conference sessions, the guestrooms establish the private comfort level of the overnight guest. Many corporations establish small room sizes, partly to save on expenses but also to encourage mingling among the participants. While this move is well intentioned, small, cell-like rooms are distasteful to guests and meeting planners alike. Rooms smaller than 250 square feet (23.2 square meters) should be built only as a last resort—not only due to their effect on the guest, but, as noted earlier, because they are not as adaptable to double occupancy and to other markets that the center may try to attract in the future.

The recommended guestroom dimensions at different types of conference centers (see Table 9–1) are based on common solutions for the layout of the furnishings and the plan of the bathroom and entry. Actually, to a large degree, these issues can be considered separately; most room layouts can be paired with nearly any bathroom design. Both, however, must be carefully conceived to meet the needs and expectations of the principal market or markets.

The room design considerations are somewhat different than those for hotels. After matching the bed type to the typical guest, the most important concerns are the size of the work area, the comfort of the chair, and the capabilities of such special equipment as the phone and computer systems. The dresser and closet capacities must be suited to the typical guests' length of stay; corporate and university centers, for example, often host single conferences for several weeks at a time, and Harvard

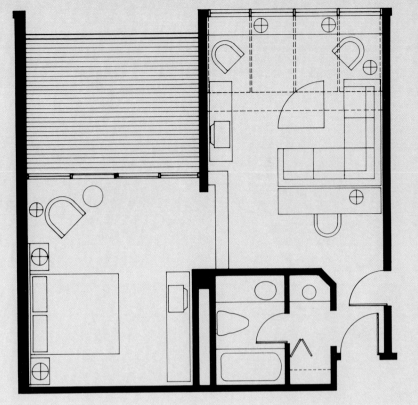

Scanticon-Denver suites (top) are equal to two standard rooms; the sleeping area is raised two steps and the living room features a sloping glass window-wall, creating a memorable space. (Design: Klenow Deichmann and Overbye.)

Suites at the Resort at Squaw Creek (bottom left), over 600 square feet (56 square meters) each, feature two rooms side-by-side and save width by the creative design of the bathroom—dressing area and angled dividing wall. (Design: Simon, Martin-Vegue, Winkelstein, Moris.)

Northland Inn suites (bottom right), about 500 square feet (46 square meters) each, are of the "front-to-back" type, with a living room off the atrium corridor—some are furnished as breakout rooms—an oversized bathroom with a whirlpool tub, and a separate bedroom at the exterior wall. (Design: Wudtke Watson Associates.)

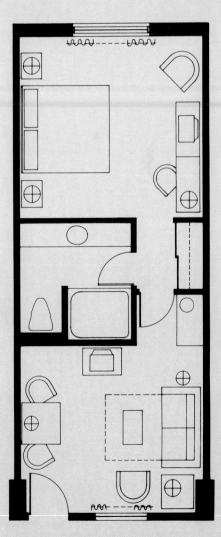

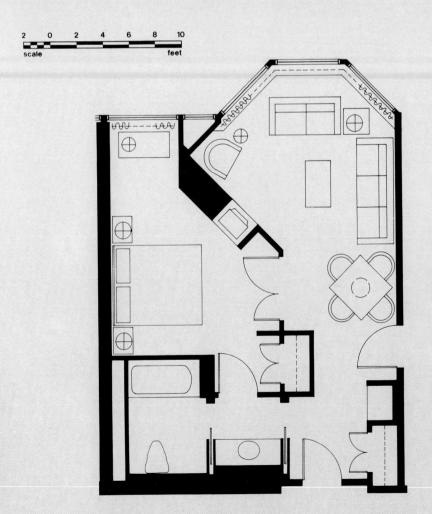

scale feet

Conference center guestrooms meet widely differing requirements based upon anticipated market, occupancy, and projected budget. Clockwise from above right: Executive Residence, University of Michigan (photo: Christopher Lark); IBM-Palisades (photo: Mick Hales); Hotel Macklowe (photo: Elliott Kaufman); The Resort at Squaw Creek (courtesy of Benchmark Management); Four Seasons Hotel and Resort (photo: Jaime Ardiles-Arce).

Scanticon-Denver, Englewood, Colorado. Some
executive and resort centers provide VIP or club
floors that include extra room amenities, a lounge
serving continental breakfast and cocktails, and
concierge services. (Architect: Friis Moltke Larson
with RNL; interiors: Klenow Deichmann and Overbye; photo: Ron Solomon.)

operates a number of 12-week advanced programs, necessitating ample storage capacity.

Furnishings. Conference center rooms, in addition to accommodating the basic functions of sleeping, reading, television viewing, bathing, and dressing, usually are used for a substantial amount of evening study or work, necessitating a large desk or table, and perhaps room for a computer. Conference centers anticipating double occupancy (usually not-for-profit centers, more price–sensitive continuing education facilities and low-level training centers) should have a considerable number of rooms furnished with two oversized twin beds. Resort and executive conference centers attract weekend leisure business that leads to a high percentage of double occupancy, but this can be accommodated with queen or (more frequently) king beds. Centers attracting only single attendees often provide a single lounge chair and ottoman with a table or floor lamp; those accommodating two guests need additional casual seating.

The work area must include an oversized desk to accommodate a large amount of paperwork. More and more participants are bringing computers, and the desk must provide for the lower-height keyboard shelf. Centers with computers installed in the guestrooms must include custom work areas to accommodate the keyboard and CPU. In addition, the computer (usually installed in a low cabinet) requires adequate ventilation, and the guest must have easy access to the disk drives. Lighting must be suitable for both typical paperwork and computer work.

Equipment. Conference center guestrooms often feature such additional equipment as computers, VCRs, and state-of-the-art telephone systems. When possible, phone lines are positioned at the desk and at an alternative location, such as by the bed or the lounge chair, to provide for both communications and computer use. If a computer is permanently installed, careful consideration of ergonomic design issues, chair selection, and lighting are warranted. Printers still are uncommon in guestrooms (although they may be located in sound-insulated closets off the corridor). VCRs are provided primarily in university and resort centers, where they are intended to support

the very different conference and leisure markets. New centers are adding more sophisticated telephone systems. Some corporate centers install an office voice-mail system, through which each room is capable of receiving direct incoming calls and the guest has the ability to record and play back individual messages; as centers grow internationally, this feature will become more common, permitting easy communication in any language.

Bathroom Design. The design of the bathroom contributes in large part to the attendee's general satisfaction level with the guestroom. While the basic design of the bathroom can be fairly straightforward, smaller details can establish its ultimate success or failure. Does the faucet design cause the guest to bang his or her knuckles when turning the faucets? Is the towel rack unreachable from the shower? Is the ventilation inadequate to prevent fogging of the mirror?

Centers should provide a standard three-fixture bathroom with a combination tub–shower and a large vanity counter. The common arrangement fits into a five-by-eight–foot (1.5-by-2.4–meter) space. However, the virtues of this model must be balanced against the needs and expectations of the anticipated leisure and transient business markets. For example, a small number of corporate conference centers have substituted an oversized stall shower for the bathtub, so far with no reported complaints. Although a few university and not-for-profit centers might benefit from the savings in floor area accrued by this move, guestrooms without bathtubs are not recommended for most centers.

Designers and developers should seek out bathroom features and design details that add to the comfort without substantially increasing costs. For example, a dimmer for the mirror lights allows guests to set the light level to their needs, and abrasive-coated ceramic tile increases the safety level; in both cases, the added cost is nominal.

Some resort rooms and suites, which may host more upscale guests, should have larger and more luxurious bathrooms. They might include a fourth fixture—either a separate stall shower or a second sink—a whirlpool bathtub, a separate toilet compartment, a built-in dressing area, or marble finishes.

CHAPTER 10

Planning the Public Facilities

Conference centers today are much more than simply meeting sites with a few additional amenities. Developers and operators are paying increasing attention to the design and management of the public facilities: the lobby and registration areas, the food and beverage outlets, and the various lounges. These—along with the recreational facilities (see Chapter 14)—provide the "living and leisure" accompaniments to the learning focus of the center. At the more market-driven properties, (essentially the executive and resort conference centers), the design of these public facilities is essential to attracting customers and assuring their satisfaction and return business. At the corporate and university centers, on the other hand, the program and design of the public facilities is more closely matched to the specific needs of the individual project—continuing or executive education, middle-management training, executive development, and so forth—allowing the design to reflect the needs of the specific market segments that the center serves.

Among the development team's first steps is to establish the operational program to meet these requirements, usually with the help of a hospitality management company. Many such firms specialize in conference centers; alternatively, specialized consultants in such areas as food service, audiovisuals, computers, and recreation planning can be retained to deal with the individual design, operations, and equipment issues.

The operational program should address the full range of necessary decisions (Table 10–1). The task is simpler if the conference center operation is broken down into departments or similar units. For example, the team might collectively work through the arrival sequence, considering dropoff and parking, luggage handling, reception, guestroom access, and the associated equipment and communications needs of the front desk and administrative offices. Separately, the team could outline the food and beverage requirements, including conference dining, alternative dining, beverage and entertainment lounges, banquet and special events spaces, conference refreshment service, and room service. A similar step-by-step approach could apply to each department.

Designers should try to understand the attitude of the participants throughout the design of the public areas. Many guests approach a

Westfields International Conference Center, Westfields, Virginia. The elegant Westfields caters to suburban Washington conferences and social and transient business. The interiors combine classical elements with architectural details reminiscent of Virginia estates; the lobby lounge offers a quiet place to sit and enjoy continental breakfast, afternoon tea, or cocktails. (Architect: Perkins and Will; interiors: Chandler & Cudlipp; photo: Peter Vitale.)

TABLE 10-1. PUBLIC FACILITIES OPERATIONAL CHECKLIST

Area	Factors to Consider
Lobby and reception areas	☐ Height of the porte cochere
	☐ Number of vehicles at entrance
	☐ Provision of separate entrances for the conference center and hotel lobby
	☐ Provision of preregistration service
	☐ Need for concierge
	☐ Retail requirements and corresponding staff
	☐ Special security precautions
	☐ Guest access to administrative offices (sales, catering, general manager, safe-deposit, etc.)
	☐ Luggage and coat storage requirements
	☐ Food and beverage requirements in the lobby
	☐ Provision of meeting registration service in the lobby
Conference and alternate dining rooms	☐ Choice of buffet or servery configurations
	☐ Choice of dedicated or multipurpose buffet units
	☐ Provision of exhibition cooking
	☐ Provision of other food displays (wine room, bakery, etc.)
	☐ Provision of semiprivate sections
	☐ Desirability of floor-level changes
	☐ Provision of outdoor dining
	☐ Table mix
Lounges	☐ Orientation to public or conferees
	☐ Provision of food service
	☐ Provision of entertainment and/or dance floor
	☐ Capacity at bar, tables, and for standing
Game room	☐ Orientation to public or conferees
	☐ Types of games and amenities
	☐ Proximity to food and beverage outlets or recreation areas

conference program confidently; others may have serious reservations. For example, new corporate trainees, attending their first company session or middle-management employees being sent to a first-tier business school may be apprehensive about the experience, concerned with their ability to succeed in the highly competitive environment. The facility design, beginning with the approach and entrance and continuing with the public areas and the conference space, should allay any such fears and make the guest or participant feel comfortable and at ease. At the same time, it must establish an architectural character and ambience appropriate to a conference facility and meet a number of highly specific functional requirements. This balance between the businesslike and the comfortably inviting should be a major architectural goal throughout the public areas.

While conference centers must satisfy many of the operational characteristics of more typical hotels, the overriding feel must be of an educational center. As a result, the planning and design of the public areas must reflect generally recognized objectives and, in addition, accommodate the peculiarities of the type of conference center and of the particular developer or institution. One way to approach the planning of the lobby areas, restaurants, and lounges is to identify and highlight their distinctions from corresponding areas in hotels. One major need, which underlies practically all types of conference centers, is to provide the same level of comfort and service for both the resident guest and the nonresident, day meeting attendee.

The public areas encompass about 10 percent of the total conference center area, or slightly more than 100 gross square feet (9.3 gross square meters) per guestroom. There is substantial variation among the different types of conference centers however; the lobby, restaurants, and lounges at corporate centers alone can vary from as little as 50 to over 200 square feet (4.6 to 18.6 square meters) per room. These areas have large associated capital costs, and the suitability of their design and the efficiency of their planning enhance and support the operation of the entire conference or training center.

PLANNING THE LOBBY AND RECEPTION AREAS

Many hoteliers believe that the lobby makes the single greatest impact on the guest. Lob-bies of corporate training centers for blue-chip Fortune 100 companies may project an ambience of permanence and stability; university centers often attempt to build in the character of the campus; many not-for-profit centers are more rustic and establish a feeling of informality.

Program Considerations. In developing the lobby program and its design, the designers need to meet a number of practical requirements. The lobby serves as the registration area, the central point of assembly, the circulation heart, and perhaps even houses the restaurant or auditorium foyer. Frequently, it is the nucleus, with the conference areas to one side, the guestrooms to a second, and the restaurants and lounges to a third.

This central location offers the architect an opportunity to envision a space with a special character. The Scanticon lobbies reinforce the Scandinavian flavor that pervades each property; those at mountain resort conference centers, such as The Resort at Squaw Creek, use natural materials—stone fireplaces and laminated wood beams, for example—to introduce a rugged ambience entirely appropriate to their settings.

The conference center lobby program establishes a space of about 14 to 18 square feet

Harrison Conference Center at Lake Bluff, Lake Bluff, Illinois. The restored and expanded center, situated on a 45-acre (18.2-hectare) estate, includes 84 guestrooms and 11 meeting rooms, each with special architectural features. The living room offers a quiet lounge for informal gathering. (Architect for renovations: Hansen Lind Meyer; photo courtesy of Harrison.)

(1.3 to 1.6 square meters) per guestroom and an additional component for the related support functions (sundries shop, public toilets and phones, and luggage storage), bringing the total for the lobby to 18 to 22 square feet (1.6 to 2.0 square meters) per room. Establishing a precise limit to the lobby size may prove inconsequential—the question of whether the lobby is, say, 3,000 or 5,000 square feet (279 or 465 square meters) is not as important as the feel and aura that it contributes to the project. Some operators simply require that the reception space be "of ample space and character appropriate to its function of welcoming guests and serving as a popular meeting place," rather than stating a defined program area.

In most hotels, the front desk is centrally located in the lobby. At conference centers, however, because guests may be staying several weeks, the reception function is de-emphasized, and the desk may positioned to one side in a less conspicuous lobby location, allowing the guests and visitors a more direct route to the conference space. There should be easy access to the principal administrative offices, often located adjacent to the front desk, although many of the executive and sales functions, even accounting, can be in a more remote location.

Another practical consideration is the provision of group seating in the lobby area. The design should allow enough for six to ten people at the least, depending on the overall program and arrangement of functional areas, but much more of the social gathering and informal meeting occurs in other locations, so ample seating is not warranted.

The largest of the necessary adjunct areas is the sundries shop, which stocks newspapers and magazines, toiletries, candy and snack items, and local souvenirs. Its area usually is in the 200- to 500–square foot (18.6- to 46.5–square meter) range. At smaller conference centers, the shop may be located adjacent to the front desk, allowing the desk staff to oversee the sales. Despite the shop's importance and necessity, there is little reason to keep it open during the morning and afternoon meeting periods, given the daily conference schedule, even at larger centers. Resorts and executive centers, which attract more transient business and outside food and beverage sales, may be able to justify a larger outlet and longer hours.

Other lobby support areas include the public rest rooms, coat areas, and telephone alcoves—which might be combined with similar areas nearby, such as at the restaurant or banquet rooms—as well as the luggage storage, bellman stand, valet parking office, and fire-control rooms. In addition to establishing the area program requirements for these areas, each type of conference center has particular operational needs.

Executive Conference Centers. The market-driven executive centers, which compete most directly with other lodging properties, need to duplicate many of the typical hotel lobby features. Practical considerations, such as the location of the front desk, guest elevators, seating, retail, concierge, bellman, and luggage storage are little different from those in hotels. The route to the conference and meeting spaces must be obvious, though. The conference services desk should be prominent, and the meeting directory visible. In short, guests arriving for a meeting should not need to ask directions.

The lobby area requirements at executive centers are similar to the general rules already discussed, with the lobby and support functions requiring no more than 22 square feet (2 square meters) per room. Of course, if additional activities, such as a lobby lounge or conference restaurant, exist within the lobby space, the total floor area may be considerably larger. Executive conference centers frequently include a lobby bar, increasing the revenue-generating potential of the lobby, swelling the level of activity, and offering additional opportunities for informal gathering.

Resort Conference Centers. The tendency is for resort conference centers to be designed with slightly smaller lobbies—about 12 to 15 square feet (1.1 to 1.4 square meters) per guestroom—in part because much of the social gathering occurs at other locations (often outdoors or at the recreational areas). Also, at resort centers like Kingsmill or Cheyenne Mountain, where the guestrooms are built in, scattered, low-rise buildings, smaller lobbies are sufficient because there is considerably less traffic through any central area. The guests usually park their cars at their residential units and can enter the conference rooms, restaurants, and recreational facilities directly from the grounds without having to pass through the lobby. Many of the resort conference centers have more extensive retail areas (Squaw Creek devotes 7,000 square feet, or 651 square meters), which generate substantial revenues to the operator through store leases.

Resort lobbies need to be designed to ac-

Minaki Lodge, Minaki, Ontario. Located 150 miles (241 kilometers) from Winnipeg, this 120-room wilderness conference resort features a central granite structure whose main rotunda rises over 50 feet (15 meters) to a pitched ceiling of cedar logs. Originally built by the Canadian National Railway in 1914, the lodge was totally renovated in 1982. (Photo courtesy of Four Seasons Hotels.)

IBM Technical Education Center, Thornwood, New York. The technical training center houses 250 guestrooms in a 285,000 square foot (26,505 square meter) facility. The lobby offers a secure reception area leading to wings containing the training rooms and lodging, which face each other across a landscaped courtyard. (Architect: RTKL; photo courtesy of RTKL.)

commodate the requirements of the applicable recreational orientation or resort setting. Scanticon-Denver, for example, features an outdoor swimming pool surrounded by paved terraces on several levels, the highest of which is directly off the ballroom assembly space. The successful juxtaposition of pool, terraces, prefunction area, and ballroom has generated great interest in catering, which in turn afforded the operator the opportunity to make the sales offices more obvious. As a result, the catering sales offices have been moved to the lobby. The local clientele, initially drawn to the facility for conference or food and beverage business, now finds it easy to book private functions.

Other lobby support functions may be increased slightly over the basic requirement found in executive centers. For example, the program should identify the need for temporary storage to accommodate golf bags, skis, and other sports equipment, in addition to the more extensive luggage resort guests commonly bring.

The porte cochere at resort centers may have additional requirements as well. All lodging properties need to provide a covered dropoff, of course, to give protection from the weather for loading and unloading luggage. But, at resorts, there may be additional vehicles around the entrance—shuttle bus service to and from the airport, van service to the more distant residential units, and group excursions to nearby attractions—which may necessitate regular access by larger buses.

Corporate Conference and Training Centers. Many corporate centers are restricted entirely to in-house use. The sponsoring company may design a project to house a limited number of specialized training programs with known durations and closely scheduled arrival and departure dates. One result is that the lobby, needed only to handle peak functions for a few hours each week (Sunday evening checkin and Friday afternoon checkout, for example), might be drastically reduced in size. The preliminary plans for the 450-room training center designed for Digital Equipment incorporate an extremely compact lobby—less than 2,000 square feet (186 square meters)—which also serves as the entrance for a large number of day conferees.

Security is an important consideration at many corporate centers. Accordingly, several include a 24-hour security office at the front entrance to check guests' identification badges. Nonguest visitors must have an appointment to gain entry, especially at the more security-conscious, higher-technology computer and telecommunications companies. (Similar security is present at the service entrance, where vendors must be announced and met by the operator.) The security function typically includes an office for two or three people, badge-printing equipment, and close-circuit TV monitors. Often the security personnel are cross-trained to provide front desk services during the night shift.

Because of the highly regulated training schedule, other functions, such as baggage handling and storage, occur at peak times. Because the training center can expect a 100 percent turnover in a single day, with a required checkout before the morning sessions, departing guests need to store their luggage, or procedures must be established for center staff to retrieve it during the morning. Similar peak activity occurs on Sunday evening, or whenever the group arrives. To fully accommodate this and prevent luggage from piling up in the lobby, as much as 2 square feet (0.18 square meters) per room may be required for storage.

University Conference Centers. University executive education facilities generally are designed for very particular programs, often combinations of one- and multiweek courses along with weekend MBA sessions. Therefore, the need for registration, checkout, luggage storage, and so forth can be accurately projected. There are two models for the typical 100- 120-room facility, designed for two to four concurrent programs of 30 to 50 participants each: One has a lobby of 800 to 1,000 square feet (74.4 to 93 square meters), essentially to accommodate the front desk functions and little else; the other features a lobby of 2,500 square feet (232.5 square meters), providing a more gracious hotellike space. Because of the nearby campus store and shops in the adjoining community, very little retail space is needed other than for a small sundries shop. Luggage storage for 100 percent turnover should be provided.

Nonresidential Conference Centers. The nonresidential centers, of course, do not need to accommodate the same types of registration functions as residential centers do. However, reception activities, similar to what might occur for day users of other centers, still take place. Essentially, the nonresidential centers need to provide a conference foyer, including the conference services desk, and such support functions as toilets, coat room, and telephones. Because participants

are arriving from off-site, the coat room must be large enough to accommodate winter overcoats and, potentially, luggage, because many attendees may be staying at a nearby hotel.

Because most meetings held at nonresidential centers are one-day conferences, a high percentage of the participants are unfamiliar with the layout of the facility. It is therefore important for the designers to incorporate clear signage and visual clues into the center. At the Shearson Leahman Brothers facility near Wall Street, video monitors are built into the wall at one end of the elevator foyer, cluing visitors to turn in that direction.

Design Considerations. Once the guests have registered, the lobby may serve more as a transition space than as a reception area. The position and design of the front desk may be secondary, in fact, to circulation routes between guestrooms, dining areas, and the conference center. Therefore, the position and layout of the front desk, seating areas, sundries shop, and other support functions need to reinforce and focus on the daily routine of the conference program, rather than on the usual lobby functions.

Finishes. The lobby area should incorporate many of the finishes and decorative touches found throughout the rest of the center. In fact, it should establish an expectation level for finish quality that the guest will encounter during his or her stay. This may include marble or granite floors and wood paneling in the more upscale centers, or more informal materials, such as flagstone flooring and open-beam trusses, in the resort and more casual university and not-for-profit facilities. In each case, however, the guest should understand the quality level of the operation immediately upon arriving by the look and feel of the lobby finishes and furnishings.

While hard surfaces are convenient (they may be easier to maintain), their use should be limited so that the public areas have better acoustics and a less harsh look. Large expanses of glass need to be softened by drapes, blinds, or shutters. Area rugs (at seating areas or in front of the registration desk) and fabric or vinyl wall sections create a variety of materials, textures, and colors, add visual interest, and reduce the scale of larger, undefined surfaces. The designers should strive to attain this variety without the design becoming overly busy.

Maintenance and durability issues need to be considered from the outset, including such factors as heavy pedestrian traffic through par-

Kellogg Center, Michigan State University, East Lansing, Michigan. The remodeling of this early-1950s conference center included minor additions and the upgrade of public areas. The designers enlarged the guest entry, made it handicapped-accessible, and reconfigured the front desk and support facilities. (Interiors: DiLeonardo International; photo: Warren Jagger.)

ticular routes (front door to front desk to elevator, for instance), additional wear caused by baggage carts, and damage to walls and corners from carts and hand-carried luggage. Many operators and designers eschew such visually unpleasant solutions as corner guards and tile floors, preferring to specify more attractive materials that can be quickly replaced or easily repaired (carpet tiles or wood moldings, for example).

Furniture and Artwork. The lobby, although relatively small in area, offers an opportunity for placing special furnishings and artwork that set the character of the conference center. Again, the choice must be in keeping with the rest of the project, but the designers might consider choosing large scale, bold signature pieces covered with leather or other special materials, to catch the attention of the visitors. In addition, artwork should be selected for the lobby (and throughout the property) to carry out some nominal theme, be it abstract pieces or local landscapes by emerging regional artists, works by employees or alumni, or the artistic efforts of some particular group.

Fixtures and Equipment. The architect, designers, and other consultants need to collaborate on the design and selection of the lobby fixtures and equipment, including such elements as the front desk, public telephone areas, storefronts, and service counters. The front desk design is the most obvious example. Cooperation is required among the architect (for planning the space), the interior designer (for detailing the top and front of the desk and the back wall), the lighting designer (for conceiving the lighting concept), computer systems and telephone consultants (for selecting the equipment), fire-protection specialists (for positioning the alarm systems), and so forth. Smaller, seemingly insignificant elements must be carefully designed and positioned: metal fire-hose cabinets should not end up in a paneled wall; thermostats should not be on walls where artwork is anticipated; baseboard heating and enclosures should not interfere with draperies. The fixtures therefore require the collaborative design attention of the entire team.

Even the smallest conference centers should have two work stations at the front desk—essentially one for registration and one for the cashier. The architect should add an additional station for each 100 guestrooms over 150. The lobby and desk should not be designed for short peaks of activity; if the entire facility turns over in a single day; therefore, it may be necessary to set up temporary tables in the lobby or conference foyer. The operational program should identify just such specifics of the conference center schedule and establish recommended design and management solutions.

PLANNING THE DINING FACILITIES

The experience of the conference center operator is essential to the early conceptual and programmatic decisions regarding the food and beverage operations. Rather than basing the dining capacity solely on the maximum numbers anticipated in the conference rooms, or on the number of guestrooms, the food and beverage program must anticipate how participants will move through the educational programs.

The primary outlet, of course, is the conference dining room, incorporating either an extensive buffet setup or an adjoining servery. The dining room usually is designed to accommodate the maximum number of conference guests plus a small number of additional people. The designers should consider a variety of approaches to varying the ambience from breakfast to lunch to dinner.

For programs lasting more than a week, it is essential to have a second dining room within the project in order to offer the guests more variety. Also, some centers have two or more distinct categories of users—conference guests and transients, or company employees and customers, for instance—and may desire to maintain separate dining facilities for each.

The size of the food and beverage facilities varies depending on the type of conference center. Most of the executive facilities provide between 40 and 50 square feet (3.7 and 4.6 square meters) per guestroom in restaurant and lounge space. Resorts are generally similar, although those with multiple sports-oriented outlets may contain as much as 80 square feet (7.4 square meters) per room. Corporate centers, on the other hand, provide less space, due to the frequent lack of an alternate dining room and the reduced number of lounges. The total food and beverage space in many corporate centers falls between 25 and 45 square feet (2.3 and 4.2 square meters) per room, with a few of the smaller management development centers at about 60 square feet (5.6 square meters) per room.

Comparing the food and beverage space to net meeting space may be a better indicator. For example, in executive centers, the total area devoted to the restaurants and lounges is about 40 to 50 percent of the conference and training room space. The comparative figures for other types of conference centers bracket this normal range. Resort conference centers are somewhat higher, because of their additional restaurant and lounge outlets and, generally, somewhat less conference space; the area in the food and beverage outlets equals approximately 55 to 60 percent of the conference rooms. University centers, because of the limited amount of meeting space needed for highly defined executive education programs, show figures of 50 to 70 percent. Corporate centers exhibit an interestingly wide range: for most facilities, the total restaurant and lounge area is about 35 to 50 percent of the total conference room area; however, in projects with much duplication of training rooms, the food and beverage facilities represent as little as 15 percent of the training space.

Conference Dining. The foodservice consultant or experienced operator will establish the conference dining program early in the conceptual phase. One of the principal questions to be answered deals with the type of service, usually a choice between a buffet setup in the dining room or a servery. A comparison of the two service styles shows that each has strong support from varying segments of the industry. Most executive and resort conference center operators select the buffet, because the food display greatly adds to the ambience of the whole facility; corporate, university, and nonresidential centers often opt for a servery, which, while owing a lot to its cafeteria-line origins, practically duplicates the variety and artistic display of the buffet in a more convenient location and format for the operator.

The operational program must also call for the number of seats, the designated meal periods, types of amenities, and so forth. Also important is the architectural program, addressing area requirements (usually about 17 to 20 square feet, or 1.6 to 1.8 square meters, per seat, excluding the buffet or servery), adjacencies, degree of separation, and interior design criteria. Each conference center type has its fairly typical solutions to the program statement for the conference dining room (Table 10–2).

Executive Conference Centers. The conference dining room at these centers is a useful amenity for competing with commercial hotels. Most centers accommodate the full

normal capacity of the conference core. Typically, the dining room's capacity is about equal to the number of guestrooms, and its area is approximately 20 percent of the conference core's. At conference centers with large banquet rooms this figure may be about 15 percent; at properties with one or two other restaurants, such as Westfields and the two Scanticon executive properties, the dining room is slightly smaller, about 12 to 18 square feet (1.1 to 1.6 square meters) per room.

Executive center dining rooms are distinguished by their spectacular buffet setups. Benchmark has established a particularly successful program at their centers: they feature three individual buffets—one for hot entrées, one for salads (or fruits, yogurt, and juices at breakfast), and one for desserts (cereal at breakfast). In addition, they install a grill station, which prepares specialty items. These permanent units provide tremendous flexibility for the three meal periods and allow great creativity by the chef and food and beverage director.

Resort Conference Centers. Similar to the executive centers in many ways, the resort conference centers place an equally large value on high-profile food and beverage operations, including the three-meal or conference dining room. Resort centers usually attract a smaller percentage of conference business—more of the guests are staying for personal or other business reasons—and, as a result, the capacity of the dining room can be reduced. Also, many of these transient visitors utilize room service or dine in one of the several alternative outlets. For example, at Kingsmill, although the 360 condominium units are available for conference groups, many are occupied by golfing guests who are likely to eat at the golf club or sports center. Therefore, the main dining room (3,450 square feet, or 320.8 square meters) has less than 10 square feet (0.93 square meters) per room—half that of a typical executive center's dining room. However, because resort centers have somewhat less extensive conference cores, this smaller dining room provides about the same ratio of conference dining to total conference room area as in executive centers.

Corporate Conference and Training Centers. The dining operation in corporate training centers differs in two primary ways from the food and beverage programs in the two previous categories of centers. First, instead of a buffet, corporate facilities usually incorporate a servery (although a buffet is common in the smaller management development centers), which offers operational advantages in terms of reduced staffing levels and

Cheyenne Mountain Conference Resort, Colorado Springs, Colorado (above right). The 216-room resort offers dramatic views from the two restaurants, the lounge, and the conference foyer. The restaurant is divided into more intimate sections, allowing diners in the rear to enjoy some additional privacy. (Architect: Richardson Nagy Martin; interiors: Wudtke Watson Associates; photo: Peter Vitale.)

Doral Arrowwood, Rye Brook, New York (below right). Originally the Citicorp training center but now a resort facility, Doral Arrowwood features a lobby overlooking the lower-level conference dining room. (Architect and interiors: The Hillier Group; photo: Ashod Kassabian.)

TABLE 10-2. CONFERENCE DINING ROOM PROGRAM COMPARISON

	Conference Dining Room		Guestrooms Comparison		Conference Area Comparison	
	Net Area[a]	Capacity	Number of Rooms	Dining Seats per Room	Conference Net Area[a]	Dining Area as a % of Conference Area
Executive conference centers						
Hamilton Park	4,000 (372)	204	219	0.93	19,600 (1,823)	21
Scanticon-Minneapolis	4,300 (400)	250	240	1.04	23,850 (2,218)	18
Peachtree	5,025 (467)	245	254	0.96	17,873 (1,662)	28
Westfields	4,250 (395)	340	342	0.99	29,000 (2,697)	14
Resort conference centers						
Doral Arrowwood	5,800 (539)	250	276	0.91	24,370 (2,266)	24
Kingsmill	3,450 (321)	230	360	0.63	10,120 (941)	34
Scanticon-Denver	7,200 (670)	270	301	0.90	31,100 (2,892)	23
Lansdowne	5,000 (465)	220	305	0.72	27,800 (2,585)	18
Corporate conference and training centers						
GTE	3,300 (307)	160	118	1.33	14,000 (1,302)	24
Aberdeen Woods	4,950 (460)	250	150	1.67	41,350 (3,845)	12
IBM-Palisades	4,925 (458)	300	206	1.46	30,825 (2,867)	16
Merrill Lynch	6,400 (595)	240	350	0.71	22,300 (2,074)	29

[a]Figures shown in square feet (square meters).

food waste and increased numbers of guests per time period. Second, because many corporate centers house participants two to a room and include a large training staff, the dining room capacity is greatly increased in terms of the usual bedroom ratio.

At the smaller centers like GTE and General Electric, the single conference dining room has 24 to 28 square feet (2.2 to 2.6 square meters) per room. This larger allotment is partly the result of the high quality level of the two centers, but also reflects the fairly large number of corporate staff who use the dining rooms. In those corporate centers with large amounts of specialized training space, the dining room can be as little as 15 percent of the classroom area.

University Conference Centers. The conference dining rooms at the university centers are similar to those at the training centers. The more prestigious universities, along with those dedicated to the smaller business school executive education programs, tend to feature a buffet, usually somewhat more limited in scope and choice than those at the executive centers; the larger operations often utilize a servery or cafeteria line, although this tends to be of a much higher level than is found at the usual college student dining area.

Often the conference dining room is the only restaurant in the university centers; based on there being fewer guestrooms and meeting rooms, the capacity tends to be smaller, the furnishings less luxurious, and the menu offers fewer choices. But on a per-room basis, the size and capacity need to be larger than for the other types—commonly about 30 to 35 square feet (2.8 to 3.2 square meters) per room (at Michigan, a 3,550 square foot [330 square meter] room serves 96 guestrooms, while at Duke a 3,700 square foot [344 square meter] restaurant supports a 113-room facility). This is because the dining room generally is used by the instructors and executive education staff as well as by the participants.

In a number of university centers, the planning of the conference dining shows an interesting divergence from many of the other types of centers. Rather than being located in a separate wing or floor, the dining room is more fully integrated into the conference area. At the Steinberg Center at Wharton and The Center for Executive Education at Babson, the dining room is surrounded by teaching spaces. Here the participants move freely between classes and meals without interrupting their discussions. Whatever approach is taken, the

FOUR SEASONS HOTEL AND RESORT

The resort–spa–conference center in Irving, Texas, includes elegant interiors throughout the public areas and guestrooms. The Café on the Green overlooks the eighteenth hole of the golf course and offers an informal buffet and a complete à la carte menu. The game bar features billiards, cards, and other games. The specialty restaurant provides a menu for the health-conscious in an intimate space, with hand-painted murals of fruit and vegetables. (Architect: HKS; interiors: Wilson and Associates; photos: Jaime Ardiles-Arce.)

educational programmers should consciously determine the location of the conference dining in the schematic design.

Nonresidential Conference Centers. The nonresidential centers offer a lower-profile conference dining room, usually much simpler in design and operation because it is used only for lunch—it is harder to justify the expense of more luxurious appointments when dinner is not being served. The dining room tends to be supported by only the simplest of pantries, further reducing the menu choice and guest expectations.

Nevertheless, the importance of this dining room should not be underestimated. Some corporate nonresidential centers have found their fairly standard cafeterias to be a source of frequent complaints from a number of sources: employees assigned to classes want to be treated to more than the simplest lunch; staff members working at the center want more choice; and outside users expect a higher quality level.

Not-for-Profit Conference Centers. The type of conference center with the greatest variability in its dining operations is the not-for-profit center. The developer must consider the needs of the organization and guests and develop a program that meets these expectations. For example, the small think tank center operated by Battelle Seattle serves only seventy-five, while the YWCA facility on Monterey Peninsula has a dining room for 850.

Alternate Dining. The larger centers usually offer a specialty restaurant and, occasionally, a gourmet dining room. Resorts, in addition, may introduce casual outlets related to the sports and recreational facilities; Kingsmill, for example, operates a dining room in the golf clubhouse and a separate lounge in the sports club. Additional food operations include refreshment service to the conference rooms, employee dining, and, possibly, room service. The detailed food and beverage program should provide a description of such outlets and operations. Consultants, such as Cini-Little International or Ricca & Associates, may be asked to develop detailed concepts including operational and architectural criteria, budgets for kitchen and other equipment, staffing levels, and utilization projections, all of which are extremely useful as the team modifies and refines the operational concept.

Most executive and resort conference centers will have some type of alternative dining, most likely an upscale speciality restaurant.

These may be small, only sixty to ninety seats, but they nonetheless offer the guests an opportunity to move beyond the usual fare of the conference dining room. Corporate training facilities, where the length of stay may be considerably longer, are likely to have a more casual dining alternative.

The size of the second outlet falls into two distinct categories. The most common are smaller restaurants or informal dining rooms of about 1,800 square feet (167.4 square meters); less frequent are larger outlets, usually in executive conference centers, with 180 to 200 seats and approximately 3,500 square feet (325.5 square meters). These outlets should be serviced from the main kitchen whenever possible, rather than from a satellite pantry, which adds substantially to the capital and operating expenses.

The size and orientation of the specialty restaurant depends on the surrounding community. Executive centers in wealthy suburban communities might anticipate the demand for a gourmet restaurant; those sited within office parks should expect heavy luncheon demand for a good quality specialty dining room. Westfields, in Virginia, featuring tableside Russian service and an impressive wine list in the exclusive Palm Court, draws from the nearby residential areas; Scanticon-Princeton, located in the heavily developed Forrestal Center, attracts substantial midday business from the surrounding Fortune 500 offices to its elaborate buffet in the Tivoli Gardens Restaurant.

Resort centers frequently incorporate similar specialty restaurants but may, in addition, offer one or more outlets at the recreational areas: The Four Seasons in Irving, Texas, includes a 180-seat restaurant in the sports complex; Scanticon-Denver features a 140-seat grille room adjoining the golf pro shop and lockers; and Kingsmill offers a 100-seat restaurant and bar in the fitness center.

Although many of the corporate training centers do not provide an alternate dining room, those that do—generally, the larger ones—establish a casual alternative to the conference dining room. Center operators report that after a few days of three complete meals—all you can eat, at that—and continuous coffee breaks, guests will seek out informal dining options; some even may hunger for junk food. Eagle Lodge, the CIGNA corporate training facility now open to the public, has a lounge on the top level of the pool building where it offers its long-stay groups the option of, say, hamburgers one day and a barbecue or theme

TABLE 10-3. DINING ROOM DESIGN CHECKLIST

Design Aspect	Criteria
Operational concept	☐ Menu
	☐ Capacity
	☐ Operating hours
	☐ Style of service
	☐ Outdoor dining possibilities
	☐ Food merchandising options
	☐ Separate lounge area provisions
Architectural concept	☐ Location
	☐ Image
	☐ Plan configuration
	☐ Size of space
	☐ Interior–exterior orientation
Interior design concept	☐ Entry sequence
	☐ Food and wine displays
	☐ Self service and buffet issues
	☐ Decorative treatment
	☐ Seating type and mix
	☐ Lighting
	☐ Floor-level changes
	☐ Tabletop design
	☐ Uniforms

party the next; Merrill Lynch includes an informal restaurant on the mezzanine, directly above the conference dining room; and the IBM customer training center features a casual room near the guestroom wing, overlooking the pool, and adjoining the game room and health complex. Often, the corporate operators request that guests choose if they want the alternate meal half a day ahead, so that the staff can better plan the production and service.

Private Dining. Many groups staying a few days or longer will request a special dinner—maybe a graduation function or theme party. As a result, the private dining facilities should be sized according to the conference program, with rooms designed to accommodate the usual class size. The designers should understand that these rooms need to be somewhat larger than a hotel might provide for the same function: cocktails may be served before dinner begins, meeting planners might request

any of several table arrangements—not just the standard banquet rounds—or there might be some type of audiovisual presentation.

These private dining rooms have been designed as minor elements in most conference centers: a room off the conference or specialty restaurant, perhaps, or banquet rooms near the larger ballroom. But some centers with as much as 800 square feet (74.4 square meters) in private dining areas find their space inadequate. One corporate center utilizes only its largest private dining room for conference groups, with the smaller rooms relegated to breakouts or small working dinners; another center combined its two private rooms into one to make it more functional. This suggests that developers of new conference projects perhaps should provide more private dining space than is first projected. A midsize project might include two rooms at 800 square feet (74.4 square meters) and one or more larger rooms, which could be sections of the main ballroom.

If space and cost are primary concerns (and they usually are), the conference dining room should provide opportunities for creating separate private dining areas. The conference dining room at the Macklowe, in New York City, divides into four private rooms, which can be used in any configuration. At Kingsmill, Cornell's Statler Hotel, and Wharton's Steinberg Center, the conference dining room includes a smaller ancillary dining area, which can be sold separately for private functions.

Design Considerations. The food outlets offer many design and operational opportunities for furthering the mission of the conference facility. So much of the informal learning and networking occur during the meal periods that the food and beverage operations should be carefully designed to go beyond culinary excellence and enhance the overall educational experience. Table 10–3 identifies many of the operational design criteria for restaurants and private dining rooms. The restaurants need to achieve a balance between continuing the center's architectural and decorative theme and establishing a separate presence of their own. They should, however, refrain from the heavy-handed themeing so prevalent in the hotel and restaurant industries.

Finishes. Most conference center restaurants try to establish a quiet, restful feel, offering the opportunity for comfortable conversation, a respite from the active learning environment, a retreat. The typical approach is to carpet the floor and provide relatively simple, straightforward walls and ceiling, without much added decoration. In the conference dining room, tile or hard-floor materials should be limited to areas around the buffet lines and the servery; in upscale restaurants, decorative materials might be used at the entry or at such features as an open grill, a fountain or pool, a wine room, or a dessert display. The carpet should be selected to resist and hide stains, tolerate frequent and hard cleaning, offer acoustic benefits, allow for selective replacement of damaged sections, and meet such special operational needs as accommodating wheeled serving carts.

Wall surfaces have many of the same design criteria. The designer needs to determine what materials and level of decorative detail is appropriate to the conference center environment. Most prefer some middle ground between the crispness of a blank wall and the variety of a highly decorated design. Some conference centers extend the main architectural material—brick, for instance—into the restaurant interiors to maintain consistent palettes of materials and colors. Color, perhaps is most noticeable on the walls—certainly more so than on the floor or ceiling planes—although upholstery, table linen, and tabletop selections add substantial accents.

Furniture. Early in the design phase, the design team must develop the dining room layout and the seating mix—the relative number of tables for two, four, six, or more. This should be done in conjunction with the operator or the ownership group, who need to establish objectives for this design. At many of the corporate centers, the goal is simply for the attendees to meet as many other participants as possible—even those in other programs. Thus, the design might include a large number of tables for six or eight and none for two. University centers, especially those emphasizing the case study method in their executive courses or assigning groups of six or eight to work together, may encourage these groups to sit at a single table. On the other hand, executive centers and resorts, with a high proportion of nonconference business, need many more smaller tables.

Seating provisions should be flexible because the requirements may change over time. The designer might arrange deuces (tables for two) and fours along a banquette, allowing the manager to group tables together for larger parties; freestanding square tables for four can

TABLE 10-4. LOUNGE DESIGN CHECKLIST	
Design Aspect	*Criteria*
Operational concept	☐ Market description
	☐ Financial projections
	☐ Bar and lounge emphasis
	☐ Entertainment provisions
	☐ Capacity
	☐ Operating hours
	☐ Availability of food and snack service
	☐ Provision of an adjoining food outlet
Architectural concept	☐ Location
	☐ Image
	☐ Size of space
	☐ Interior and exterior space issues
Interior design concept	☐ Entry sequence
	☐ Bar location
	☐ Seating mix
	☐ Provision of a stage and/or dance floor
	☐ Special entertainment requirements
	☐ Floor-level changes
	☐ Sound system

be combined, whereas round tables cannot.

The designer's selection of dining chairs, tables, and their upholstery and finish helps set the mood and character of the outlet. The designers and operators of centers with only a single three-meal restaurant need to consider how they can change the mood and formality of the room and the tabletop from breakfast to lunch and from lunch to dinner. Often, this entails separate china or it may be as simple as moving from a paper placemat at breakfast to a cloth placemat or runner at lunch and to full table linen at dinner.

Fixtures and Equipment. Experienced operators have established basic equipment lists to accommodate the varying needs of the different meal periods, so that a buffet, for instance, can easily adapt from breakfast to lunch and dinner. Some operators will carefully design each of the individual buffet units to accommodate specific menu items. One unit may contain a series of hot wells for the main entrées; another, chilled compartments for juices, salads, and fruit; and third, a uniform top with a raised platform for condiments. Other operators prefer the flexibility of permanent but undefined buffet units that can be used in a variety of ways depending on the meal period, season, or type of theme dinner. All these buffet units should include storage for table linen and other daily supplies.

Other millwork may be required, such as for a host stand, a service station, sliding panels between rooms, and banquettes or islands to separate the seating. Here, as elsewhere, the designer and operator need to work together to ensure that the concepts reinforce the overall food and beverage program and that they do not limit future adaptability, such as for using the room for special functions.

LOUNGES AND RELATED AREAS

Most hotels and resorts have a variety of lounges located in a number of different areas: lobby lounge, wine bar, cocktail lounge, pub, nightclub, and so forth. Lounges are important for enhancing the leisure aspects of a meeting program and encouraging informal discussions among the participants (Table 10–4). However, the social orientation, while valuable, may run counter to the educational focus of corporate training and university executive education programs. In fact, many companies prohibit alcohol on their properties, and many universities, which are increasingly sensitive to student drinking, minimize beverage areas or locate them in restricted areas. The designers must assess the perceived relative value and prominence to be placed on lounges throughout the conference center.

Cocktail Lounge. The executive and resort conference centers often provide two beverage areas: a centrally located lobby lounge and a bar adjoining or connected to the game room. In some properties these are combined, reducing the necessary staff and providing the conferees with a flexible lounge operation. At the Northland Inn, an all-suite atrium conference center, the lobby lounge is sheltered under a gazebo in the main lobby space but supports the activity in the game room, which is located immediately adjacent under the guestroom structure. At the Merrill Lynch center, where the game room is located on a mezzanine immediately above the lobby (and, in fact, is part of the main circulation route between the guestrooms and the conference and dining areas), the cocktail lounge is immediately below, and conferees actively move between the bar and the game room in the evening.

Scanticon-Minneapolis, Plymouth, Minnesota. The Partners Pub next to the conference dining room continues the property's Scandinavian theme and attracts active crowds before and after dinner. An elevated section offers pool, darts, and wide-screen television. (Architect: Friis Moltke Larson with BRW Architects; interiors: Klenow Deichmann and Overbye with Daroff Design; photo: Ron Solomon.)

IBM ADVANCED BUSINESS INSTITUTE

The customer training center in Palisades, New York, provides a core of recreation and informal facilities at the connection between the 206 guestrooms and the public areas. The casual dining room overlooks the pool, while the adjoining game room forms a bal-cony above the racquetball courts. The conference dining room is reached via a grand stair from the lobby and features skylit seating with access to a terrace and views of the pond. (Architect and interiors: Mitchell/Giurgola; photos: Mick Hales.)

The Statler Hotel and Marriott Executive Education Center, Cornell University, Ithaca, New York. The browsing library, located on the lower level near the conference dining and faculty lounges, overlooks the main campus avenue and provides a quiet space for reading newspapers and current periodicals or checking basic reference works. (Architect: The Architects Collaborative; interiors: Kenneth E. Hurd & Associates; photo: Ed Jacoby.)

The resorts, of course, organize beverage outlets close to the sports centers, and a few conference centers also include some type of pub or entertainment area. The Resort at Squaw Creek includes a café designed for high-volume lunch business, including skiers. The room features an exhibition cooking grill, bar, dance floor, and space for a disc jockey. The nearby pub bar is oriented more toward the golfers and summer pool activity, and includes the standard game room amenities, a large-screen television, and an area for a small band.

In a few projects the lounge is more remote, somewhat removed from the lobby and the main activity. For example, at Wharton's Steinberg Center, the cocktail lounge is located on the fifth floor—the top guestroom floor, also housing the small fitness center. No beverage activity is visible on the two public floors. The executive education facility at Babson College includes a lounge at the connection between the conference area and guestrooms, where it is used during the day for informal gathering between sessions and in the evening for relaxation.

Game Room. Practically every conference center contains a game room with some combination of pool or billiards, lounge seating, card tables, large-screen television, newspapers and magazines, and related amenities. As the previous discussion has illustrated, the game room often is closely associated with the lobby lounge or pub. But there are other equally common solutions, and as architects and developers discuss the relationships inherent in the schematic organization for a new conference or training center, they should assess the benefits and drawbacks of the various solutions and determine the primary criteria for the particular project.

Many developers place the game room within the recreation core, where it is a more passive complement to swimming, racquetball, or an exercise regimen. Eagle Lodge contains a three-story sports complex with the game room and racquetball anchoring the central level, the pool and lockers downstairs, and the pub upstairs. The IBM Advanced Business Institute positions the game room near the guestrooms as part of a casual dining and recreation cluster.

In a few projects, the game room is more directly associated with the conference core or the guestrooms. The GTE Management Development Center places the social lounges, including a game room, on the same floor as the conference rooms, emphasizing the association of leisure with the primary learning focus. The Pitney Bowes training center, Aberdeen Woods, locates the game room in the guestroom structure as a specialized type of commons space.

Other Lounge Areas. Each project has its individual requirements for the development team to meet creatively yet economically. Many of the university projects, for example, include a reading room or browsing library. These contain comfortable seating, newspapers and periodicals, reference books, works by faculty or alumni authors, and perhaps a public-access computer for reference or data base searches. At Wharton, the library adjoins the lobby and doubles as a small breakout room or a lounge, where, for example, faculty and staff can host or interview a visiting dignitary. At Cornell, the library adjoins the conference dining room and offers participants the opportunity to check an assortment of national newspapers or take a brief post-lunch break from the classroom routine.

Some specialized lounges should be considered. Given the increasing concern and regulatory action limiting smoking in public areas, for example, some conference centers are providing separate smoking lounges. Additional lounge space might also be provided specifically for day conferees—other participants can steal a few minutes in their guestrooms, but the non-residential guests need some chance to get away from the bustle of the main assembly spaces; a specialized lounge offers them a quiet place to sit, work, make phone calls, and so forth.

CHAPTER 11

Planning the Meeting Facilities

One key difference between hotels and conference centers, and certainly the one that center developers and operators feel is most central to their success, is the planning and design of the conference and training areas. The conference center industry has grown around providing a superior meeting product, including better service, fewer distractions, and an all-inclusive price. However, these attractions give little real advantage if the meeting facilities design does not provide sufficient dedicated conference space organized for effective meetings.

The earliest conference centers developed a core of meeting space balanced between multipurpose rooms to meet the varying needs of different users and single-purpose spaces dedicated to conferences, audiovisual presentations, private dining, and so forth; developers eventually learned which types of rooms established the most salable mix between these two divergent approaches. Today, most conference center operators emphasize the single-purpose spaces, further strengthened by increased marketing and management abilities. Also, over the last two decades, operators have found that attendees want and expect more generously sized rooms, and so space requirements have escalated. For example, breakout rooms that might have been 250 square feet (23.2 square meters) a decade ago are now 400 square feet (37.2 square meters); meeting rooms for thirty participants have increased from 750 to 1,000 square feet (69.7 to 93 square meters). As a result, among the most important decisions is to evaluate the expected conference user, and to design rooms for their specific needs.

ESTABLISHING THE CONFERENCE SPACE PROGRAM

The architectural program for salable conference and meeting spaces is essential to defining the conference center product. This can best be done in three steps:

1. Consider the types of general- and special-purpose rooms that are required.

2. Determine the optimum and maximum capacity for each.

3. Establish the number of each type.

The difference with hotels is obvious. Convention hotels contain one or more large ballrooms and a number of smaller meeting and banquet rooms, usually multipurpose and

Kellogg Center, Michigan State University, East Lansing, Michigan. A third phase in the Kellogg Center renovation in 1989 included doubling the size of the multipurpose Big Ten Room and providing additional breakout rooms and support areas. (Designer: DiLeonardo International; photo: Warren Jagger.)

subdivisible; not much space is dedicated to high-quality small and midsize meetings. The current standard for conference centers, on the other hand, is to provide many more conference rooms, few or none of them subdivisible, a high number of small breakout rooms for working groups, and such dedicated rooms as amphitheaters, auditoriums, and computer facilities. In addition, assembly and refreshment spaces, conference services staff offices, and projection and audiovisual needs are essential to meeting customer expectations. Because different developers and management companies use varying terminology (for example, an "auditorium" may be a large, multipurpose conference room or a sloped-floor theater), it is necessary to define the terms used generally throughout the conference center industry.

Auditorium. The auditorium is a sloped-floor, theaterlike room for formal presentations, sometimes with additional balcony seating. It generally includes a stage and front-screen (and occasionally rear-screen) projection capability. Auditoriums are most common in corporate training facilities, with room capacities of 150 to 300, and in university continuing education centers, with capacities as high as 1,000. Space requirements: 8 square feet (0.7 square meters) per seat for the auditorium seating and aisles; 10 to 12 square feet (1.1 square meters) per seat overall, including the stage and a small projection room.

Amphitheater. The amphitheater is a tiered room incorporating built-in work surfaces, which are often curved to focus seating on the speaker or horseshoe-shaped to allow better eye contact among attendees. It features front-screen projection in university executive education centers and rear-screen projection in executive facilities. Capacity at university centers is limited to between 40 and 60, depending on the class objectives, and between 90 and 125 at executive conference centers. Space requirements: 25 square feet (2.3 square meters) per seat.

Multipurpose Conference Room. This is a large, flexible meeting room, often with subdivisible partitions, a flat floor, and a 200- to 500-seat capacity. The character of this room can vary greatly, depending on the type of conference center, with some more resembling a junior ballroom and others little different from a standard conference room. Most incorporate either front- or rear-screen projection. Space requirements are 16 to 24 square feet (1.5 to 2.2 square meters) per seat for executive theater and classroom setups.

Conference Rooms. These dedicated conference rooms for twenty to fifty people form the majority of the meeting facilities. They have flat floors, simple built-in systems, including writing and tackable surfaces, projection screens, and presentation rails. Some include front-screen projection. Space requirements: 18 to 26 square feet (1.6 to 2.4 square meters) per seat for executive theater and classroom setups; 34 to 42 square feet (3.1 to 3.9 square meters) per seat for hollow square and U-shaped arrangements.

Breakout Rooms. Breakout rooms are small conference rooms for up to twelve people with limited features, usually including tackable walls, a whiteboard, and a projection screen. Space requirements: 25 square feet (2.3 square meters) per seat; larger rooms are often used, but still for no more than ten to twelve people.

Boardroom. The boardroom is a special, upgraded conference room with a fixed table, executive chairs, high-level finishes, front- and/or rear-screen projection, and a private lounge or anteroom. Usual capacity is about sixteen to twenty-four. Space requirements: 40 square feet (3.7 square meters) per seat, increased by 50 percent when providing a projection room, pantry, or anteroom.

Computer Room. This special training room, found mostly in corporate and university centers, incorporates several rows of work stations, each with the capability of exchanging information between the instructor and the students. Many of these rooms are part of a larger building or campus network. Space requirements: 30 to 40 square feet (2.7 to 3.7 square meters) per seat.

Of course, the exact number of each room type and its respective capacity will be the result of the market study and operational objectives of the owner and operator. For example, the program may call for many similar 40-person conference rooms and 10-person breakout rooms designed to meet a general set of design criteria. In addition, it may establish specialized requirements for individual larger rooms, or for those with distinctive audiovisual or computer requirements. A computer company, for example, certainly will have different requirements for a presentation room in a training center than a university business school will have for its executive education case study room—both of which may essentially be a tiered-floor amphitheater for thirty people.

ESTABLISHING THE ASSEMBLY AND SUPPORT AREAS PROGRAM

In addition to determining the necessary conference and training spaces, the team must establish the program for the prefunction areas and such support functions as conference services, audiovisuals, coffee pantries and, in corporate and university projects, offices for faculty and program directors. The assembly spaces are of several types, from a separate lobby for day attendees, to major prefunction areas outside the larger rooms, to smaller refreshment areas and outdoor terraces. The assembly areas should total between 30 and 50 percent of the salable conference space.

The support areas add further complexity to the program definition. The principal components include:

☐ *Conference services:* Space is needed for offices for the conference concierge, the conference service manager, and conference planners, and a lounge for meeting with clients; some operators include an audiovisual display room and work areas adjacent or nearby.

☐ *Audiovisuals:* Rear- and front-screen projection rooms, the latter being the more common; office and workrooms for the audiovisual technicians; a "head-end," or central distribution room.

☐ *Graphics:* Reproduction capability for handout material is essential; larger centers provide a complete print shop to reproduce course materials, signs, name badges, and so on, and include a full photographic darkroom.

☐ *Storage areas:* Space is needed for conference room furnishings, including tables, chairs, lecterns, and risers; portable audiovisual equipment; food service supplies; and client materials sent in advance of meetings.

☐ *Coffee pantry:* Include a service area for brewing coffee and tea, holding cold drinks, preparing and holding pastries and fruit, storing soiled dishes, and so on.

☐ *Faculty and trainer offices:* Requirements include offices, staff workrooms, and resource rooms for the instructors and program managers. These are most common in university executive education and corporate training centers; executive and resort conference centers may provide two or three small offices for the client meeting planner.

If there are no extensive offices for instructors, the support areas range from about 15 to 30 percent of the salable conference space. The major variant is the amount of audiovisual support space required for projection rooms and the central audiovisual–graphics services. Throughout the program phase, the owner and operator must fully discuss whether added capabilities and service levels justify higher capital expenses (for both space and equipment) and the eventual correspondingly higher payroll cost. And a separate audiovisual program should address the equipment duplication implied by a major investment in audiovisual support space.

DEVELOPING THE CONFERENCE AREA SCHEMATIC PLAN

Once the space program is established, the planning of the conference section offers the architect and developer an opportunity to create a lasting impression on the customer, ensuring return business, and influencing the operating efficiency for the life of the building. The goal is to provide a design solution offering a series of public assembly, meeting, and support spaces that meet specific educational and conference objectives, that have a consistent architectural character, and that contribute to the overall operational objectives.

The team must resolve several principal considerations for planning conference center meeting space during the schematic design (Table 11–1). The first is the relation of the conference core to such other major elements as lodging, food and beverage, and recreation; these were discussed in Chapter 8. Part of this process is recognizing the routes employees, customers, and guests will take to enter the center—not only do meeting attendees arrive from the hotel lobby and guestrooms, but many are day participants who need to enter directly from parking lots, corporate employees who might be arriving from the adjoining office complex, university students or employees coming from elsewhere on campus, or instructional faculty entering from their nearby offices. Equally important are the service connections between the conference core and the kitchen, the audiovisual support, furniture storage, housekeeping, and the like.

Other planning assessments include whether the conference program is better suited to a single floor or should cover two or more levels; if a separate satellite conference core can contribute increased business; and how the individual program spaces should be organized.

TABLE 11-1. CONFERENCE FACILITIES CHECKLIST

Conference Area	Requirements
Conference and training rooms	☐ Separate structural system (not confined by guestroom or other structural modules)
	☐ Column-free spaces
	☐ Separate entrance for day participants
	☐ Convenient access from lodging and dining areas
	☐ Convenient access to outdoor terraces
	☐ Separate conference core from recreation and other potential distractions
	☐ Exterior orientation for natural light and views
	☐ Possible provisions for future expansion or adaptation
	☐ Few or no subdivisible rooms
	☐ Two-story volumes or high-ceilinged spaces
	☐ Elevated projection booths with control for two or more rooms from a single booth
	☐ Room proportions that maximize utility for different furniture configurations
Assembly and break areas	☐ Central conference foyer for day guests
	☐ Number of assembly and break areas
	☐ Support functions (rest rooms, coats, telephones, etc.)
	☐ Access to outdoor terraces
	☐ Concept and menu for refreshment areas
	☐ Electricity and plumbing for break kiosks
	☐ Program for conference lounges
Conference services	☐ Strategy and location for conference support offices
	☐ Program for audiovisuals, graphics, and projection rooms
	☐ Access to the kitchen and other back-of-house areas
	☐ Storage convenient to conference rooms
	☐ Duplicate support areas for large or spread-out facilities

One-Floor vs. Multiple-Floor Plans. Conference operators have strong opinions about how the conference and meeting rooms should be organized. Most, however, favor a plan with most or all of the meeting space spread over a large area on one floor, rather than a more compact plan on two or three floors. The single-floor organization provides easy access among the rooms and between the conference area and the other functional elements. If the conference area is built on grade, this plan imposes few structural or mechanical constraints, permits total freedom in the planning of the rooms, allows for access from the refreshment break areas to outdoor terraces and patios, and—given sufficient land—permits easy expansion as the market grows. Scanticon-Princeton, for example, was expanded efficiently by extending its one-story conference wing onto an adjacent lawn.

A multiple-floor plan offers a more compact scheme but puts guests at the mercy of stairs and forces service functions (food, furniture, equipment, etc.) to be dependent on elevators. There are some advantages to consider. The additional floors help define the separation between large and small conference rooms or between the conference core and restaurants; a grand stair, as is featured at Kingsmill, can provide a visual theme for the conference center.

In addition, adding floors provides the opportunity to create higher-ceilinged rooms, locate break areas projecting over lower foyers, and organize the service functions efficiently around a vertical core. In addition, more than one floor of meeting space makes it easier for management to separate different groups using the center.

Separate Executive Meeting Areas. Occasionally a developer or corporation may find it advantageous to provide a satellite conference area for high-level meetings, yielding greater privacy and confidentiality. Doral Arrowwood, for example, in addition to having a main core of seventeen rooms covering about 30,000 square feet (2,790 square meters), has two separate meeting clusters, each with two conference rooms featuring built-in audiovisual systems, four breakout rooms, and private coffee lounges. Also, Merrill-Lynch's 350-room conference and training center includes sixty-two guestrooms in a separate executive center, complete with its own lobby, dining, and seven conference rooms—a self-sufficient minicenter within the larger one. The executive center initially was planned for the highly intensive and confidential senior management assessment programs. The minicenter also is marketed to other Merrill-Lynch divisions as well as to outside companies who prefer the privacy of the separate facilities.

This separate meeting center has great potential if it can be used flexibly. It is important that is can be separate at specified times and fully integrated with the main conference center at others, and the developer and operator should carefully consider the best mix of meeting, lodging, and other facilities to make this possible. If too many elements are duplicated by the main and satellite centers, especially those with high operating expenses (such as lobby registration and food preparation), the minicenter will detract from the financial potential of the conference center.

Determining the Optimum Location of the Conference Rooms. Once the conference core is sited during the early schematic design, the architect must give careful thought to the relative positions of the conference and meeting rooms. In most centers, these are organized either along a single prefunction corridor or in a loop, with a block of meeting rooms, service areas, or a courtyard in the center. In the first case, the guests have only one route to the farthest meeting rooms, and a busy day may lead to heavy congestion. The

circular organization provides an alternate route, which is especially useful for bypassing crowded break areas.

Consider the various room planning options: Should staff offices be in the meeting core or part of the larger executive office suite? Should the breakout rooms be grouped together or spread among the larger conference rooms? Should they all be in the conference core or should some be within the lodging section or near the banquet area, where they might double as private dining rooms? As the planning progresses, the design team should at least consider certain basic issues.

Auditorium. The auditorium is most common in corporate training centers, where it is used for presentations to employees and class groups. Frequently, senior management takes part in the presentation. Also, many of the corporate training facilities make serious efforts to reach out to the community, and one result is that the auditorium is available to community organizations for presentations, public hearings, and charitable events. If this is anticipated, it is logical to position the auditorium close the main entrance. In companies where security is a great concern, as it is with many computer and high-tech firms, the control function might best occur beyond the more public lobby and auditorium.

The auditorium requires the associated foyer, coatroom, toilets, telephones, and audiovisual support. Frequently, the "head end," or main audiovisual distribution room, is nearby or is combined with the auditorium projection room. The architect needs to consider the local handicap access requirements and confirm that they are fully met—especially in terms of the sloped floor, fixed seating, and stage.

Amphitheater. The amphitheater, incorporating built-in work areas for the participants, is the primary teaching space in many of the university executive education centers, where the business curriculum emphasizes case study discussion. Therefore, amphitheaters are prominently positioned, often the first rooms that the visitors reach. Because they are used for primary meetings before the groups break into smaller rooms, amphitheaters often are centrally located and directly accessible from the main prefunction and refreshment break areas. At the Thomas Center at Duke University's Fuqua Business School, for example, the large, parabolic amphitheaters define the center of the education and lodging core and simultaneously dominate the residential courtyards.

UNIVERSITY PLACE
CONFERENCE CENTER AND HOTEL

Connected to a 278-room hotel, this conference center, at Purdue University at Indianapolis, is totally self-contained except for the dining areas. The siting of the hotel and conference center creates a semiprivate courtyard used for breakouts and informal gathering. The two floors of the conference center, interconnected by a circular grand stair, contain a 338-seat auditorium equipped with front- and rear-screen projection and translation capability, two tiered classrooms and ten other conference rooms, most with built-in projection booths, a dedicated computer room, and numerous breakout rooms and client offices. Teleconferencing equipment, full video flexibility, and press and media capability are available in the facility, in part because of the adjoining offices for the Big Ten sports conference. (Architect: Edward Larrabee Barnes with Howard Needles Tammen & Bergendoff; photos: Richard Kline.)

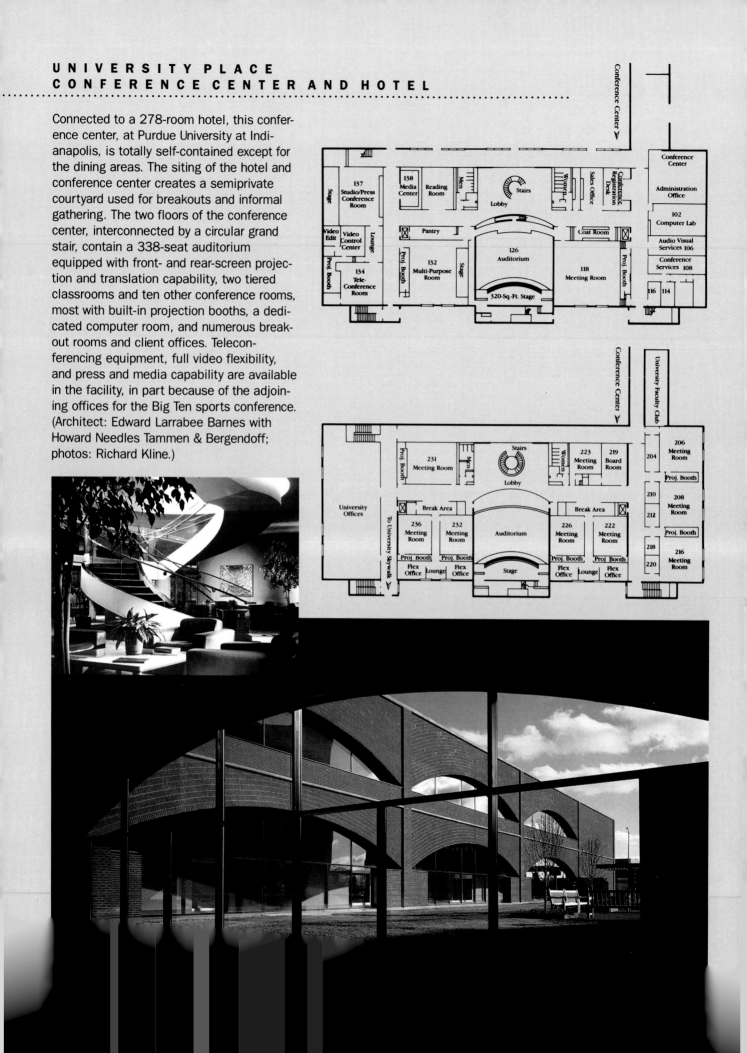

Multipurpose Conference Room. The largest meeting room serves different primary functions. In some centers it is a junior ballroom, essentially a banquet space, equipped with projection capability for major meetings; in others it may be a large subdivisible conference room, providing the flexibility unavailable in the solid-walled, more soundproof meeting rooms. Scanticon has been successful providing a large, flat-floored room, 5,000 to 7,000 square feet (465 to 651 square meters), which can be used more flexibly—and more often—than a fixed seat auditorium. Such a multipurpose room is best located near the entrance to the conference core.

Conference Rooms. The more common 800 to 1,500 square foot (74.4 to 139.5 square meter) conference rooms usually are clustered in several areas to help separate groups and to reduce traffic congestion and noise. The architect should provide entrances to these rooms off small vestibules or hall alcoves, rather than directly off the noisy prefunction space.

As noted earlier, most conference center operators disdain movable partitions; therefore, the architectural planning must accommodate the more popular furniture setups. One management company dictates not only conference room area but the exact dimensions, based on proven success in other properties.

Scanticon provides a projection room between every two conference rooms; most other conference center developers and operators satisfy video or projection needs with portable equipment, or by scheduling groups requiring audiovisual support into one or two specific rooms.

Breakout Rooms. These smaller conference rooms, intended for groups of no more than twelve people, become more and more in demand as conferences break into small problem-solving or case study sections during the day. University centers, where the education program includes constant small-group sessions, may have more breakout rooms than the total of all the other conference rooms combined. In some projects, these may be located in the residential building or on guest-room floors.

Corporate conference and training centers follow two patterns. Properties with a training focus tend toward 1,000 square foot (93 square meter) rooms with very few small breakout rooms; those with a management development thrust, on the other hand, may have only a few large rooms and as many as two dozen

breakouts. And even this is not always enough—several operators have remarked that their primary functional problem is a lack of sufficient breakout space.

Boardroom. The conference center boardroom usually is located at the most remote end of the meeting core, to assure a minimum of interruptions and distractions. The most common arrangement is for a large, fixed table seating about sixteen, although Scanticon has found wide acceptance of U-shaped arrangements, which accommodate more people and still permit good eye contact and a feeling of close involvement.

To enhance the boardroom experience, there should be an accompanying lounge or private prefunction space, toilets, and telephones—all exclusive to the room, if possible. The owner must indicate whether a projection room is desirable; although such support is useful, some clients worry that confidential discussions might be compromised with outside staff present.

ASSEMBLY AND SUPPORT AREAS

Coincident with the schematic planning of the conference and training rooms, the architect and other members of the development and design teams must develop the plan for the several assembly areas and the conference support functions, all of which will be crucial to the center's overall success. The assembly areas include more than simply wide corridors for prefunction areas—many centers provide a separate conference foyer for day guests, serving much the same architectural function as the conference center residential lobby. Practically all centers include specially designed coffee and refreshment lounges with permanent food display units supported by nearby pantries. Other centers add special private lounges, where customers or staff can meet. And conference center boardrooms often incorporate private anterooms for gathering before or during a meeting without the congestion of the public break areas.

The conference assembly and support areas must be dealt with early in the design phase—the space requirements are substantial and the organizational issues paramount to a well-functioning center. In most centers, these areas total approximately one-third to one-half of the net floor area of the conference and training rooms—an amount equal to the training rooms in corporate properties. This may represent 15,000 square feet (1,395 square meters) in an executive center or, because of the large number of training offices and significant amount of technical support, as much as 40,000 square feet (3,720 square meters) in a corporate center.

The planning of the assembly and support areas should be carefully paired to the particular needs of the conference center. Developers, corporations, and institutions establish very different objectives for the meeting space, the circulation and break areas, and the conference services and audiovisual support. Independent developers, for example, use these areas to help market the projects—large foyers, extravagant refreshment displays, and exhaustive audiovisual support may attract high-end business meetings; corporations expect their employees to mix and network, but this may be accomplished in the conference dining room or the recreational facilities; institutions, which run the university centers (and some nonresidential and not-for-profit projects), often are constrained by tighter budgets and lower CMP rates, and so their foyer areas are smaller, refreshment breaks more restrained, and services and technical support more limited.

The conference support functions further differentiate the conference center from competing lodging properties. Foremost are the conference services offices, usually centrally located within the meeting core. More variable among the centers is the extent of audiovisual, graphics, and projection services. Also, the conference rooms and break areas are supported by food pantries and various storage areas.

Prefunction and Break Areas. Because of conference centers' emphasis on informal discussions, the assembly and other foyer spaces are critically important. The better centers include large amounts of prefunction space, spread throughout the conference core, so that attendees have every opportunity to meet casually and continue the program discussions. Unfortunately, too often the prefunction space is no more than a wide corridor (albeit equipped for refreshment breaks). Excluding corridors, the various assembly areas—the prefunction, break, and lounge areas—should be between 30 and 40 percent of the total net area of the conference and training rooms. This compares favorably with hotels, which normally provide a prefunction foyer of about 25 percent of the ballroom area and very little additional assembly space for the other banquet and meeting rooms.

Refreshment Break Areas. Many developers and operators believe that the best approach is to provide one central prefunction space, convenient to the auditorium, amphitheater, or multipurpose conference room, and two or three additional smaller break areas for the clusters of conference and breakout rooms. Having too many prefunction lounges requires the staff to constantly monitor and replenish the break areas, while too few results in crowding and delays as beverages and snacks are resupplied. Doral Arrowwood has two major break areas, each with permanent coffee stations, supported by fully equipped independent pantries; additional refreshment centers are located in the smaller satellite conference areas. Kingsmill also features two coffee break and refreshment lounges, in addition to the ballroom prefunction area. These are tile-floored, sunlit corner rooms, with views over the golf course and grounds and direct access to terraces. The lounges are magnets, drawing people from the conference rooms and corridors during the breaks and leading to informal conversations throughout the day. The Pitney Bowes training center, Aberdeen Woods, on the other hand, features a grand, two-level prefunction corridor with small self-service pantries at either end. Between sessions, guests move first to one of the contained coffee and refreshment counters, then migrate to the adjoining sunlit lounge.

In these resort and corporate conference center examples, the developers and management chose a configuration directing the participants to a limited number of break areas. This subtly coerced mixing, enhancing the social and recreational focus at resorts or the company networking at corporate centers, suits the goals of the respective center types.

Other conference facilities, however, consciously seek to provide multiple break areas, so that each group has a private area. One of the most striking, the IBM Advanced Business Institute in Palisades, New York, has ten small coffee pavilions, which allows each class its own break area and permits the staff to provide an upgraded refreshment setup for a VIP group. Similarly, some of the nonresidential centers are planned with a series of small, private coffee lounges for the different meeting groups.

Conference Lounges. Many conference centers include private lounges programmed and planned to meet special functions. These are furnished with comfortable seating and

include a refreshment setup, computer, telephone, and other amenities. Often, the lounge adjoins the conference services offices, where it functions as a business center (with computer, fax, and a private breakout), library (with basic reference books and current periodicals), green room (as a lounge to meet a presenter), or simply a place for the management staff to meet with customers.

In addition, many of the more exclusive and higher-priced centers provide an anteroom or private lounge for the boardroom. The intimate space is sized for small receptions and breaks for the twelve to twenty boardroom occupants—often no more than 300 square feet (28 square meters). University centers may include a separate browsing library to complement the scholarly atmosphere of the campus setting, but these usually are located off the lobby or adjacent to quiet lounges rather than integrated with the conference core.

Assembly Support Areas. The architects should carefully plan the public rest rooms, coat rooms, telephones, and so forth, which all too often are inadequate or poorly located. While hotel developers sometimes hesitate to provide sufficient support areas for peak occupancy, specialized conference center developers should recognize these areas' importance and provide support functions equal to about 5 to 8 percent of the total conference room area. Designers should assume that a given meeting population could be either all

men or all women and size the rest rooms accordingly, not resorting to the 50–50 assumption that is usually for programming.

Most designers try to group these ancillary functions together near the approach to the conference core, which makes them easy to locate. Alternatively, rest rooms and coat areas might be centrally positioned within the conference area, although this may force guests to pass through other foyers to reach the facilities.

The design team should assess whether a central coat room will require a coat check clerk to assure adequate security; increasingly, developers instead are providing individual coat closets at each conference or training room. Telephones should be generously spread throughout the center and designed into small alcoves to reduce the surrounding noise level. Where possible, the designers should provide individual kiosks or separate telephone rooms for increased privacy.

Conference Support Areas. The several conference center management groups fall into two camps in terms of how they plan support space and deliver support service. Although both schools of thought provide for a conference concierge and a high level of audiovisual support, they diverge on the point of how much backup should be given to each function and the question of locating the support staff within the conference core or elsewhere in the building. (In addition, of course,

Nikko Hotel, Chicago, Illinois (above left). Support functions, such as the conference services desk, toilets, coat rooms, and telephones, require detailed design attention. These telephone rooms offer an important amenity to conference guests. (Interiors: Mingis Design; photo by author.)

Hamilton Park Executive Conference Center, Florham Park, New Jersey (below left). Conference services often are located at the entrance to the conference core, where visitors can seek out information and directions. Some centers provide multiple television monitors, message boards, and other audiovisual systems at this central location. (Architect and interiors: Richard J. Cureton; photo: Jerry Pecknold.)

Scanticon-Denver, Englewood, Colorado (right). The plan of the conference support areas illustrates the cluster of offices and lounges behind the conference concierge and the major provision of technical support areas—including graphics, audiovisual, and central control rooms—located on a mezzanine between the two large multipurpose conference rooms. (Architect: Friis Moltke Larson with RNL.)

all serious conference centers provide substantial reinforcement to the conference services function by allocating sufficient space for conference storage, coffee pantries, and related service functions.)

Conference Services. One organization plan places the conference services desk, conference manager, work area, and audiovisual display and control room at the entrance to the conference core; this concept requires 600 to 800 net square feet (55.8 to 74.4 square meters) of space. Guests can easily receive directions, request assistance, leave messages, or whatever. The audiovisual systems are visible—often the developer lines up banks of monitors behind a display window—and guests may be enticed to make use of extra services. The individual conference planners assigned to each client work out of the administrative offices, where they are near the sales staff and can, together, coordinate the details of upcoming conferences.

The second approach provides greater service but at substantially larger staff and space costs. Under this scheme, the conference services desk functions much as it does in the first model, but the several conference planners are housed in adjacent offices, placing them closer to the customers during the meeting. This organization typically encompasses 1,000 to 1,500 square feet (93 to 139.5 square meters) for the conference concierge, coordinators, workrooms, and lounge.

In this configuration, the conference coordinators have considerably less direct contact with the sales department. More significantly, the audiovisual services are substantially expanded—to as large as 3,000 square feet (279 square meters)—including some or all of the following elements:

☐ *An audiovisual control room*, for transmission and distribution of all audiovisual systems throughout the center

☐ *An audiovisual workroom*, for preparing and editing tapes and for equipment storage

☐ *Audiovisual office*, for the manager and technicians

☐ *A graphics room*, for document printing, duplicating, handout preparation, and so on

☐ *A photographic darkroom*, to support the printing operation

The audiovisual control room often doubles as the projection booth for the ballroom, auditorium, or major multipurpose conference room, and includes the necessary equipment to record, transmit, or distribute images and signals, both within the building and to remote sites. The room usually is secure from the guests (although at Doral Arrowwood the entire audiovisual operation is visible). The audiovisual workroom and offices should be close to the control room. The graphics operations should be located nearby, since they are supervised by the same manager, but if the

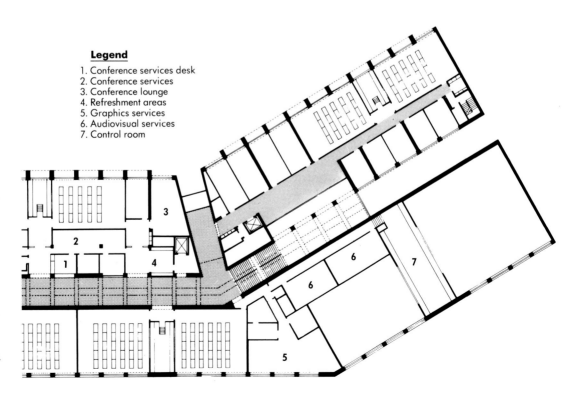

Legend
1. Conference services desk
2. Conference services
3. Conference lounge
4. Refreshment areas
5. Graphics services
6. Audiovisual services
7. Control room

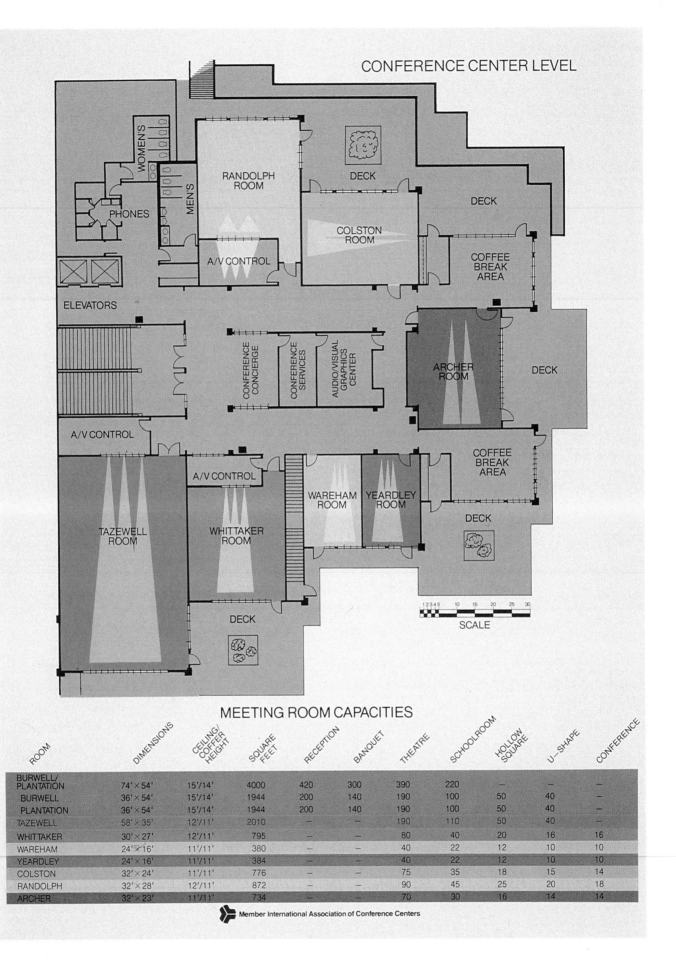

CONFERENCE CENTER LEVEL

WOMEN'S

PHONES

MEN'S

RANDOLPH ROOM

DECK

DECK

COLSTON ROOM

A/V CONTROL

COFFEE BREAK AREA

ELEVATORS

CONFERENCE CONCIERGE

CONFERENCE SERVICES

AUDIO/VISUAL GRAPHICS CENTER

ARCHER ROOM

DECK

A/V CONTROL

COFFEE BREAK AREA

TAZEWELL ROOM

A/V CONTROL

WHITTAKER ROOM

WAREHAM ROOM

YEARDLEY ROOM

DECK

DECK

1 2 3 4 5   10   15   20   25   30

SCALE

MEETING ROOM CAPACITIES

ROOM	DIMENSIONS	CEILING/ COFFER HEIGHT	SQUARE FEET	RECEPTION	BANQUET	THEATRE	SCHOOLROOM	HOLLOW SQUARE	U—SHAPE	CONFERENCE
BURWELL/ PLANTATION	74' × 54'	15'/14'	4000	420	300	390	220	—	—	—
BURWELL	36' × 54'	15'/14'	1944	200	140	190	100	50	40	—
PLANTATION	36' × 54'	15'/14'	1944	200	140	190	100	50	40	—
TAZEWELL	58' × 35'	12'/11'	2010	—	—	190	110	50	40	—
WHITTAKER	30' × 27'	12'/11'	795	—	—	80	40	20	16	16
WAREHAM	24' × 16'	11'/11'	380	—	—	40	22	12	10	10
YEARDLEY	24' × 16'	11'/11'	384	—	—	40	22	12	10	10
COLSTON	32' × 24'	11'/11'	776	—	—	75	35	18	15	14
RANDOLPH	32' × 28'	12'/11'	872	—	—	90	45	25	20	18
ARCHER	32' × 23'	11'/11'	734	—	—	70	30	16	14	14

Member International Association of Conference Centers

audiovisual control and production areas are remote, the graphics areas are better positioned more convenient to the conference services offices.

Projection Rooms. Closely associated with the audiovisual areas are the several projection rooms. Scanticon locates a front projection room between every two conference rooms. Most other developers plan only the two or three larger rooms with front or rear projection, or, as an alternative, may provide one or more rooms with ceiling video projectors.

Most projection rooms are accessible from the corresponding conference room itself; however, many meeting planners prefer that the technician be able to leave the booth without walking through the room and disturbing the session. IBM-Thornwood addresses this issue by neatly incorporating a vestibule to many conference rooms, offering independent access to and from the control booth.

Front-projection rooms can be very small—under 100 square feet (9.3 square meters). They need to be elevated slightly above the floor of the conference room to ensure projection over the participants' heads. Rear-projection rooms, on the other hand, must be deep enough to create a sufficiently large projected image. This can be facilitated with special projector lenses, or with mirror arrangements that reflect the image onto the rear screen. Unfortunately, rear-projection rooms require quite a bit of space—the average size is about 300 square feet (27.9 square meters)—and most operators therefore try to economize by searching for configurations that allow the lower few feet to be used for chair and equipment storage. Separate access should be provided for technicians.

Conference Storage. The storage requirements for conference centers parallel those for other types of lodging properties. Developers attempt to provide storage space equal to at least 5 to 10 percent of the conference and training rooms. The most substantial storage requirement is for furniture, especially the executive chairs (which are standard features and required for membership in IACC), which do not stack; in addition, conference tables, lecterns, and risers must be stored.

The architect should provide a series of additional rooms convenient to the conference core for nonfurniture storage needs. Alternatively, these might be provided in a larger room, subdivided with lockable wire cages, to separate functions and provide better security. At least one space needs to be provided for portable audiovisual equipment, such as overhead and slide projectors, easels and flipcharts, and for expendable items like markers and erasers. If the conference rooms are spread over more than one floor, then additional audiovisual storage rooms should be provided near each conference area.

The corporate conference centers generate a massive amount of printed materials in the form of training manuals, workbooks, and related instructional items. At the public conference facilities, on the other hand, most of this material is produced off-site by the meeting planner or instructor and sent to the center prior to the meeting. Locked space convenient to the conference core is needed for storing this material until the beginning of the session, when it is usually moved to the meeting planner's office or to individual closets in the appropriate conference rooms.

Coffee Pantry. It is helpful to provide satellite refreshment pantries at the conference core. Supported by the main kitchen, the staff uses the pantries to brew coffee and tea, make ice, store food, beverage, and snack items, and hold dirty dishes. Occasionally the pantry will handle warewashing, although most operators prefer to take care of this at the kitchen.

Here, as elsewhere, look for ways to stay current with contemporary concerns: one corporate center, due to the recent environmental concern over solid waste, has constructed a new pantry in order to use china instead of disposable paper products.

CHAPTER 12

Designing the Conference and Training Rooms

The planning of the meeting facilities establishes the framework for the design of the individual conference and training rooms—the essential reason for the conference center's development in the first place. Each individual room must not only meet the practical needs of the users—the meeting attendees, meeting planners, and presenters—but should meet or even exceed the users' functional and aesthetic expectations. The center's design must ensure that the participants leave with entirely positive impressions. While the architectural and functional planning discussed in the previous chapter are important, the design of the individual conference rooms is even more critical to the complete experience.

First, the conference rooms must meet a number of general criteria. They must be designed suitably for the market and the conference center type, with the sufficient floor area, furnishings, finishes, audiovisual capability, and so forth. An executive boardroom does not belong in a rustic not-for-profit retreat; a multimedia rear-screen projection system is not required in a university executive education facility. Moreover, the project budget, including construction, site improvements, fur-

nishings, equipment, and other costs, must be appropriate to the market potential for generating revenues and profits.

CONFERENCE ROOM DESIGN REQUIREMENTS

Each conference and training room must be programmed and designed with a particular meeting need and capacity in mind. In addition, each must meet a large number of general architectural criteria (Table 12–1), many of them essentially the same as for hotels and other lodging types—an absence of columns, adequate sound proofing, sufficient ceiling height—although some criteria may be considerably more stringent.

Many of these issues elicit strong opinions for and against (windows, subdivisibility); others are widely accepted as essential (elimination of columns); some carry major cost implications (increased ceiling height); and a few are important only in special situations (floor loading, such as for when a room might be used for exhibit purposes).

The earlier chapters identified the differences in the needs for various types of conference and training rooms among the several conference center categories. The architect's

Evergreen Conference Center and Resort, Stone Mountain, Georgia. An amphitheater, like this one, can be expensive to construct and furnish, but many resort and university conference centers find it to be a valuable feature nonetheless. (Architect: Chapman Coyle Chapman; interiors: DiLeonardo International; photo: Rion Rizzo, Creative Sources.)

TABLE 12-1. CONFERENCE ROOM DESIGN CHECKLIST

Project Aspect	Requirements
Programmatic Requirements	☐ Provide for both typical and special rooms
	☐ Establish room capacities
	☐ Establish preferred seating configurations
	☐ Define audiovisual requirements, including needs for audiovisual distribution and projection booths
	☐ Define support needs, including storage and conference services
Architectural Requirements	☐ Determine room dimensions
	☐ Confirm ceiling height
	☐ Establish need for divisibility
	☐ Evaluate desirability of windows
	☐ Provide column-free space
	☐ Establish soundproofing standards
	☐ Confirm any needs for unusual floor loading
	☐ Develop interior design criteria
	☐ Confirm building code and exiting requirements
	☐ Confirm handicapped requirements
Mechanical and Electrical Requirements	☐ Provide separate systems for each room
	☐ Provide cooling and ventilation for peak demand
	☐ Provide dimmable lighting
	☐ Calculate power requirements for special systems or computers
	☐ Install jacks for audio, video, telephone, etc.
	☐ Provide phone to control room and conference services

first tasks include a careful assessment of the prospective uses of the conference and training spaces and the establishment of precise program requirements for their size and features. The conference room criteria vary depending on the type of meeting and the preferred furniture setup. Many sources identify area-per-person standards for each room configuration, but, it is important to realize that the seating efficiency of any layout is dependent on the relative size of the conference room (Table 12–2). Because of the space required for the speaker at the front of the room, as well as the inefficiencies caused by placing standard furniture in rooms of particular dimensions, increasing the room size correspondingly increases the efficiency in terms of the amount of floor area per person. For example, note that Table 12–2 establishes 14 and 16 square feet (1.3 and 1.5 square meters) per seat for theater seating in ballroom and large meet-

ing rooms, 18 (1.6) in medium meeting rooms, and 20 (1.8) in small rooms—the per-seat space requirements go up as the room size goes down. By comparison, hotels often list theater capacity at 8 to 10 square feet (0.7 to 0.9 square meters) per person, using smaller banquet chairs and attempting to show maximum capacity rather than a reasonable optimum use.

Spatial Requirements. In addition to understanding function and related capacity, architects and developers must deal with a number of basic design criteria. Among the most controversial are the inclusion of windows and the desirability of divisible walls. The proponents of windows, such as Scanticon and many of the resort operators, cite the benefits and restful quality of natural light and the advantages of emphasizing the setting. The opposing view holds that windows create distractions and make light control for audiovisual presentations difficult and expensive.

As for the issue of subdivisible rooms, one distinct feature of conference centers is their dedicated, single-purpose rooms intended only for conferences, breakout sessions, seminars, and so on. These rooms do not double as banquet and reception rooms; therefore, the space program should include few, if any, subdivisible rooms, except for the larger function rooms used for banquets and social events rather than for meetings. Where subdivisible conference rooms are desirable, they function best at the smaller end of the scale. For example, an 800 square foot (74.4 square meter) conference room could be divided into two breakout rooms; in such a case, there is little likelihood that the conversation from one room will disturb the participants in the next.

The most notable exception to this concept is Westfields International Conference Center outside Washington, D.C., which contains three subdivisible ballrooms (creating eleven individual conference and banquet rooms), an amphitheater, and seven small conference rooms; in the social and association-oriented Washington market, such a program decision is sensible. Also, it is not unusual for resorts catering to incentive groups but seeking to attract high-level conferences to build large, flexible meeting and function space. The Keystone Resort in Colorado recently added a freestanding conference center featuring a mammoth 16,000 square foot (1,488 square meter) grand ballroom for 1,100 people.

Other architectural criteria must be developed in conjunction with the context of each individual room. The ceiling height must be sufficient for the room dimensions and also take into account the audiovisual requirements. For example, in the fairly common 1,000 square foot (93 square meter) conference room where the attendees in the back may be sitting in the eighth or tenth row, the projection screen must be raised above the heads of the audience. In these rooms, forty to fifty feet (12.1 to 15.2 meters) long, standard practice requires an eight-by-eight–foot (2.4-by-2.4–meter) screen, and, therefore, about a 12-foot (3.6-meter) ceiling. Larger rooms, and those with adjoining projection rooms, require substantially higher ceilings. One shortcoming of many hotels is that the medium and small conference rooms have insufficient ceiling height for satisfactory slide- or video-projection use.

Soundproof meeting rooms are essential. What is significant in most cases is not that the rooms protect privacy and confidentiality, but that the participants are not disturbed by outside activity. The relative ability of a wall to isolate sounds is represented by a sound-transmission class rating, or STC. STC ratings of 60 or higher should be achieved between conference rooms (52 or higher where subdivisible partitions are used).

Accessibility Requirements. There is a growing awareness of the obvious need to provide facilities that are accessible to people

TABLE 12-2. CONFERENCE ROOM SEATING STANDARDS[a]

| | Theater-Style | | Classroom-Style | | | | | |
	Executive Setup[b]	Maximum Setup[c]	Executive Setup[b]	Maximum Setup[c]	Hollow Square Setup	U-shaped Setup	Conference Setup	Banquet Setup
Ballroom	14 (1.3)	11 (1)	22 (2)	18	NA	NA	NA	14 (1.3)
Large conference room	16 (1.5)	13 (1.2)	24 (2.2)	20	40–45 (3.7–4.2)	50–55 (4.7–5.1)	NA	14 (1.3)
Medium conference room	18 (1.7)	15 (1.4)	26 (2.4)	22	34 (3.2)	42 (3.9)	40 (3.7)	NA
Small conference room	20 (1.9)	15 (1.4)	30 (2.8)	24	32 (3)	38 (3.5)	35 (3.3)	NA
Breakout room	NA	NA	NA	NA	NA	NA	25 (2.3)	NA
Boardroom	NA	NA	NA	NA	32 (3)	NA	40 (3.7)	NA
Amphitheater	NA	NA	25 (2.3)	NA	NA	NA	NA	NA

[a]Figures represent optimum square feet (square meters) per person.
[b]Executive setup includes executive conference chairs and 24- to 30-inch (61–76 cm) wide tables.
[c]Maximum setup includes stacking banquet chairs and 18-inch (46 cm) wide tables.

IBM Advanced Business Institute, Palisades, New York. The several types of conference rooms at the customer facility are located on two floors in the educational wing, with training offices on the third floor. Three amphitheaters extend to one side, partially buried on the rolling site. The other conference rooms—all with rear-screen projection—are located in a central block with foyer and break spaces around them. Most classrooms provide oversized individual work stations, comprehensive audiovisual and computer systems, and highly detailed custom millwork finishes. (Architect and interiors: Mitchell/Giurgola; photos: Mick Hales.)

with restricted mobility. Although every American jurisdiction addresses some aspects of handicapped accessibility, many codes are insufficient to meet the real need, and many other countries' regulations are far behind those in the United States. Table 12–3, excerpted from a handbook published by the Paralyzed Veterans of America with assistance from the American Hotel and Motel Association, highlights many of these concerns, which go far beyond general accessibility to include such issues as adequate knee space, the height of writing boards and lecterns for dis-

abled speakers, and visual and acoustic considerations.

Other criteria aren't as likely to be consciously identified by guests as concerns but nonetheless often influence the user's relative satisfaction with the center. For example, consider the issue of access to and from a meeting room: Should the doors be at the front, rear, or side of a room? Should there be direct access to outdoor terraces? Should there be a connection to a service corridor? Should double or oversized doors be installed for moving furniture, refreshments, or displays? The confer-

---

TABLE 12-3. HANDICAPPED RECOMMENDATIONS FOR CONFERENCE FACILITIES

Reception Lobbies
- ☐ Connect reception area to the main lobby by an accessible route; provide separate and accessible entrance and dropoff
- ☐ Provide accessible public facilities (drinking fountains, telephones, and rest rooms) convenient to the reception area; provide comfortable seating for waiting
- ☐ Design accessible built-in or portable reception desks for guests in wheelchairs

Meeting and Conference Rooms
- ☐ Provide access to seating locations and the speaking area for participants with restricted mobility; provide wheelchair knee space at conference tables; coordinate the seat height of chairs with the table height
- ☐ Have available portable or built-in audiovisual systems, such as amplification systems and television monitors, for attendees with restricted vision or impaired hearing
- ☐ To reduce background noise, provide sound-insulated meeting room walls; use sound-absorbent materials for finishes and furnishings within the room
- ☐ Provide well-lit presentation areas in conference rooms; include accessible display boards and microphones

Lecture Rooms and Amphitheaters
- ☐ Provide accessible seating at dispersed locations for attendees in wheelchairs, with sightlines comparable to those from other seats
- ☐ Provide level wheelchair seating spaces, 2′–9″ × 4′–0″ (0.8 × 1.2 m) deep for front or rear access and 5 feet (1.5 meters) deep for side access
- ☐ Provide sufficient knee space and footroom for desks in amphitheaters; add individual lights at each seating location
- ☐ Make speakers' platforms accessible to people with restricted mobility
- ☐ Provide theater seating with swing-up armrests at aisle seats

Listening Systems
- ☐ If an audio-amplification system is provided, include a listening system, such as induction loops, wireless FM, or infrared systems, to assist persons with severe hearing loss
- ☐ If a listening system is provided for fixed seats, provide such seating within 50 feet (15.2 meters) of the speakers' platform

Visual Systems
- ☐ Provide visual systems, such as large screens or television monitors, to aid guests with restricted vision

Source: Davis, T. and Beasley, K. (1988). *Design for Hospitality, Planning for Accessible Hotels and Motels.* New York: Nichols.

ence room, of course, must meet individual building codes, which usually require two separate means of egress for rooms with a capacity above fifty people. But beyond that there are a number of operationally oriented criteria that need careful consideration.

Mechanical and Electrical Requirements. Early in design development, the architectural and engineering consultants establish the environmental criteria for heating, ventilation, and air conditioning. The designers adjust standard criteria to match the room configuration, anticipated maximum number of people, and such details as whether the users may add computers or other equipment. No-smoking regulations in many parts of the country help reduce the need for extreme amounts of ventilation.

Among the biggest complaints of conference attendees and meeting planners is the inability to control the meeting room climate, and so each room must have separate controls to allow users to regulate the room's temperature; in centers with subdivisible rooms, added controls should be incorporated allowing each room to be controlled individually or as one. In addition, the noise level of the mechanical systems must be reduced as far as possible. In short, the goal is to design a system that runs so effectively that the guests are unaware of its existence.

TYPES OF CONFERENCE AND TRAINING ROOMS

Each of the typical conference rooms has a number of unique planning criteria to consider early in the design. These require the collaborative effort of all members of the design team, especially the architect, interior designer, audiovisual consultant, and operator. A room-by-room examination now follows.

Ballroom. The ballroom in conference centers serves dual functions as the principal banquet room and, for larger groups, as the meeting room for general sessions. Its design, therefore, includes sophisticated audiovisual systems, one or more projection booths, increased ventilation, larger foyer and breakout areas, and high-quality soundproof divisible partitions. Many of the decorative touches common in hotel ballrooms (the expansive chandeliers, delicate wall sconces, or boldly patterned carpet) are absent, but the conference center ballroom still offers the potential for attracting weekend social business, and so

should have enough design character to capture this secondary market.

The ballroom's "split personality" raises a number of difficult planning and design questions: Should the ballroom be located in the conference core or nearer the restaurants? How should it be decorated? Does it need the same sophisticated systems of the largest meeting rooms? Each project team needs to assess the anticipated conference market and determine where the ballroom falls on the continuum between function room and meeting room. For example, Westfields' three large subdivisible ballrooms, discussed earlier, each offer highly sophisticated computerized audiovisual systems, and the management provides the full range of conference services at each one.

Several resort properties include two ballrooms oriented to different uses: One is designed principally as a function room, the second equipped as a large meeting room, including rear-screen projection. Although, either room can be used for any type of meeting or function, the developers established a primary use and designed and equipped the rooms accordingly.

Large Conference Room. Large conference rooms (those greater than 1,500 square feet, or 139.5 square meters) are most often used for presentations requiring little audience involvement through discussion or questions. These rooms are set up theater- or classroom-style, in straight rows facing the speaker. Because the room depth usually exceeds fifty feet (15.2 meters) and the rows number at least ten (often twenty or more), it may be necessary to provide a stage or riser. This is an important consideration because it influences the design of the front presentation wall and, as a result, the planning of such support areas as a rear-projection room.

Unfortunately, the larger rooms often are subdivided, an alteration that creates significant difficulties because these rooms have the greatest need for sophisticated audiovisual and sound reinforcement systems. Audiovisual capability often is compromised, or redundant systems are required in subdivisible rooms. These rooms more often have specialized audiovisual presentations, and it is therefore imperative for the speaker to be able to darken the room with a minimum of effort; if the rooms include windows, it is important to provide electronic blackout shades or drapes.

Also, the larger rooms require substantially

Scanticon-Princeton, Princeton, New Jersey. Scanticon offers a large multipurpose conference room that can be arranged flexibly (although most often theater- or classroom-style), additional conference rooms (usually with classroom or U-shaped layouts), fixed-table boardrooms in an unusual open-square configuration, and breakout rooms. Every room has natural light and full audiovisual services, including connections to the central control room. (Architect: Friis and Moltke with Warner Burns Toan and Lunde; interiors: Friis and Moltke with Enicho Deichmann; photos: Ron Solomon.)

DESIGNING THE CONFERENCE AND TRAINING ROOMS   217

greater ceiling heights, which influences the rooms' location in the building. Rather than combining higher and lower ceiling spaces in the same zone (resulting in unusable volume above the finished ceiling of the smaller rooms), the larger rooms frequently are located in a low structure extending beyond the guestroom tower, or on a lower level that can accommodate the two-story volume.

Medium Conference Rooms. These rooms, in the 1,000 to 1,500 square foot (93 to 139.5 square meter) range, are the mainstay of today's properties. For example, among the corporate projects, the Pitney Bowes training center includes thirty out of forty-six conference rooms at this size, and the IBM Advanced Business Institute has eighteen of twenty-one. These midsize rooms, used for highly interactive training, management development, marketing, and executive education, need to allow practically any type of room arrangement: theater, classroom, hollow square, U-shaped, or small-group configurations. In addition, these rooms require a variety of permanent and portable equipment and audiovisual systems. At a minimum, they need a whiteboard, projection screen, tackable walls, an overhead projector, and at least two easels. Beyond these basic requirements, which apply to all types of conference centers, the operator must assess the need for slide, video, audio recording, and other systems.

Some conference center operators establish very precise requirements for these midsize conference rooms, based on their experience and knowledge of the types of furniture to be specified. For example, when planning a new project, the Benchmark program establishes not only conference room areas but the exact *dimensions*. This is in order to accommodate the maximum number of people with the more generous executive furnishings. For instance, a conference room 28 feet (8.5 meters) wide comfortably holds four 5-foot (1.5-meter) conference tables and two 4-foot (1.2-meter) side aisles; a narrower room would force the elimination of one table in each row or would require a single center aisle. A slightly wider room would provide more generous aisles but no increase in capacity.

Small Conference Rooms. Centers expecting to attract groups of twenty to thirty people may program a large number of smaller conference rooms in the 500 to 1,000 square foot (46.5 to 93 square meter) range. While these

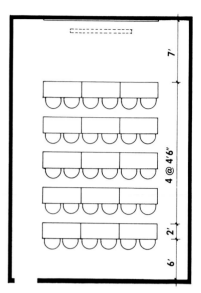
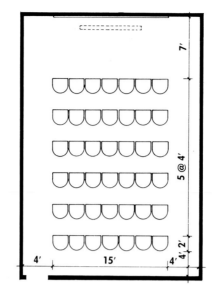
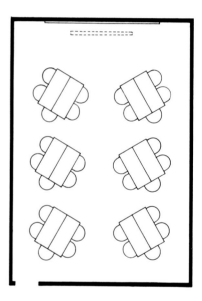
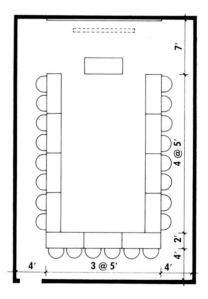

Conference room layouts. Conference center operators are alert to the potential variations in capacity of different layouts. The illustrated rooms, 23 by 33 feet (7 by 10 meters) or 760 square feet (70 square meters) show maximum seating and fairly tight spacing, especially between seating and the walls. Theater layout (top left) offers the most seats; classroom (top right), U-shaped (bottom left), and cluster (bottom right) arrangements accommodate about equal numbers but will vary slightly depending on the room dimensions.

smaller rooms offer less flexibility and may encourage crowding of slightly larger groups, many operators bemoan the lack of a sufficient number of smaller rooms. A careful analysis of the needs of the primary users and of competitive centers may establish the right mix for a new project.

These rooms should be equipped similarly to midsize rooms. Each space should have a permanent projection screen, whiteboard, and walls that can accommodate sheets torn from a flip chart. Some operators install a hanging rail, offering wide flexibility to meet the needs of each client.

Breakout Rooms. Another distinguishing feature of conference centers is the provision of a high number of breakout rooms, often equalling the total of the other conference rooms. The size of these rooms varies dramatically among centers, some allowing no more than an office-sized space, say 150 to 200 square feet (13.9 to 18.6 square meters); other operators insist on breakout rooms large enough for groups of eight to twelve and set a minimum size of about 400 square feet (37.2 square meters). The recent addition to Scanticon-Princeton included seven breakout rooms of 450 square feet (41.8 square meters) each. The larger rooms are more flexible, of course, accommodating larger groups as well as those needing to work on extended projects, bring in computers or video equipment, role-play, or otherwise spread out.

Breakout rooms require the same minimal equipment as do smaller conference rooms. Most have little specialized audiovisual equipment; executive centers may provide audio and video jacks to accommodate transmissions to or from a central control room.

Boardrooms. Most executive and resort conference centers include one or two boardrooms. The developer needs to determine whether a boardroom is desired as a marketing tool or is necessary to meet actual demand for such a room. While the boardrooms require relatively little floor area (500 to 800 square feet, or 46.5 to 74.4 square meters, for the room itself), many developers choose to add private lounges, toilets, projection rooms, and other accessory areas, which increase the space program. In addition, the boardroom is expensive to furnish and equip, often running two to three times the cost of a standard conference room. Much of this expense comes from the additional millwork: movable wall panels,

to hide writing and tackable surfaces or coat closets, oversized custom tables, built-in buffets, and similar luxuries.

If security is a major concern, the boardroom may need to be physically separated from the other conference rooms, fully soundproofed, and totally private; for example, switches may be installed to cut off audio transmissions to the central control room. Such characteristics need to be defined early in the programming phase.

Amphitheater. Many resort and university centers include an amphitheater. These custom-designed spaces are expensive to provide, in part because they are not sufficiently flexible for different types of seating arrangements, which means groups that are the right size for the amphitheater may not choose to use it because they prefer a different layout. In fact, instructors who like one design (the horseshoe shape common in business school case study rooms, for instance) often refuse to use the slightly curved amphitheaters found in resort and executive centers because of the lack of eye contact among the participants. In addition, amphitheaters' construction, furnishings, and equipment costs are high because of the change in floor levels, ceiling articulation, millwork counters and railings, special lighting, upgraded executive chairs, and audiovisual and computer connections. The feasibility study should establish early on whether there is legitimate need for an amphitheater.

An amphitheater, if eventually programmed, requires about 25 square feet (2.3 square meters) per seat, or about the same amount of space as a more typical conference room. Most rooms will have either a front- or rear-projection room equipped for most media, including slides, video, and film at the very least. If multimedia or multiple-image presentations are anticipated, the front wall needs an oversized screen.

One of the most difficult design tasks is the organization of the amphitheater's presentation wall, which needs to accommodate a writing surface (business schools may require multiple whiteboards), tackable surface, presentation rail, projection screen, and speakers. Scanticon provides two or more screens, one for the projection systems and a second that can be tilted for use with overhead projectors. Some presenters may want to combine two systems—showing slides and, at the same time, writing notes on the board, for example.

Controls need to be positioned at several locations. Room lights are switched at the door; the other systems, including lights, projection, audio, window drapes, and so on, are controlled at the lectern (which often is connected into a floor box), at the front wall, and in the projection booth. Wireless remote control is possible for most applications.

The design of the tiered seating and work surfaces varies tremendously among conference centers. Some are as simple as standard conference tables bolted to the stepped levels; others include a fairly simple work surface and modesty panel; a few feature carefully crafted custom millwork units incorporating such details as electrical outlets, microphones, computer and translation jacks, leather writing inserts, undershelves and narrow slots for displaying participant name boards. The relative values of these features should be established at an early meeting and incorporated into the design criteria.

Auditorium. Corporate training centers frequently include a large, 150- to 300-seat auditorium for major class presentations, other presentations by company executives, and community use. Because of this public role, the auditorium usually is located near the main entrance, off the conference center lobby, rather than within the main conference core.

A few of these auditoriums are equipped and finished with permanent work areas; most, however, are typical theaters with a sloped floor, a stage, a balcony, and projection capability. Translation booths may be provided if the need is identified early enough.

Computer Rooms and Special Classrooms. Some centers will include specialized spaces to meet their individual market needs. Many of the university executive education facilities, for example, feature a computer room, which is used both for instruction and as a student resource when classes are not being conducted. Generally these are limited to fifteen to twenty stations because of the difficulties of conducting computer exercises for larger groups.

The program should allow at least 35 to 40 square feet (3.2 to 3.7 square meters) per person to accommodate the computer stations and the associated printers, reference materials, software, and supplies. Most computer rooms are designed so that the instructor's computer display is projected on the front wall. More sophisticated arrangements allow

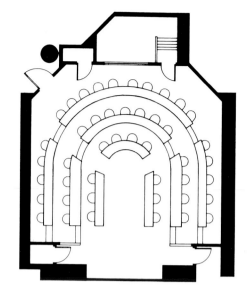

Amphitheater layouts (left). Special-purpose rooms offer less flexibility but may be essential for particular instructional objectives; many centers provide amphitheaters—either gently curved or horseshoe-shaped—to enhance participation among the attendees. Top: Steinberg Center, University of Pennsylvania (architect: The Hillier Group); bottom: IBM-Palisades (architect: Mitchell/Giurgola).

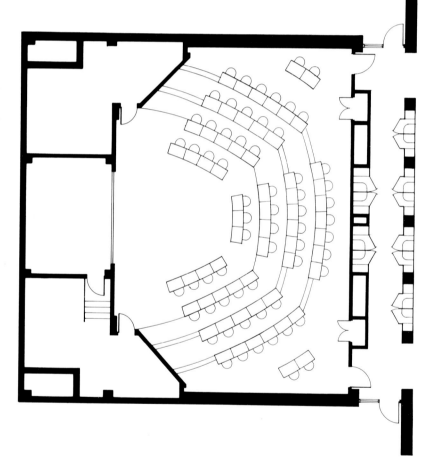

Amphitheaters (facing page). Top: Steinberg Center, University of Pennsylvania; (photo © Mark Ross, 1988); bottom: Mount Washington Conference Center, Baltimore, Maryland (photo: Ron Solomon).

Merrill Lynch Conference and Training Center, Princeton, New Jersey. Merrill Lynch includes a number of specialized telephone labs as well as more flexible octagonal conference rooms, breakout rooms, and a large two-level amphitheater. The typical rooms provide rear projection, other computer and audiovisual capability, closets, indirect lighting, and 42-inch—wide (1.1-meter—wide) individual student tables. (Architect: The Kling-Lindquist Partnership; interiors: Daroff Design; photos: Tom Crane, courtesy of Harrison Conference Centers.)

the instructor to retrieve any student's work onto his computer or onto the projection screen for discussion and comment. Ambitious centers may include a computer network, so that the software and instructional systems are available at each classroom and even in the individual guestrooms.

Other centers feature unique rooms equipped for highly specialized needs. Merrill-Lynch has installed five telephone laboratories at their conference and training center in Princeton, where financial consultants are trained in telephone sales techniques, cold prospecting, and closing deals, a three-week course that follows a 14-week field program. Designed like a computer lab, the multipurpose phone lab features rows of carrels with adjustable front and side panels which provide the flexibility of open, semi-private, or full carrel configurations.

CONFERENCE ROOM INTERIORS

Much of the success of conference centers is based on the high quality of their meeting rooms, partly a reflection of the rooms' dedicated character and generally large size, but also the result of the superior level of finishes, furnishings, and equipment, which contribute to much more than simply the aesthetics of the space. Design criteria for the surface finishes, standards for tables and chairs, and specifications for instructional equipment all add immeasurably to the potential for a successful conference, and the design team must begin to establish interiors criteria early in the schematic phase; it is inadequate to "decorate" and equip the rooms in the months preceding the opening.

The interior designer and operator should prepare outline specifications of the conference room finishes, furniture, and equipment. In addition, the architect and designer need to coordinate their respective responsibilities for the selection and budgeting of special finishes. Although the furniture can be selected later, it is necessary for the team (and especially the operator) to approve the meeting room layouts early on, to confirm the space planning. Similarly, the equipment purchases could be delayed until midway through construction, but the operator, audiovisual consultant, communications expert, and other team members must develop early equipment standards; these will influence the design of the rooms and establish cabling requirements that will be used throughout the rest of the facility.

Conference Room Finishes. Floors at conference centers are almost universally carpeted, with the material choice based on acoustic, visual, and aesthetic qualities and comfort; only occasionally, in certain corporate training centers with special-purpose classrooms, is resilient tile or another material substituted (for example, an insurance company training center may have fire labs, where carpeting would be inappropriate). The carpet pattern should be very simple, if not a solid color, in order to limit distractions. Some operators prefer carpet tiles, which allow easy replacement for soiled or damaged sections but may result in a slightly uneven color due to differences in wear and age.

Much of the discussion of conference room finishes is related to the walls, which most often are painted, vinyl-covered, or tackable. Instead of using tacks, however, many instructors prefer simply to tape sheets of paper, torn off the easel, to the walls, and a substitute criterion might therefore be for a "tapeable" surface that permits the easy removal of masking tape. As with the floors, most designers specify the walls to be a relatively light, solid color or subtle pattern, rather than dark or strongly patterned. Window coverings should meet similar criteria.

Lighting, sound systems, HVAC, fire protection systems, and so forth can be integrated into the ceiling, much of which should be acoustic tile to reduce reverberation within the space. The tile may be combined with a frame of painted gypsum board or other material.

Conference Room Furniture. The second element of the conference room interior design is the furniture selection, which essentially means the tables and chairs. Obviously, these contribute substantially to the success of the design and the comfort of the participants. One critical decision to be made when planning a conference center is the type of meeting room chair to be used throughout the property. The IACC requires its member centers to use eight-hour chairs in the conference rooms, rather than the banquet chairs most often found in hotels. These executive chairs are fully upholstered, swivel-and-tilt armchairs that are particularly comfortable for full-day meetings. Their use, however, has other implications. In addition to their substantial expense ($300 and more), they create a major storage problem since they do not stack. Many operators will turn one upside down on another and store them two high. Large centers

Doral Arrowwood, Rye Brook, New York. The typical conference room shows a U-shaped arrangement and the simple but effective and flexible treatment of the side and front walls. (Architect and interiors: The Hillier Group; photo: Jim D'Addio.)

may build a chair storage room with a wood platform raised about four feet (1.2 meters) above the floor, creating a deck for storing a second pair of chairs.

The other main decision involves the size of the conference tables, which influences guest comfort (in terms of the amount of room given each attendee) and to some degree establishes the conference room dimensions. The operator who selects tables eight feet (2.4 meters) long will have limited options: for example, in a room between 20 and 28 feet (6 and 8.5 meters) wide, there will be insufficient room for anything other than two tables (16 feet, or 4.8 meters) and an aisle. Shorter tables provide many more options for configuring the meeting room. Rather than selecting furnishings for a given room after its dimensions are set, however, the team should establish a preferred table size based on guest comfort and then develop ideal room sizes. Specifying a table five feet (1.5 meters) long gives two participants 30 inches (76 centimeters) of space each, a 6-foot (1.8-meter) table gives two participants 36 inches (91 centimeters) each or three people 24 inches (61 centimeters) each, and so on.

With the executive chairs expected at most conference centers, 27 inches (68 centimeters) should be the minimum acceptable space per person and 28 to 32 inches (81 centimeters) is preferred. Most common is a 5-foot (1.5-meter) table providing 30 inches (76 centimeters) for each participant. It is unacceptable to expect meeting attendees to sit at the edge between two tables, straddling the table legs and writing on the crack. Table 12–4 outlines the potential for different table sizes.

Similarly, the developer and operator need to determine the optimum table width. Hotels often used tables 18 inches (46 centimeters) wide, barely acceptable for classroom setups; conference center tables should have a width of 24 inches (61 centimeters), deep enough to comfortably accommodate reference materials and a writing pad or notebook; 30 inches (76 centimeters), which provides extra space, is even better but may be a luxury. Occasionally, a center will specify a small number of trapezoidal tables, with ends cut at a 30- or 45-degree angle. This offers two advantages: the ability to provide roughly an open circle and the opportunity to combine two tables for cooperative or group sessions.

Conference Room Fixtures and Equipment. A third aspect of the interior design is the conference room equipment, most of which is directly related to the teaching or meeting objectives of the center and the particular room. Often the equipment is divided into two categories—permanent and movable. The permanent equipment includes such items as the whiteboards or other writing surfaces, tackable panels, hanging-rail systems, and built-in stages. Mobile elements include lecterns, portable projection screens, easels, carts, and so forth.

Whiteboards. All medium and small conference rooms and breakout rooms should be equipped with permanent writing surfaces. The traditional blackboard is now usually a white surface designed to take colored dry-erase markers. Surface-mounted systems, which gang two or three boards together with tracks, allow panels to be raised or lowered either electrically or manually, providing considerably more writing area.

Easels. The majority of the small confer-

TABLE 12-4. CONFERENCE ROOM TABLE SIZES

Table size	Utilization	Comments
42 inches (107 cm)	One person @ 42 inches (107 cm)	Excessive space, inflexible
48 inches (122 cm)	Two people @ 24 inches (61 cm)	Unacceptable
54 inches (137 cm)	Two people @ 27 inches (69 cm)	
60 inches (152 cm)	Two people @ 30 inches (76 cm)	Optimum
66 inches (168 cm)	Two people @ 32 inches (81 cm)	
72 inches (183 cm)	Two people @ 36 inches (91 cm)	Comfortable, slightly excessive
	Three people @ 24 inches (61 cm)	Unacceptable
84 inches (213 cm)	Three people @ 28 inches (71 cm)	Table unwieldy and heavy

GTE Management Development Center, Norwalk, Connecticut.
There are only three types of conference rooms at the influential GTE Property: two amphitheaters, four meeting rooms, and six breakout rooms. The flexible conference rooms are carefully proportioned for different seating configurations, and all rooms offer variable lighting, complete audiovisual services, and custom finishes. (Architect: Hellmuth, Obata & Kassabaum; interiors: Kovacs McElrath; photos: Martin Tornallyay.)

ences are still using writing boards, overheads, and easels with newspads. The most common arrangement utilizes freestanding easels, which the instructor can place anywhere in the room. The hanging-rail systems provide similar flexibility, although the tablets can only hang on the wall surfaces; this frees up floor space, however. Harrison Conference Services designed and uses a larger two-sided easel–cart, which can be rolled to any position and accommodates two oversized tablets.

Tackable Panels. Facilities anticipating a large amount of group work, brainstorming, and case-study exercises should expect conference leaders who will want to tack or tape paper to the room walls or to individual cork or fabric panels. Sometimes the writing surface at the front of the room will be flanked by a pair of tackable panels, but this limits the location for display. Tackable or tapeable walls or a hanging rail are better options.

Projection Screen. Among the standard features in practically every conference room is a permanent projection screen, often recessed into the ceiling and electrically operated. Larger rooms may require two screens, so that one can be lowered for slides, video, or overheads while portions of the front whiteboard remain available to the instructor.

Even the smallest breakout rooms should be equipped with screens; these may be surface-mounted on the wall or ceiling. Operators should avoid portable screens because of the labor expense involved in moving them and their relative flimsiness.

Projected images become distorted when the projector is not perpendicular to the screen surface; to correct for this, many operators install screens that can be tilted.

Hanging Rail. Suppliers are designing new systems for the meetings industry. Many centers now use a hanging rail, mounted about seven feet (2.1 meters) above the floor, from which the operator can suspend individual writing boards, tackable panels, easels, projection screens and so forth. This arrangement permits the instructor to choose which side of the room is the front, to direct breakout groups to work in clusters around the room perimeter with their own easel or whiteboard, or to add extra writing surfaces when needed. While the system offers total flexibility in mounting particular units, it also has its limitations. Some instructors may want easels in the center of the room, or desire larger undivided surfaces than the three- to four-foot (1- to 1.2-meter) width of the individual panels. If not carefully thought through, the hanging rail might be too low (making viewing over heads difficult), or two high for shorter instructors. If such a system is used, a small amount of additional portable equipment should be purchased and available to the instructor and meeting planner.

Stage or Riser. Additional equipment may be necessary to properly set up a conference room. Larger spaces may benefit from a stage or platform to elevate the speaker or panel above the audience. Except in the largest function rooms, these should be portable, allowing the operator and meeting planner great flexibility in room configuration. In midsize and small rooms, risers should not be necessary, especially if the instructor will be moving around the space to engage the participants. If a platform is expected to be used in a given room, designers should consider increasing the height of electrical outlets and audiovisual jacks and providing raisable writing surfaces and projection screens.

Portable Equipment. Conference centers are equipped with a large amount of additional portable equipment. Much of this is audiovisual equipment; the rest includes floor and table lecterns, mobile carts, registration or refreshment tables, message boards, and so forth. Wherever possible, some of this equipment should be permanently assigned to each room to reduce the need for transportation. Storage must be convenient for the equipment that is frequently moved.

Clocks. Differences of opinion rage over the advisability of including wall clocks (standard in classrooms, uncommon in hotel meeting rooms) in conference center rooms. Clock proponents argue that clocks allow the instructor and participants to stay on schedule, take breaks and lunch at established times, and help keep tabs on guest presenters who would otherwise run over their allotted time; opponents feel clocks encourage participants to watch the time rather than concentrate on the presenter. Obviously developers of new projects will have to draw their own conclusions and plan accordingly.

Signage. Proper graphics and directional signage are important for facilities with many new guests each day, as is the case in conference centers. Consider the prospect of over a hundred new arrivals headed for a half-dozen or so rooms within a few minutes on a Monday morning, and the need for signage becomes clear. Wall or video directories at the center entrance should list the room designation for each meeting; maps or highly legible signs should direct the participants; and room signage outside each room must list the name of the appropriate conference. Of course, the signage system should be consistent with other graphics in the conference center.

Four Seasons Hotel and Resort, Irving, Texas. The resort—spa and conference center offers a variety of conference rooms, the larger ones directly off a major skylit prefunction area. The 96-seat amphitheater uses front projection, including a ceiling-mounted video projector. Many of the typical rooms, located on the first two floors, provide video projection, in-room storage closets, and adjoining breakout rooms. (Architect: HKS; interiors: Wilson and Associates; photos: Jaime Ardiles-Arce.)

CONFERENCE ROOM LIGHTING

Meeting planners cite lighting as the single most important element in the selection of conference and training space. The optimum conference room will combine incandescent downlights (with dimming capability) and fluorescent lamps, providing a wide range of lighting flexibility. The incandescent lights allow the instructor to lower the light level at particular locations—in the front of the room, for example, when slides or overheads are used—and create a warmer feel; the fluorescents provide general room illumination, either directly or by indirect systems reflected off the ceiling. In addition, there may be wall washers lighting the vertical surfaces, spotlights over the lectern or buffet, or fluorescent fixtures highlighting the writing surface.

The design team, perhaps in consultation with a professional lighting designer, should deal with the following lighting requirements:

☐ Overall room illumination, which can vary depending upon the anticipated type of instruction and can be direct or indirect

☐ Dimming capability, which may vary in circuits from the front to rear of room

☐ Wall washers highlighting the room perimeter

☐ Task lighting on the writing board, tackable walls, and student work surfaces

☐ Accent lighting on the speaker, wall displays, and, if present, such features as a built-in buffet

☐ Control of unwanted light from the corridor and projection booth

These requirements must be carefully integrated to create a unified lighting design for the entire conference room. The designers should consider the effects of daylight on the room and execute appropriate methods to control excessive glare. Systems should be individually controlled throughout the conference core and the individual meeting rooms, so that, for example, downlights illuminating only the front presentation wall can be turned off when the projection screen is lowered. Related audiovisual and control systems are discussed more fully in the next chapter.

CONFERENCE ASSEMBLY AREAS

Although the conference and training areas are the principal spaces influencing the success of a particular conference center, the design of the associated assembly and support areas is important to the functioning of the conference core. Many meeting attendees, having encoun-

AT&T Executive Conference Center, Chesterfield, Missouri (above left). AT&T operates a number of product-marketing centers, which include theaters, hospitality rooms, demonstration rooms, and conference rooms. This unusual multimedia theater utilizes freestanding chairs and drum tables on a three-level raised platform for participant seating. (Interiors: Cole Martinez Curtis and Associates; photo: Anthesis/WEM.)

The Center for Financial Studies, Fairfield University, Fairfield, Connecticut (below left). In addition to a subdivisible amphitheater, the center provides eight flexible conference rooms equipped with a variety of instructional media. Portable equipment includes the oversized custom flipchart stand. (Photo courtesy of Harrison Conference Services.)

Indigo Lakes Resort & Conference Center, Daytona Beach, Florida (right). Conference centers feature all-day refreshment displays, often set up on permanently installed kiosks incorporating refrigerated compartments, beverage units, and drains, with storage below. (Architect: Greening & Sayers; interiors: William H. Dodson; photo: Meisel Corporation.)

tered the guestrooms, lobby, dining room, reservations, staff, and so on, already have strong impressions of the conference center's quality before attending their first session. Their initial impressions, which should, of course, be positive, must be further confirmed and reinforced by the design of the assembly areas, or else the initial positive impressions will be wasted and forgotten.

Most assembly areas serve a number of functions, each of which must be anticipated, accounted for, and accommodated in the design. For instance, these areas are used for meeting registration, and therefore must have sufficient space for temporary tables as well as the communications and data systems for phones, computers, television, and so forth. Also, the prefunction areas are used for cocktail and other receptions requiring food and beverage service, necessitating decorative and accent lighting and a connection to the back-of-house areas.

Because the foyers are constantly crossed by guests and meeting attendees who may need to sit and briefly discuss this or that, a balance should be struck between permanent and flexible furnishings, bright and subdued lighting, and hard and soft materials, all of which will allow the foyer to take heavy traffic at specific times but provide a sense of luxury and relaxation at others. The more intimate and smaller-

scaled coffee break spaces have somewhat the same use but undergo steadier, less severe wear.

Conference centers feature a number of other public areas within the conference core. Special lounges are furnished to offer a quiet place to sit and talk, and the more elegant boardroom lounge offers comfortable seating and includes some type of buffet or bar for coffee, refreshments, and cocktails, individual telephone alcoves, and private restrooms. The finishes here may be upgraded—for example, a wood parquet or marble floor, an Oriental carpet, wall paneling, or a coffered ceiling with indirect lighting. The furniture compares with that in the best suites: leather-upholstered seating, marble-topped tables, quality artwork, and numerous accessories.

The designers should develop millwork concepts for a number of specialty fixtures, including the conference services desk and the various refreshment kiosks. Because these have very definite functional requirements for accommodating communications and computers on the one hand, and electricity, plumbing, heated and chilled compartments, and so forth on the other, experienced operators have established standard designs to meet their operational procedures. Designers for new properties should study these elements and apply what they learn to their own projects.

CHAPTER 13

Conference Center Technology

The availability and increasing use of sophisticated audiovisual and communications systems is a major reason why many clients select conference centers over traditional hotels for management, training, and other meetings. Most modern properties offer a broad menu of systems, many of which are available in practically every room, from the most advanced auditorium to the simplest breakout room. These systems include front and rear projection of videos, slides, and film; full recording, editing, and transmission capability of conference sessions or other events; and a variety of technical services, including teleconferencing, computer systems, and specialized communications equipment.

Even clients who do not expect to need video or closed-circuit television can benefit from the technical features that most conference centers provide, such as multiple writing surfaces, flexible lighting systems, and tiltable projection screens for use with overheads. None of these requires advanced technology, special wiring, or the assistance of audiovisual staff, and each should be standard in every meeting and conference room.

Many of the other more technical audio-visual and related systems, however, require careful programming and planning from the outset, to ensure that they are appropriate for the expected clientele, meet budget constraints, and can be accommodated by the building and systems design.

AUDIOVISUAL SYSTEMS

The goal of any audiovisual program is to provide for the initial needs of the operator and meeting instructor and be sufficiently flexible to allow for expansion and future enhancements to the system. The design team should approach the audiovisual program from several directions. First, they should develop a description of the characteristics of each type of conference room and its audiovisual and communications needs. At the same time, they should identify the general level of systems to be provided throughout the center—for example, video transmission between rooms, rear projection in the major conference areas, or complete remote-control capability at each space. An important aspect of this is to clearly state whether specific equipment will be dedicated to a particular space (either permanently installed or assigned), portable, so that it can be shared with other conference rooms, or not

Scottsdale Conference Resort, Scottsdale, Arizona. Elaborate conference center technology systems often are controlled from one central room. (Photo: Peter Vitale, courtesy of International Conference Resorts.)

present but provided for in the basebuilding design, so that it can be acquired later.

Basic conference equipment and systems should be permanently installed or dedicated to each conference room so that it can function independently; it should not be necessary to transport such commonly used, portable items as easels or projection screens each day. The instructor should be able to start a video, advance slides, and adjust lighting without help. Although duplicate controls in a projection room or central control room may be used during a formal presentation, many meeting planners insist on the instructor's operation and control of the basic systems.

Also, because several conference rooms may need to be used together, the audio, video, and communications systems should be able to interconnect them. Many operators will propose establishing a program for the basebuilding requirements that will allow for a myriad of future additions—even systems as yet undeveloped. To better enable this, a control or head end room should be provided in every project, perhaps doubling as the projection room for the major auditorium or amphitheater, with the main function of controlling all audio and video signals throughout the property, including television distribution to the guestrooms. Table 13–1 lists the scope of the most common audiovisual systems.

The Scanticon properties provide the most complete audiovisual systems of any developer or management group. Essential elements in their conference centers include:

☐ A high percentage of the equipment inventory dedicated to individual conference rooms
☐ Remote control for all systems in each room
☐ Front-projection rooms adjoining each conference room
☐ Audio and video transmission between every room
☐ Recording capability from head end room for every room
☐ Audio and video program availability in guestrooms

Most project developers can define their audiovisual and other systems requirements by reviewing the most comprehensive programs and deleting the equipment and systems that do not meet their needs and/or exceed their budget. The team must be careful not to provide so little equipment that the rooms function poorly or, on the other hand, more than can be effectively utilized. Tables 13–2 and

TABLE 13-1. AUDIOVISUAL SYSTEMS	
System Type	*Components*
Control systems	☐ Lighting systems (raise, lower, preset, off)
	☐ Blackout shades (raise, lower)
	☐ Curtains (open, close)
	☐ Projection screens (raise, lower, tilt)
	☐ Video (on, off, forward, reverse, pause)
	☐ Slide projectors (on, off, forward, reverse, focus)
	☐ Sound system (raise–lower volume)
	☐ Intercom/telephone (on–off bell)
Screen/display systems	☐ Central front projection screen
	☐ Side front projection screens (tiltable)
	☐ Rear projection screen
	☐ Writing boards (single, multiple, movable)
	☐ Tackable (or tapeable) walls
	☐ Easels (portable)
	☐ Hanging-rail system
Projection and video systems	☐ Video and computer projection (floor, ceiling, or rear location)
	☐ Video monitors (permanent, portable)
	☐ Slide projection (floor, projection booth, or rear location)
	☐ Film projection (floor, projection booth, or rear location)
	☐ Video recording
	☐ Video transmission and playback
	☐ Video editing and production
Audio systems	☐ Speech reinforcement (live sound)
	☐ Audience microphones
	☐ Program speakers (recorded sound)
	☐ Audio recording
	☐ Audio transmission–playback
	☐ Audio editing and production

TABLE 13-2. FULL-FEATURED CONFERENCE AUDIOVISUAL SYSTEM

	Control Systems	Screen and Display Systems	Projection and Video Systems	Audio Systems
Ballroom	Lighting controls for each ballroom division; screen, video, and slide controls; electrically operated blackout shades; remote control for all systems	Electrically operated screen at end and one side of room	Projection booth at one end of room; video jacks in walls and floor boxes; remote control availability from floor boxes at each subdivision	Speech-reinforcement system; program speakers; audio jacks in floor (for audience microphones) and walls (for recording); telephone
Large conference rooms[a]	Fully adjustable lighting systems; electrically operated blackout shades and curtains; remote control for videos, slides, and sound system	Electrically operated central projection screen and two tiltable side screens; multiple movable writing boards; tackable walls	Video projection in ceiling; slide and film capability in front projection room; video jacks around room perimeter	Same as for ballroom
Midsize and small conference rooms[b]	Same as for large conference room	Two projection screens, one tiltable; multiple movable writing boards; tackable walls	Portable video monitors; slide and film capability at back of room; video jacks in walls	Same as for ballroom
Breakout rooms	Lighting controls at entry	Pull-down projection screen; writing board; tackable walls; easels or hanging-rail system	Video jacks in wall and floor box	Audio jacks in wall and floor box; telephone
Boardroom	Fully adjustable lighting system; electrically operated blackout shades and curtains; electrically operated projection screen; remote control for slides and videos	Electrically operated projection screen; writing board behind custom millwork paneling; tackable walls	Same as for breakout rooms	Audio jacks in floor box and walls; switch to eliminate audio recording capability; telephone
Amphitheater	Fully adjustable lighting system; electrically operated projection screen; remote control for slides and videos	Rear-screen display; front projection screen for overheads; writing board with movable panels; tackable walls	Rear-screen slides and videos; overhead from beside lectern; video jacks in walls and floor box	Speech reinforcement system; audience microphones; program speakers; audio jacks in wall and floor box; telephone
Auditorium	Same as for amphitheater	Electrically operated front screen; mobile writing and display unit	Front projection booth and head end room at rear of space; overhead from beside lectern; video jacks in walls and floor box	Same as for amphitheater

[a]Larger than 1,500 square feet (139 square meters).
[b]Between 500 and 1,500 square feet (46 and 139 square meters).

TABLE 13-3. STANDARD CONFERENCE AUDIOVISUAL SYSTEM

	Control Systems	Screen and Display Systems	Projection and Video Systems	Audio Systems
Ballroom	Lighting controls for each ballroom division; screen, video, and slide controls	Electrically operated screen at one end of room	Projection booth at one end of room; video jacks in walls and floor boxes	Speech-amplification system; program speakers; audio jacks in floor (for audience microphones) and walls (for recording)
Large conference rooms[a]	Fully adjustable lighting systems; electrically operated projection screens; remote control for videos, slides, and sound system	Central projection screen; multiple movable writing boards; tackable walls	Slide and film projection from projection room; video projector installed as required; video jacks around room perimeter	Same as for ballroom
Midsize and small conference rooms[b]	Fully adjustable lighting systems; remote control for videos, slides, and sound system	One projection screen; multiple movable writing boards; tackable walls	Portable video monitors; slide and film projection at back of room; video jacks in walls	Audio jacks in floor and walls
Breakout rooms	Lighting controls at entry	Pull-down projection screen; writing board; tackable walls; easels or hanging-rail system	Video jacks in wall	Audio jacks in wall and floor box
Boardroom	Fully adjustable lighting system; electrically operated blackout shades and curtains; remote control for slides and videos	Electrically operated projection screen; writing board with millwork trim; tackable walls	Same as for breakout rooms	Same as for breakout rooms
Amphitheater	Fully adjustable lighting system; electrically operated projection screen; remote control for slides and videos	Electrically operated front projection screen; writing boards, tackable walls	Front projection booth or platform at rear of space; overhead at lectern; video jacks in walls	Speech-reinforcement system; program speakers; audio jacks in walls
Auditorium	Same as for amphitheater	Stationary front screen (permanent)	Front projection booth and head end room at rear of space; overhead from beside lectern; video jacks in walls and floor box	Same as for amphitheater

[a]Larger than 1,500 square feet (139 square meters).
[b]Between 500 and 1,500 square feet (46 and 139 square meters).

13–3 identify sample programs for two levels of audiovisual support. The first describes an optimum full-service system, perhaps about 90 percent of the ultimate program; the other illustrates a more moderate audiovisual concept, essentially the minimum system acceptable for a modern professional center.

Conference Room Layout. The design and configuration of each conference or training room has an effect on the need for and provision of audiovisual services. For example, the presence of windows, the height of the ceiling, and the layout of the conference tables all influence the type of projection system and its location, either in the meeting room or in an adjoining projection room. Windows, for example, provide a welcome amenity to conference spaces, but either some degree of blackout capability must be added to ensure sufficient contrast for video and slide presentations or the system designers should select a rear-screen projection format. Similarly, ceiling height dictates the utility of a projection room and establishes the maximum size of the projected image. When the ballroom is used for video presentations, the ceiling height and chandelier placement must be coordinated with the projection system. And, obviously, room layout is critical; the designers should indicate the room orientation and the systems must account for viewing angles and distances, the location of the lectern and aisles, and so forth.

Control Systems. Perhaps the most critical of the audiovisual system's individual elements is the set of controls available to the conference instructor or to the technicians assisting with the meeting. Planners prefer a space where they or the instructor can supervise the lighting, HVAC, sound, and projection systems. Central controls, which often are inaccessible, or those placed in awkward locations (the adjoin-

ing service corridor is among the worst) are untenable to today's clients.

A simple way to establish the outline for the necessary control systems is to "walk through" a typical meeting mentally. First, upon entering the room, which lights or specialized systems should be controlled from the doorway? Next, as the instructor sets up the room and projection systems before beginning the session, how (or with whose assistance) does he or she cue up slides or a videotape? Who sets the lighting, projection screens, and window shades? How does the instructor or a technician adjust lights, sound levels, and equipment during a presentation? As the team answers these questions, the program for the control system becomes clear and a consultant can begin to assess the impact such criteria may have on the design of the conference rooms, the audiovisual and equipment budget, and the eventual need for technical staff.

The general rule is to place a complete set of controls at the lectern or front wall, as well as in the projection room (if one exists). Selected switches, such as for room fluorescent lights, should be duplicated at the entry. In addition, many of these might be incorporated into a remote-control console available to the speaker. Scanticon uses a wireless control that fits into the top of the lectern but can be removed and set on a table or another location as desired. Whatever control setup is used, it should control a number of systems.

Lighting. The electrical plan should include switches at the room entry for the overhead fluorescent lights. This is more economical for when the room is not being used for meetings, such as during setup and cleaning. Additional switches should be located at the front wall, to the left or right of the central screen and writing board, controlling these lights as well as each group of downlights or track lights. The projection booth should have full control of all lights, as well. It is advisable

Remote control. The portable remote control unit used at Scanticon conference centers can be recessed in the lectern or placed anywhere in the meeting space. It controls lights, projection screen, drapes, and audiovisual systems. (Photo by the author.)

to include one or more presets for slide or video projection, controls for which should also be available at the lectern; to provide full flexibility, these might be provided in a floor box alongside the podium.

Window Coverings. Blackout shades and decorative curtains must be provided to darken the room for video or slide presentations. In larger rooms and such upscale spaces as executive boardrooms, these coverings should be electrically operated. The front wall, lectern, and projection booth should have identical controls.

Projection Screens. The larger conference rooms require electrically operated projection screens. Each screen should be controlled by the instructor as well as from the projection room.

Projection and Video Systems. The most important controls are those for the slide, video, and other projection systems. These should allow the instructor to turn power on or off, advance and reverse the equipment, pause a videotape, and focus slides. Dual controls for left and right images is standard. While controls at the lectern offer advantages to the stationary speaker working from notes, the system also should accommodate instructors who prefer to move about the conference room. Most presenters and operators prefer wireless remote systems.

Audio Systems. The podium or front wall panels should control the volume of the front-mounted speakers, which function as the sound system for films, slide shows, video presentations, and audio recordings. Most systems also control the volume of the instructor's own speech reinforcement system, utilizing ceiling-mounted speakers.

Screen and Display Systems.
The display systems consist of projection screens, writing boards, and other equipment for displaying written work. Large rooms need multiple projection screens because of the variety of projection equipment that might be used, sometimes simultaneously. There continues to be discussion concerning the advantages of front- versus rear-screen systems in different types of conference rooms. Generally, front-screen systems provide more flexibility in terms of both equipment choice and screen location, offer a sharper and richer image, and require considerably less space in the front projection booth. But outside light (even from the door to the corridor) must be controlled and the speaker must stand beneath a spotlight in the otherwise-darkened room.

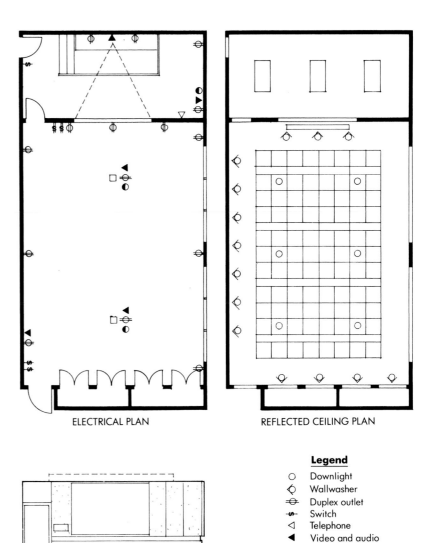

ELECTRICAL PLAN

REFLECTED CEILING PLAN

FRONT ELEVATION

Legend
○ Downlight
◇ Wallwasher
⊖ Duplex outlet
⊸ Switch
◁ Telephone
◀ Video and audio
□ Floor box
◖ Data (computer)

Conference room audiovisual and electrical layout. The plan illustrates a standard conference room, including separate lighting controls at front and rear; dual floor boxes for power, data, audiovisuals, and telephone; a combination of fluorescent and incandescent downlights, including wall washers on the tackable side wall; and a rear-projection room.

Rear-screen systems offer poorer image resolution—a serious problem with slides but sometimes acceptable for videos—and require a substantially larger projection and equipment room. Its main advantage is that the room need not be darkened, allowing the participants to take notes, continue active discussion, and communicate with the instructor.

Projection Screens. Front-screen systems should be used in most conference and meeting rooms. They can be used for all types of projection equipment and allow additional screens to be added for special multimedia presentations. A large central screen, electrically operated, should be used for most formal presentations. Many conference centers will add one or two smaller screens, mounted two to three feet (0.6 to 1 meter) from the front wall, that can be tilted back to prevent "keystoning" of overhead images. Rear-screen systems include a permanent opaque panel with a projection room immediately behind it.

Writing Boards. All midsize and small conference rooms should include permanent writing surfaces or utilize a hanging-rail system allowing individual boards to be hung as needed. In rooms with rear projection, the design of the front wall should incorporate movable writing boards that can be pushed aside to reveal the screen. New England Telephone's training center instead utilizes a three-by-five–foot (1-by-1.5–meter) rear-projection screen, located slightly off-center, with permanent writing surfaces beside it. Most centers use dry-erase marker boards.

Other Display Systems. The ability to display pages from a flip chart during an interactive meeting is crucial. Most rooms have individual panels or entire walls that are either tackable or designed to take masking tape without damage. The display equipment includes portable items as well, including easels and the various hanging panels that accompany the rail system.

Projection and Video Systems. Projection systems are another point of differentiation between conference centers and hotels, and, in fact, between different types of centers. At corporate and university centers, which are designed for specific types of meetings, the projection systems can be precisely defined to meet the needs of the training staff or of the executive education curriculum. But at executive and resort centers, the technology must be much more flexible, to meet the varying needs of a wider clientele.

Central Control Room. Conference centers must include a central control room, often adjoining the largest conference room, auditorium, or amphitheater, for receiving outside cable and video signals, recording conferences and meetings in the center, distributing audio and video throughout the facility, and, if teleconferencing capabilities are provided, transmitting programs to other locations.

Most control rooms are furnished with several bays of audio and video equipment, allowing a technician to monitor the events in any of the rooms. All conference and training rooms, including the smaller breakout rooms, should be connected to the control room—under this setup, any two rooms can be interconnected.

Television Distribution System. Nearly every conference center installs a central radio-frequency (RF) distribution system, originating from the central control room, to furnish each room at the property with a television signal. Virtually any type of programming can be distributed, including broadcast television from a commercial cable feed, prerecorded video programs, conference proceedings, live events taking place in the center (or elsewhere on the university campus or within the corporate office), or other programs received via satellite. The RF system also is used to feed video and audio signals from other locations in the conference center back to the central control room. The RF system outlets should be located in each conference and breakout room, as well as in the prefunction foyers, lounges, elevator lobbies, and so forth. Monitors might be placed at such remote locations as the recreational center and outside the conference dining room.

Most centers also utilize closed-circuit television for in-house programming, such as news, meeting schedules, and messages. When not used in the conference center, these additional channels can distribute other programming to any location in the property.

Audio Systems. The fourth part of the audio-visual program is the audio system, which governs voice amplification, recording, and playback. These three components are integrated into one structure that starts with a speech reinforcement system, consisting of a number of speakers evenly spaced throughout the ceiling. This is required in midsize and large conference rooms, amphitheaters, auditoriums, and ballrooms. If individual audience microphones are included, the participants' voices can be amplified as well as the speaker's.

Scanticon-Minneapolis, Plymouth, Minnesota. Executive and resort conference centers provide dramatic audio-visual control rooms, sometimes visible to the public but more often located on a mezzanine above the largest conference room or amphitheater, or adjoining a production studio. (Photo: Ron Solomon.)

Second, a separate set of speakers is provided at the front of the conference room for films, videos, and other audio recordings. One design problem here is the integration of this speaker system into the front presentation wall, which must also be equipped with multiple writing and tackable surfaces and projection screens. Two speakers, positioned high on the front wall and recessed to the left and right of the screen behind decorative fabric panels, is the usual solution.

Third, many centers incorporate an additional audio system to record the proceedings. The more technologically advanced centers install microphones in the ceiling for this purpose, while other centers provide audio jacks for portable microphones. Additional types of audio systems may be available in certain conference centers. For example, very few facilities in North America offer simultaneous translation capability, although such systems are standard in many other parts of the world. Modern equipment for such a system includes lightweight radio receivers, so that the audience earphones do not require hardwire connections. Similar equipment is available for the hearing-impaired, using a wireless FM broadcast or infrared systems.

Although the systems capability exists, few conference centers are actively pursuing full teleconferencing opportunities. One part of the system, receiving the satellite downfeed, is fairly simple, and most projects are so equipped; but only a few are able to broadcast. Instead, centers may contract with an outside vendor or cable television company to rent a broadcast truck for a teleconference meeting.

COMMUNICATIONS SYSTEMS

Communications systems are evolving faster than audiovisual systems, thanks to advances in computer technology and fiber optics. Telephone networks are making increasingly sophisticated features available to conference center developers and operators at reasonable costs. Some properties are choosing to provide open conduits in the basebuilding system design to allow for flexibility in the future. University and corporate centers generally provide two separate telephone lines to each bedroom, enabling guests to use computers either on the conference center's own dedicated data network or via modem to public systems or the guests' home or office systems.

It is likely that we will see an increase in voice-mail systems as the features become easier to access and more conference attendees become familiar with their operation. The GE Management Development Center already has a system that allows guests to receive incoming calls directly—without going through the center switchboard—and record personal messages. At properties that attract a high number of international customers, whose callers may leave lengthy messages in different languages, the voice-mail system offers a valuable amenity.

CHAPTER 14

Planning the Recreational Facilities

When comparing conference centers to hotels, one of the largest areas of differentiation is in the provision of recreational facilities. Conference centers place a much greater emphasis on this area, an emphasis that is evident not only in terms of the amount of space or extent of facilities provided, but also in the integration of sports and fitness into the daily conference routine.

The preoccupation with fitness has grown substantially in recent decades. While the 1960s saw a growing emphasis on the "body beautiful," the 1970s witnessed an awareness of physical health and well-being, and the 1980s saw fitness become a way of life for millions of Americans. This trend toward fitness is exemplified by many factors, including the following:

☐ The post–World War II baby-boom generation pursues an active life-style scheduled around jogging, aerobics, and exercise programs.

☐ Corporate America has recognized the importance and potential long-term economic savings associated with promoting wellness and fitness in the workplace.

☐ The health care industry now publicly promotes preventive medicine, including regular checkups and numerous informal screenings (such as those for blood pressure).

In hotels, recreational facilities traditionally have been built for families and, perhaps, the traveling businessperson who might want to unwind in the afternoon or evening, but not for the convention or meeting groups. In contrast, with the increasing focus on fitness, it should be no surprise that conference centers, which emphasize the combination of leisure activities and intensive meetings, have developed large recreational facilities directed toward the conference attendees. This can be seen as the latest stage in a historical progression: business decisions and networking have long taken place at the golf club; now they occur in health clubs and fitness centers.

ESTABLISHING THE RECREATIONAL PROGRAM

The recreational program evolves from an analysis of customer needs and expectations and a comparison of facilities at competitive properties. The developer must be aware of current trends in fitness and recreational

Xerox International Center for Training & Management Development, Leesburg, Virginia. The dramatic gymnasium is located in a separate fitness center and used both for recreational exercise and for team-building games during long training programs. Other indoor facilities include a jogging track, racquetball and squash courts, and a weight-training/exercise area. (Architect: Vincent Kling Partnership; photo: Merrill Worthington.)

equipment, and the architect should incorporate flexibility into the design to allow the space to adapt to such trends.

The recreational facilities are about 4 to 6 percent of the total project area at most conference centers (although a number of projects, especially the university centers, have little or no recreational space, and some of the resort properties and smaller corporate centers devote a higher percentage to fitness). The most common facilities include a reception area, large indoor swimming pool (2,500 square feet, or 232.5 square meters, at executive centers; 3,000 square feet, or 279 square meters, at resort centers; 4,500 square feet, or 418.5 square meters, at corporate centers), racquetball courts (usually two to four), exercise and aerobics rooms, and lockers. Some of the corporate centers may add a gymnasium, and the resorts feature golf, tennis, or a spa complex.

Two of the suburban executive conference centers, Hamilton Park and Peachtree, have very similar recreational facilities, each of about 8,000 net square feet (744 net square meters). Both have a small reception area (500 square feet, or 46.5 square meters), an indoor pool (2,500 to 3,000 square feet, or 232.5 to 279 square meters), an exercise room (900 square feet, or 83.7 square meters), two racquetball courts (1,600 square feet, or 148.8 square meters), and lockers and toilets (1,200 square feet, or 111.6 square meters). Hamilton Park also features an aerobics room (800 square feet, or 74.4 square meters). Both fitness centers are easily reached from guest-room areas and adjoin a game room and pub. In contrast, the Scanticon center outside Min-neapolis, which accepts public memberships, is about 50 percent larger, with more spacious facilities and additional courts.

The recreational offerings at the resort centers vary tremendously depending on the location and sports orientation of the facility. Doral Arrowwood, which evolved from corporate to executive to resort conference center, includes an indoor–outdoor pool, three racquet courts, and more expansive health facilities, totaling about 10,500 net square feet (976.5 square meters); it also maintains a nine-hole golf course. At newer conference resorts, the program usually calls for at least 20,000 square feet (1,860 square meters) of facilities to accommodate larger spa facilities or a major golf club.

Many resorts feature separate sports facilities. At the Four Seasons, the spa is more or less contained within the hotel structure, but the tennis and golf complex is in a separate wing, connected by a tunnel. At Kingsmill, the sports center is located one hundred yards (109.3 meters) from the main conference center building, containing the usual complement of spaces as well as an informal restaurant.

Corporate centers provide recreational amenities similar to those of executive properties, but they are generally more numerous and spacious; the swimming pool, for example, may be 4,500 square feet (418.5 square meters), complemented by four (rather than two) racquetball courts. Several corporate centers, including Xerox, IBM-Thornwood, and the proposed Digital Equipment project, feature a large gymnasium to provide aerobics programs and encourage team sports, such as basketball.

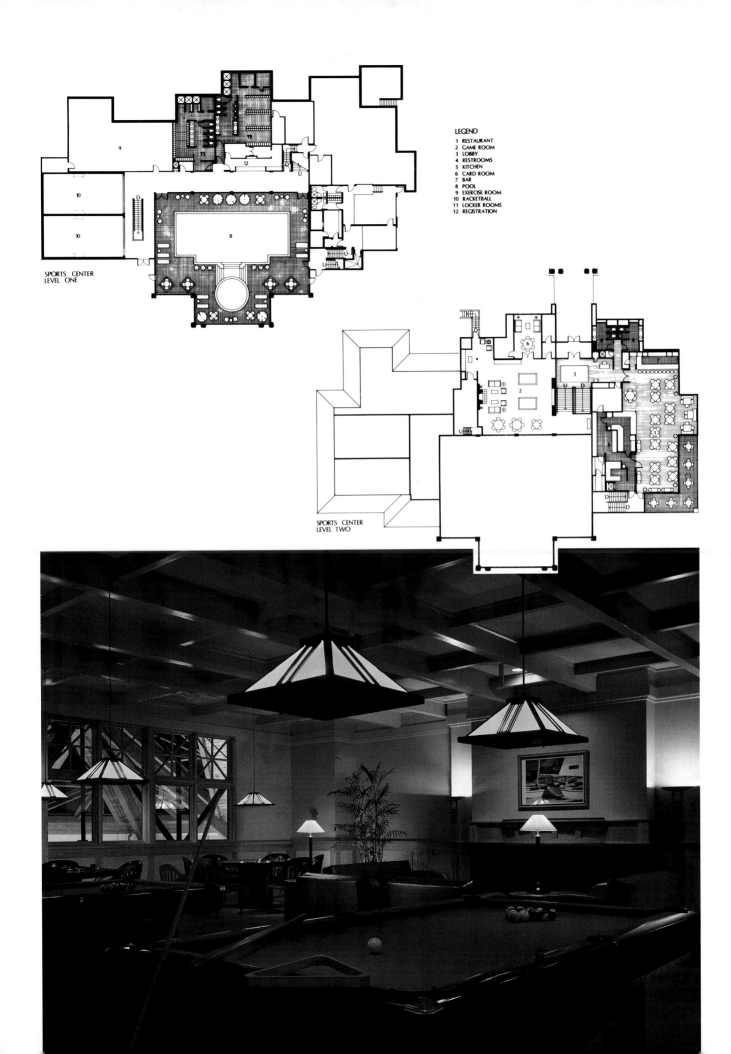

LEGEND

1 RESTAURANT
2 GAME ROOM
3 LOBBY
4 RESTROOMS
5 KITCHEN
6 CARD ROOM
7 BAR
8 POOL
9 EXERCISE ROOM
10 RACKETBALL
11 LOCKER ROOMS
12 REGISTRATION

SPORTS CENTER
LEVEL ONE

SPORTS CENTER
LEVEL TWO

PLANNING CONSIDERATIONS

The recreational facilities generally are convenient to the guestroom areas, often at the end of the residential structure, or, if there are two or three low wings, at the central junction point. Although conference and training centers emphasize informality, the objective remains to organize the circulation so that heavy sports- and fitness-related traffic does not pass through the lobby or other public areas. In addition, because the recreational areas are intended to provide a break from the intensity of the working sessions, this goal may be reinforced by locating them some distance from the conference core. This alternative also assures that the meetings will not be disturbed by the recreational activity.

Once they have generated the space program and list of facilities, the developer and management group need to consider the operational program for the sports and fitness center. They should answer the following questions:

☐ What operating hours and staff levels are expected?

☐ Are outside memberships (i.e., public access) anticipated?

☐ Will corporate employees or management staff be allowed to use the facilities?

☐ Will an outside contractor manage the recreational facilities?

☐ Is food and beverage service planned at the pool, on surrounding terraces, or at other locations?

☐ Are private parties anticipated?

☐ What are the equipment and storage needs?

The conclusions will help generate planning objectives and lead to design solutions.

Locating the recreational complex at the end of the guestroom wing, totally removed from the public facilities, offers management the opportunity to accept outside business during the day, when conferees generally are involved in meetings. This is most common at executive centers or at corporate properties where employees are permitted to use the facility at specified times. The remote location also allows the designers to include outdoor facilities, such as terraces, pools, tennis, and putting greens. These should be designed to accommodate receptions or informal dinners, providing areas for service vehicles, food storage, cooking, and cleanup.

A second common arrangement is to locate the recreational facilities centrally, near the lobby or where the guestrooms join the public areas. Often, the facilities are located on a lower level to separate them somewhat from the public circulation. At the IBM Advanced Business Institute, the recreational facilities are located at the juncture between the public areas and the guestroom structure, one level below an informal dining room and an elegant game room. Thus, they are centrally located, convenient to the residential wing, visible from the casual public areas, but totally removed from the more formal lobby, dining, and conference areas. Similarly, the architects for Doral Arrowwood located the recreational facilities on the ground floor at the center of the project; the bridges between the public and guestroom structures overlook the pool and the entrance to the health and fitness facilities.

Occasionally, the recreational facilities are separated more completely from the rest of the conference and training complex. At the Xerox training center, the fitness and recreation building is several hundred feet from the main structure; at IBM-Thornwood, the gym and sports complex are located opposite the front entrance, helping to anchor the approach and arrival sequence architecturally.

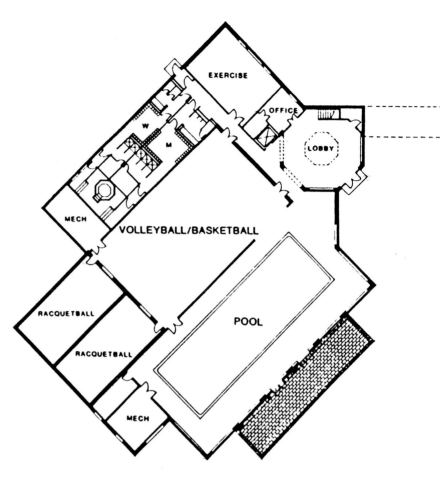

GTE Management Development Center, Norwalk, Connecticut. The corporate GTE center includes the typical facilities—exercise room, racquetball, pool, lockers, and lounge—clustered around a central gymnasium. The lap pool opens directly onto outdoor terraces. (Architect: Hellmuth, Obata & Kassabaum; plan courtesy of HOK.)

Doral Arrowwood, Rye Brook, New York. Doral Arrowwood has managed its successful evolution into a resort in large part because of the design of its fitness facilities and the prominent location of its pool off the circulation link between the public areas and guestrooms. A large reception area leads to lockers, a health club, a pool, racquetball courts, and a well-equipped exercise room. (Architect and interiors: The Hillier Group; photos: Jim D'Addio.)

Scanticon-Denver, Englewood, Colorado (above left). Golf resorts require additional food and beverage outlets, locker facilities, and a pro shop. Scanticon doubled the size of its pro shop during design development to better merchandise golf equipment, clothing, and accessories. (Architect: Friis Moltke Larson with RNL; interiors: Klenow Deichmann and Overbye; photo: Ron Solomon.)

Scanticon-Princeton, Princeton, New Jersey (left). The swimming pool at Princeton is centrally located, next to the specialty restaurant

and under an open lounge. It provides easy access from the guest-rooms and opens onto outdoor terraces through sliding glass panels. (Architect: Friis and Molkte with Warner Burns Toan and Lunde; interiors: Friis and Moltke with Enicho Deichmann; photo: Ron Solomon.)

IBM Advanced Business Institute, Palisades, New York (above right). The game room is located on a second level, adjoining the casual restaurant and overlooking the racquetball courts. (Architect and interiors: Mitchell/Giurgola; photo: Mick Hales.)

Most recreational centers include a reception area or control desk to monitor activity and to help ensure safe use of the pool and exercise equipment. Some projects include a small retail outlet selling sportswear, souvenirs, and toiletries, and a snack bar, staffed by a single person. From here guests have access to the lockers and the rest of the facilities.

The aerobics and exercise rooms, at least 800 square feet (74.4 square meters) each, require special finishes and acoustic treatment. The operator or a fitness consultant should establish the requirements for the exercise equipment before the conference center design is complete, to be certain that the room is large enough to accommodate the planned equipment. Several facilities, finding increased use of the exercise equipment, have moved some weight equipment into the adjoining aerobics room.

DESIGN CONSIDERATIONS

The recreational facilities are not usually a feature of the architectural design. Occasionally, though, individual spaces—the gym at Xerox or the pool at Doral Arrowwood, for example—are among the more memorable images of the conference center. These create a mood and ambience all their own, and the architect and designers should capitalize on such opportunities throughout the recreational complex. The less spectacular recreational areas should reinforce the design theme and materials used in the remainder of the conference center.

The design of the recreational center begins at the control desk, often a kiosk in an open area. At resort spas, the reception area is luxurious, setting the tone for the pampering to follow; at golf clubs, it is nearly as upscale, with millwork and display cabinets mirroring the quality of the championship course.

The pool areas vary from spectacular multi-story spaces with skylights or great glass curtain-walls to fairly standard tile-covered basement areas. The pool can be one of the main visual and recreational focuses for the conference center, and architects should attempt, within reasonable budgetary guidelines, to create a special space. Also, the operational program should articulate whether the pool area is intended to be a social center, used for receptions or informal gatherings; if so, the pool area requires a minimum of ten feet (3 meters) of deck space around the pool on one or two sides, and substantially more on the others, to provide space for seating areas, chaise lounges, bars, and food displays, and to allow guests to walk without fear of being splashed. Glass roofs or window walls should offer some movable panels to enlarge the space visually and offset the humid, chemical-saturated environment; in summer, the warm breezes and views to the sky further moderate the feeling of an enclosed space.

The pools themselves should be designed to allow for lap swimming and, at corporate centers, such recreational play as water polo; diving boards are inadvisable for safety reasons. If the weather is suitable, the pool might include an outdoor section, or a second pool might be constructed outdoors, surrounded by terraces. Of course, the architect must locate such a pool where it will receive unobstructed sunlight.

Other components of the recreational complex offer little opportunity to create a special architectural character. Racquetball courts, for example, tend to be fairly standard in design and finish, although designers can create second-level overlooks and a visually interesting glass corridor on the ground level.

APPENDIX A.

CONFERENCE CENTER DIRECTORY

Note: Centers marked with an asterisk (*) are illustrated in this book; each center's category is listed in parenthesis.

Alabama
Auburn University Hotel and Conference Center, Auburn (university)
Paul W. Bryant Conference Center, Tuscaloosa (university)

Arizona
Biosphere 2 Conference Center, Oracle (not-for-profit)
*Scottsdale Conference Resort, Scottsdale (resort)
*YWCA of the USA Leadership Development Center, Phoenix (nonresidential/not-for-profit)

California
*Asilomar Conference Center, Pacific Grove (not-for-profit)
*Chaminade at Santa Cruz, Santa Cruz (executive)
*LaCosta Hotel and Spa, Carlsbad (resort)
*Ojai Valley Inn & Country Club, Ojai (resort)
Pacific Gas & Electric Company Learning Center, San Ramon (corporate)
*Renaissance Meeting Center at Techmart, Santa Clara (nonresidential)
*The Resort at Squaw Creek, Squaw Valley (resort)

Colorado
The Nature Place, Colorado Outdoor Educational Center, Florissant (not-for-profit)
*Cheyenne Mountain Conference Resort, Colorado Springs (resort)
*Keystone Conference Center, Keystone (resort)
*Scanticon-Denver, Englewood (resort)

Connecticut
AEtna Institute Corporate Education Center, Hartford (corporate)
*Center for Financial Studies, Fairfield University, Fairfield (university)

*GTE Management Development Center, Norwalk (corporate)
Hamilton Heights Conference Center, Hartford (corporate)
*Harrison Conference Center/Inn, Heritage Village, Southbury (executive)

Delaware
Clayton Hall, University of Delaware, Newark (university/nonresidential)

District of Columbia
*Leavey Center, Georgetown University (university)

Florida
Sheraton Bonaventure Resort & Spa, Fort Lauderdale (resort)
The Conference Center at Dodgertown, Vero Beach (resort)
*Indigo Lakes Resort & Conference Center, Daytona Beach (resort)
Ponte Vedra Inn & Club, Ponte Vedra Beach (resort)

Georgia
*Aberdeen Woods Conference Center (Pitney Bowes), Peachtree City (corporate)
*Evergreen Conference Center & Resort, Stone Mountain (resort)
Georgia Center for Continuing Education, University of Georgia, Athens (university)
*Peachtree Executive Conference Center, Peachtree City (executive)
Southern Conference Center (Colony Square Hotel), Atlanta (executive)

Illinois
*Allen Center, Northwestern University, Evanston (university)
Center for Professional Education (Arthur Andersen & Co.), St. Charles (corporate)
Conference Center 1 (Woodfield Hilton and Towers), Arlington Heights (executive)
The KPMG Peat Marwick Executive

Conference Center, Chicago (corporate/nonresidential)
*Harrison Conference Center at Lake Bluff, Lake Bluff (executive)
*Hickory Ridge Conference Centre (AT&T), Lisle (corporate)
*McDonald's Lodge and Training Center, Oak Brook (corporate)

Indiana
*University Place Conference Center and Hotel, Indiana University—Purdue University at Indianapolis, Indianapolis (university)

Maryland
The Aspen Institute at Wye Plantation, Queenstown (not-for-profit)
*Mount Washington Conference Center (USF&G), Baltimore (corporate)
University College Center for Adult Education, University of Maryland, College Park (university)
U.S. Postal Service Management Training Academy, Potomac (corporate)

Massachusetts
Boston University Corporate Education Center, Tyngsboro (university/nonresidential)
The Center for Executive Education, Babson College Wellesley (university)
MIT Endicott House, Dedham (university)
*New England Telephone Learning Center, Marlboro (corporate)
Ocean Edge Conference Center, Brewster (resort)
World Trade Center Boston Executive Conference Center, Boston (nonresidential)

Michigan
Corporate Education Center, Eastern Michigan University, Ypsilanti (university)
Dow Leadership Development Center, Hillsdale College, Hillsdale (university)
*Executive Center and Executive Residence, University of Michigan, Ann Arbor (university)

Fetzer Business Development Center, Western Michigan University, Kalamazoo (university/nonresidential)
*Kellogg Center, Michigan State University, East Lansing (university)
Lake Country Conference Center, Big Rapids (executive)
*Marigold Lodge (Herman Miller), Zeeland (corporate)

Minnesota
IDS Oak Ridge Conference Center, Chaska (corporate)
*Northland Inn Executive Conference Center, Brooklyn Park (executive)
*Scanticon-Minneapolis, Minneapolis (executive)

Mississippi
Holiday Inn Executive Conference Center, Olive Branch (corporate)

Missouri
*AT&T Executive Conference Center, Chesterfield (corporate/nonresidential)
Doubletree Hotel & Conference Center, St. Louis (executive)
Sunnen Conference Center (YWCA of the Ozarks), Potosi (not-for-profit)

Montana
Yellowstone Conference Center, Big Sky (resort)

New Hampshire
New England Center for Continuing Education, University of New Hampshire, Durham (university)

New Jersey
AT&T Corporate Education Center, Hopewell (corporate)
*Hamilton Park Executive Conference Center, Florham Park (executive)
*Henry Chauncey Conference Center, Princeton (not-for-profit)
*Merrill Lynch Conference and Training Center, Princeton (corporate)
*Scanticon-Princeton, Princeton (executive)

New York
*American Express Conference Center, New York (nonresidential)
*Arden Conference Center (Arden House/Arden Homestead), Columbia University, Harriman (university)
Beaver Hollow Lodge and Conference Center, Java Center (executive retreat)
*Chase Development Center, New York (nonresidential)
*Doral Arrowwood, Rye Brook (resort)
*GE Management Development Institute, Croton-on-Hudson (corporate)
*Harrison Conference Center at Glen Cove, Glen Cove (executive)

*Hotel Macklowe and Macklowe Conference Center, New York (executive)
*IBM Advanced Business Institute, Palisades (corporate)
*IBM Technical Education Center, Thornwood (corporate)
*IBM Management Development Center, Armonk (corporate)
Edith Macy Conference Center, Briarcliff Manor (not-for-profit)
*Minnowbrook Lodge (Syracuse University), Blue Mountain Lake (not-for-profit)
The Rensselaerville Institute and Conference Center, Rensselaerville (not-for-profit)
*Shearson Lehman Brothers Conference and Training Center, New York (nonresidential)
*The Statler Hotel and Marriott Executive Education Center, Cornell University, Ithaca (university)
Sterling Forest Conference Center, Tuxedo (executive)
*Tarrytown House Executive Conference Center, Tarrytown (executive)

North Carolina
*Graylyn Conference Center, Wake Forest University, Winston-Salem (executive)
*Thomas Center, Duke University, Durham (university)

Ohio
Dana Center for Continuing Health Education, Medical College of Ohio, Toledo (university)
*Marcum Memorial Conference Center, Miami University, Oxford (university)
Procter & Gamble Learning Center, Cincinnati (nonresidential)

Oklahoma
*Oklahoma Center for Continuing Education, Norman (university)

Pennsylvania
*CoreStates Employee Development Center, Philadelphia (corporate/nonresidential)
*Eagle Lodge Conference Resort (CIGNA), Lafayette Hill (corporate/executive)
Great Valley Hilton and Conference Center, Malvern (executive)
*Gregg Educational Conference Center, American College, Bryn Mawr (university)
Hidden Valley Resort Conference Center, Hidden Valley (resort)
Keller Conference Center, Penn State University, University Park (university)
*Steinberg Center, University of Pennsylvania, Philadelphia (university)
Sugarloaf Conference Center, Temple University, Philadelphia (university)

Tennessee
Fogelman Executive Center, Memphis State University, Memphis (university)

Texas
*Barton Creek Conference Resort, Austin (resort)
*Dallas/Fort Worth Hilton Executive Conference Center, Grapevine (executive)
*Four Seasons Hotel and Resort, Irving (resort)
Garrett Creek Ranch Executive Conference Center, Paradise (executive retreat)
Lakeway Resort and Conference Center, Austin (resort)
*The Houstonian Hotel & Conference Center, Houston (executive)
*The Woodlands Executive Conference Center and Resort, The Woodlands (resort)

Utah
Snowbird Conference Center at the Cliff Lodge, Snowbird (resort)

Virginia
*The Kingsmill Resort and Conference Center, Williamsburg (resort)
*Lansdowne Conference Resort, Leesburg (resort)
Sponsors Hall, University of Virginia, Charlottesville (university)
*Westfields International Conference Center, Leesburg (executive)
*Xerox International Center for Training & Management Development, Leesburg (corporate)

Washington
*Battelle Seattle Conference Center, Seattle (not-for-profit)

West Virginia
The Greenbrier, White Sulphur Springs (resort)

Wisconsin
*The Council House (Johnson Wax), Racine (corporate retreat)
Westwood Conference Center, Wausau (corporate)
*Wingspread (Johnson Foundation), Racine (not-for-profit)

Ontario, Canada
Kempenfelt Conference Center, Georgian College, Barrie (university)
Gordon Centre, Queen's University, Kingston (university)
*Minaki Lodge, Minaki (resort)
Ontario Hydro Conference and Development Centre, Orangeville (corporate)

APPENDIX B.
CONFERENCE CENTER
MANAGEMENT COMPANIES

ARA Services
Gregory Wier, Vice President
Three Radnor Corporate Center
Radnor, PA 19087
(215) 687-8600

Benchmark Hospitality Group
Burt Cabañas, President and CEO
2170 Buckthorne Place
The Woodlands, TX 77380
(713) 367-5757

Conference Environments Corporation
Stanley Cox, Chairman
P.O. Box 3277
West End, NJ 07740
(201) 229-2288

The Dolce Company
Andy Dolce, President
One Madison Avenue
Morristown, NJ 17960
(201) 377-2424

Doral Hotels & Resorts
Management Corporation
Sam Haigh, President
600 Madison Avenue
New York, NY 10017
(212) 752-5700

Harrison Conference Services
Tom Silvestri, President
Dosoris Lane
Glen Cove, NY 11542
(516) 671-9500

International Conference Resorts
Richard R. Joaquim, President
7700 East McCormick Parkway
Scottsdale, AZ 85258
(602) 991-9000

Marriott Corporation
Conference Center Management
Terry Harwood, Vice President
One Marriott Drive
Washington, DC 20058
(301) 670-3142

Scanticon Corporation
Jorgen Roed, President
Princeton Forrestal Center
Princeton, NJ 08540
(609) 452-8300

Style Conferences Limited
Henry Chandler, Operations Director
Wokefield Park, Reading
Berkshire RG7 3AG
England
(0734) 332391

International Association
of Conference Centers (IACC)
Tom Bolman, Executive Director
900 South Highway Drive
Fenton, MO 63026
(314) 349-5576

BIBLIOGRAPHY

Books

Alford, Harold J. *Continuing Education in Action, Residential Centers for Lifelong Learning.* New York: Wiley, 1968.

Finkel, Coleman Lee. *The Total Immersion Learning Environment.* New York: Conference Center Development Corp., 1987.

Haigh, Sam, and Robert W. Hudson. *Understanding Conference Centers.* Fenton, MO: International Association of Conference Centers, 1989.

The Hillier Group. *A Conference Center by Design.* Fenton, MO: International Association of Conference Centers, 1990.

Hoyle, Leonard H., David C. Dorf, and Thomas J. A. Jones. *Managing Conventions and Group Business.* East Lansing, MI: The Educational Institute of the AH&MA, 1989.

Lawson, Fred. *Conference, Convention and Exhibition Facilities.* London: The Architectural Press, 1981.

Leed, Karen B., and James R. Leed. *Building for Adult Learning.* Cincinnati: LDA Publishing, 1987.

Rutes, Walter A., and Richard H. Penner. *Hotel Planning and Design.* New York: Whitney Library of Design, 1985.

Terlaga, Kory L. *Training Room Solutions.* Trumbull, CT: Howe Furniture Corp., 1990.

Magazines

Cornell Hotel and Restaurant Administration Quarterly. School of Hotel Administration, Statler Hall, Ithaca, NY 14853

Corporate and Incentive Travel. Coastal Communications Corp., 488 Madison Avenue, New York, NY 10022

Meeting News. Gralla Publications, 1515 Broadway, New York, NY 10036

Meetings and Conventions. Reed Travel Group, 500 Plaza Drive, Secaucus, NJ 07096

Restaurant/Hotel Design International. Bill Communications, 633 Third Avenue, New York, NY 10017

Successful Meetings. Bill Communications, 633 Third Avenue, New York, NY 10017

Index

Page numbers in *italics* refer to figures.

Edited by Paul Lukas
Designed by Bob Fillie, Graphiti Graphics
Graphic production by Ellen Greene
Set in 10-point ITC Garamond Light